Re-Imaging Election

Re-Imaging Election

Divine Election as Representing
God to Others and
Others to God

Suzanne McDonald

WILLIAM B. EERDMANS PUBLISHING COMPANY

GRAND RAPIDS, MICHIGAN / CAMBRIDGE, U.K.

Published 2010 by

Wm. B. Eerdmans Publishing Co.

2140 Oak Industrial Drive N.E., Grand Rapids, Michigan 49505 /
P.O. Box 163, Cambridge CB3 9PU U.K.

Printed in the United States of America

16 15 14 13 12 11 10   7 6 5 4 3 2 1

Library of Congress Cataloging-in-Publication Data

McDonald, Suzanne, 1973-
Re-imaging election / Suzanne McDonald.
p.   cm.
Includes bibliographical references.
ISBN 978-0-8028-6408-6 (pbk.: alk. paper)
1. Election (Theology) — History of doctrines.
2. Reformed Church — Doctrines — History — 17th century.   I. Title.
BT809.M39   2010
234'.9 — dc22

2010006420

www.eerdmans.com

Contents

Contents

Acknowledgments

When I began the PhD research from which this book springs I was an ordinand in the United Reformed Church in the United Kingdom, and a year and a half after completing it I crossed continents to take up my current teaching position at Calvin College. I have accumulated many debts of gratitude from the inception of my research to this point.

I am deeply grateful to the United Reformed Church (UK) for financial support during my research, and for the personal support of so many URC friends. I would also like to record my appreciation for the financial assistance I received from the Coward Trust and the Congregational Fund Board, and especially for the extremely generous grant from The Hope Trust.

My deepest gratitude goes to my supervisor, Jeremy Begbie. His encouragement while I was an undergraduate led me to embark on this enterprise in the first place, and it is my joy and privilege to have had his deep theological wisdom, abundant wit, shrewd questioning, and care for my well-being as well as my work at every step of the way. My thanks also go to those with whom I was able to share ideas at St Mary's College, the Divinity School of the University of St Andrews. In particular, thank you to Nathan MacDonald, and to Alan Torrance and the members of the Theology Research Seminar. I also appreciated being able to share some of this material at meetings of the Scottish Barth Colloquium and at the 2007 Barth Conference at Princeton Theological Seminary. Thank you also to my PhD examiners, Steve Holmes and Bruce McCormack, for their probing questions, affirmation, and encouragement to "get this out there." Circumstances have meant that it has taken a while, but here it is at last! All of you will recognize the contributions you have made to what follows — and I am sure all of you will still disagree vigorously with aspects of it!

ACKNOWLEDGMENTS

Although work on this was completed before I came to Calvin College (so no one here can be blamed for anything that follows!), I am thankful for the warm support and encouragement I have received from my departmental colleagues and the Calvin community. This enabled me to settle quickly into my new life here, and so to take steps toward publication much sooner after arriving than I had anticipated.

Many thanks also to my editorial team at Eerdmans, and especially to Jenny Hoffman, for the care taken in producing this book, and for patience with all my "first-time author" questions!

And finally, to my dear parents, whose influence on my quest to find a doctrine of election that I can indwell with integrity is more profound than they realize, love and thanks beyond words.

Suzanne McDonald

Abbreviations

CD   Karl Barth, *Church Dogmatics,* cd. G. W. Bromiley and T. F. Torrance (Edinburgh: T. & T. Clark, 1956-75)

GD   Karl Barth, *The Göttingen Dogmatics: Instruction in the Christian Religion,* vol. 1, ed. Hannelotte Reiffen, trans. Geoffrey W. Bromiley (Grand Rapids: Eerdmans, 1991)

IJST   *International Journal of Systematic Theology*

SJT   *Scottish Journal of Theology*

Works *The Works of John Owen,* ed. William H. Gould, 24 vols. (London: Johnstone and Hunter, 1850-55)

Introduction

Reforming a Reformed Doctrine of Election

To many, the doctrine of election must seem to be a peculiarly Reformed obsession. When "the doctrine of election" is mentioned, it is very often the historic Reformed account that is automatically assumed: election as individual double predestination, in which God in his sovereignty has determined from all eternity to save some in Christ and to consign others to the consequences of their sins.

Although this approach to election has a long history, it rapidly became a controversial and defining doctrine for the Reformed tradition, and we have taken it to heart with a quite extraordinary degree of tenacity (and sometimes, ferocity) ever since. It has been held forth as the supreme touchstone of right Reformed thinking; it has been the subject both of virulent dispute with other traditions and passionate internal debate; and it has been the object of popular ridicule and academic opprobrium.[1] In the midst of all the theological wrangling, adherence to the historic Reformed

---

1. Perhaps the most famous example of ridicule is the poem "Holy Willie's Prayer," by Robert Burns. Robert Burns, *Poems and Songs,* ed. J. Kinsley (Oxford: Oxford University Press, 1969), p. 56. One of the most influential scholarly critiques of the historical roots and theological consequences of this approach to election, in particular its expression in federal Calvinism, has been that of J. B. Torrance. See, e.g., his "Covenant or Contract? A Study of the Theological Background of Worship in Seventeenth-Century Scotland," *SJT* 23 (1970): 51-76; "The Incarnation and 'Limited Atonement,'" *Evangelical Quarterly* 55, no. 2 (1983): 83-94; and "Strengths and Weaknesses of the Westminster Theology," in *The Westminster Confession in the Church Today,* ed. A. I. C. Heron (Edinburgh: St. Andrew Press, 1982), pp. 40-54.

account of the doctrine has played an enormous part in shaping personal and corporate character over the centuries, for good and ill.

Even so, this approach to election has not held exclusive sway within the Reformed tradition. The nineteenth century saw several reconsiderations of the doctrine, including those of John Macleod Campbell and Thomas Erskine in Scotland, and in particular, of Friedrich Schleiermacher.[2] Above all, there follows the monumental reworking of the doctrine by Karl Barth, which has provided the Reformed tradition with its most comprehensive, sophisticated, and influential alternative to the historic account encapsulated in the Canons of Dordt.

With this plethora of options to choose from, and alternatives available from Arminian, "process," and other perspectives, the obvious question to ask of a book of this kind must be "Why?"[3] Why propose yet another way of thinking about election, and why do so from a Reformed point of view?

In part, the reason is deeply personal. I embarked on this exploration of the doctrine of election because I struggle to find a scriptural and theological place to rest, in straightforwardly upholding either historic Reformed orthodoxy or Barth's reworking of the doctrine. Yet I consider the theological contours that shape a Reformed approach to election to be fundamentally correct. So, for example, some of the basic assumptions underlying all that follows are that God's eternal electing decision determines the shape of his engagement with creation and creation's ultimate goal, and that election is entirely the expression of God's sovereign grace, unconditioned and unmerited. In election, God chooses some and not oth-

2. John Macleod Campbell, *The Nature of the Atonement* (1865; reprint, with an introduction by J. B. Torrance, Grand Rapids: Eerdmans, 1996); Thomas Erskine, *The Doctrine of Election*, 2nd ed. (Edinburgh: David Douglas, 1878); Friedrich Schleiermacher, "Über die Lehre von der Erwählung; besonders in Beziehung auf Herrn Dr. Bretschneiders Aphorismen," *Kritische Gesamtausgabe*, vol. I/10, ed. H.-F. Traulen and M. Ohst (Berlin: De Gruyter, 1990), pp. 145-222; and *The Christian Faith*, ed. H. R. Mackintosh and J. S. Stewart (Edinburgh: T. & T. Clark, 1928), pp. 536-60. For an overview of Schleiermacher's treatise and a brief account of its relationship to his discussion in *Christian Faith*, see Matthias Gockel, "New Perspectives on an Old Debate: Friedrich Schleiermacher's Essay on Election," *IJST* 6 (July 2004): 301-18. See also his *Barth and Schleiermacher on the Doctrine of Election: A Systematic-Theological Comparison* (Oxford: Oxford University Press, 2007).

3. For a recent popular discussion of a range of alternative positions, see Chad Owen Brand, ed., *Perspectives on Election: Five Views* (Nashville: B. & H. Publishing, 2006). For the development of a "process" doctrine of election, see Donna Bowman, *The Divine Decision* (Louisville: Westminster/John Knox Press, 2002).

ers, in Colin Gunton's phrase, "apart from their willing and in advance of their acceptance,"[4] and there is no capacity to love, trust, and follow God that God does not give. Again, in Gunton's terms, "both the beginning of faith and the capacity to continue in it are the gifts of God."[5] God is sovereign over our response to him.

At first glance, then, it might seem as though I am simply perpetuating the obsession. I engage with the two most prominent streams of thought on election within the Reformed tradition: that of historic Reformed orthodoxy, represented by John Owen, and that of Karl Barth. The questions and priorities that inform my quest to rearticulate the doctrine are rooted in the Reformed heritage that shapes my theology as a whole. This means that some of the questions I seek to answer will seem redundant to others, and some of the questions that arise from different ways of considering election will not be asked at all. Even the idea that inspired the whole enterprise — that it might be fruitful to explore election in relation to the scriptural and systematic relationship between election and the *imago dei* — is a reflection of the influence of my heritage upon my thinking. The Reformed tradition has always forged the closest of links between the two.

Yet, arising from my probing of the Reformed heritage and a reexamination of the scriptural contours of election and its relationship to the *imago dei* is what I hope will be an account of the doctrine that is also open to being taken up more widely. I formulate three scriptural guiding principles to shape a theological account of the doctrine and develop the conviction that "representation" — representing God to others and others to God — is a key category for understanding the nature and purpose of election. Neither the scriptural guiding principles I put forward nor the representational dynamic that I develop necessarily requires a Reformed frame of reference. I pursue them in this context because, as I have said, I happen to believe that the premises of a Reformed theological approach are correct. Nevertheless, the leading ideas of what I have come to call "election to representation" can be interpreted within theological traditions other than my own.

This is a reflection of the fact that while election may exercise a particular fascination for those of us who are Reformed, it is not a Reformed doctrine. It is a doctrine for the whole church. For all the problems raised

---

4. Colin Gunton, "Election and Ecclesiology in the Post-Constantinian Church," *SJT* 53 (2000): 212-27, 215.
5. Gunton, "Election and Ecclesiology," p. 218.

by the use (and abuse) of particular formulations, and for all the debate surrounding the various ways of understanding it, the concept of election itself lies at the very heart of the scriptural narrative of God's dealings with the world.

Reforming a Reformed Doctrine of Election:
Scriptural Themes, Pneumatological Focus

To reconsider the issue of election is especially uncomfortable at a time when the struggle to deal justly and peaceably with the tension between the particular and the universal is acute, nowhere more so than in the context of religiously motivated discourse and action.[6] Nevertheless, we cannot disregard or downplay a crucial scriptural category for the self-understanding of the people of God, and for the unfolding of God's purposes for humanity in general and the whole created order.

Lesslie Newbigin reminds us of this by making consideration of the doctrine of election central to his development of a Trinitarian theology of mission. He does so precisely *because* election is "the key to the relation between the universal and the particular" which is at the heart of the nature of mission, and also because it is a doctrine "that permeates and controls the whole Bible. . . . From the beginning of the Bible to its end we are presented with the story of a universal purpose carried out through a continuous series of particular choices."[7] To speak faithfully of who God is in relation to us, and who we are in relation to God, theology must unavoidably begin to speak in terms of a doctrine of election in which God chooses to

---

6. Even though it is now well over a decade, and a tumultuous decade at that, since the appearance of *The One, the Three and the Many,* this still serves as a powerful analysis of the wider theological, philosophical, and cultural issues at stake in the debate. Colin E. Gunton, *The One, the Three and the Many: God, Creation and the Culture of Modernity* (Cambridge: Cambridge University Press, 1993).

7. Lesslie Newbigin, *The Open Secret: An Introduction to the Theology of Mission,* rev. ed. (London: SPCK, 1995), p. 68. See chap. 7 ("The Gospel in World History") *passim* for his discussion of election in relation to the mission of the church, in which he offers an astute diagnosis of some of the reasons for contemporary discomfort with the concept. In addition to discussing ways in which he considers the doctrine to have been distorted, he associates the neglect of and distaste for the notion of election with tendencies to allow monadic individualism to dominate the conception of the self, and with the blunt assessment that the doctrine "touches the raw nerves of contemporary bourgeois guilt," in which any suggestion of apparent "elitism" is the "unforgivable sin" (p. 68).

enact his universal purposes through the singular particularity of calling out a chosen covenant people.

Contemporary theology's task in this regard is assisted by a renewed interest in election within biblical studies. English-speaking Old Testament scholarship, including work from both Jewish and Christian perspectives, has challenged longstanding presuppositions concerning the shape of Israel's election in relation to that of the church. As we shall see, this has resulted in a discernible convergence of opinion on the nature and purpose of election between various strands of Old Testament scholarship, and between elements of Old and New Testament studies, most particularly N. T. Wright's description of the Pauline reinterpretation of election in the light of the "climax of the covenant" in the life, death, and resurrection of Israel's representative Messiah.

It is in exploring these convergences and the conceptual links between election and the image of God in both the Old and New Testament that I find scriptural challenges to aspects of earlier Reformed orthodoxy and Barth's doctrine of election alike, as well as the resources for a fresh approach to election through the category of "representation."

Drawing out the implications of the scriptural witness to election in Israel, in Christ, and in the church suggests that we can speak of a twofold ontology of election: that it is intrinsic to the being-and-doing of the elect community consciously and unself-consciously to *represent God to others* and *others to God*. In particular, I explore the notion that the elect are set apart to hold the alienated and apparently rejected "other" before God, and so within the sphere of God's promised covenant blessings. I consider this representational dynamic to be at the heart of the way in which God's purposes for the rest of humanity unfold. The lynchpin of this dynamic is the work of the Holy Spirit, forger of the relationships between God and the elect — and between the elect and the rest of humanity — upon which the unfolding of the triune God's electing determination in the economy depends.

One of the major themes throughout will therefore be to trace the role of the Holy Spirit in election. This approach brings key scriptural and Trinitarian issues into sharp focus. A delicate balance between christology and pneumatology in election is essential for the full recognition that election is both "*in Christ*" and "*by the Spirit.*"

Taking a pneumatological approach also allows the earlier Reformed tradition to be heard more clearly on its own terms, rather than in having to respond defensively to Barth's account. One of the consequences of

Barth's dramatic reinterpretation of election is that christology has become the dominant category in the discussion not only of his own doctrine, but also of historic Reformed orthodoxy. Christology is the focus of Barth's innovation, and of his dissatisfaction with the earlier formulations. Not surprisingly, christology is therefore the focus of the concerted defense of the tradition mounted most notably by Richard Muller.[8] One byproduct of the intense attention given to christology is that the carefully nuanced, scripturally and trinitarianly rich election pneumatology of the earlier tradition has largely dropped from view. This is one of its profound strengths, while by contrast, the Spirit's role is recognized as one of the areas of weakness in Barth's reworking of the doctrine.

The need to give renewed attention to the pneumatology of election has not gone unrecognized. In his "Election and Ecclesiology in the Post-Constantinian Church," Colin Gunton offers a programmatic sketch for a reconsideration of the doctrine of election in which the need for a stronger pneumatology plays a prominent part. He also juxtaposes the two theologians who will be the principal Reformed interlocutors here, as uncomfortable but fruitful partners for contemporary theology's attempt to rethink the doctrine.

While not wishing to relinquish the fundamental insights that Barth's christology offers into the nature of God's election, Gunton highlights some of the problematic elements of Barth's doctrine, suggesting that what is required is a stronger eschatological orientation and a richer election pneumatology than Barth provides. He points us to the way in which Owen expresses the relationship between Christ and the Spirit (and christology and pneumatology) in Christ's election (and ours) as potential resources for reconsidering the nature, purpose, and dynamic of the church's election.

At the same time, he wishes to avoid Owen's adherence to individual double predestination and limited atonement.[9] It is at precisely this point that we are confronted with the systematic question that a focus on pneumatology will always raise for a Reformed doctrine of election. Given that the gift of the Spirit which enables response to God is precisely that — sovereign, unconditioned divine gift — Gunton gives no indication as to how it might be possible for a rich election pneumatology such as Owen's not to lead straight back to the account of election that Owen upholds.

---

8. See especially his *Christ and the Decree: Christology and Predestination in Reformed Theology from Calvin to Perkins* (Durham, NC: Labyrinth Press, 1986).

9. Gunton, "Election and Ecclesiology," pp. 221-23.

In the brief compass of this article, however, Gunton's task is simply to sketch some possible outlines. The actual shape of a renewed doctrine of election is less clear than the direction we might take in order to set about the task. He remarks that if we are to see the Spirit too as "electing God," and "if the Spirit is the one who gathers the church to the Father through Christ in order that his will be done on earth, then somewhere in that vast dogmatic minefield are to be found clues to the way we should take."[10]

To attempt to pick a way through this minefield and so to begin to set out what such a doctrine of election might look like is the aim of all that follows.

Reforming a Reformed Doctrine of Election:
Outlining the Task Ahead

Part I looks in turn at the ways in which Owen and Barth present the doctrine of election, and the links they forge between election and the *imago dei.* John Owen stands as the representative of historic Reformed orthodoxy in the Dordt tradition. His staunch defense of election understood in terms of individual double predestination, coupled with a particularly rich pneumatology and a distinctive approach to the *imago dei,* make him an ideal dialogue partner for both the analytical task and the constructive enterprise to follow.

Barth is also a highly apt dialogue partner in that he offers us *two* accounts of election — the doctrine of election he sets forth in the *Göttingen Dogmatics,* and which influences *Church Dogmatics* I/1 and 2, and his mature doctrine of election in *CD* II/2. Each has a very different understanding of the significance of the Spirit's role, and for this reason, Barth provides a fascinating test case for some of the pneumatological issues raised by a Reformed approach to election. It is through Barth's two doctrines of election, as well as Owen's account, that we are starkly confronted with the pneumatological crux for any Reformed doctrine of election. Does a scripturally and trinitarianly robust role for the Spirit in election lead only and inexorably towards the historic tradition's interpretation of the double decree? This is the "pneumatological question" which gives Part I its title.

In order to probe the possibility of formulating an account of election that is able to maintain the robust pneumatology of the earlier Reformed

---

10. Gunton, "Election and Ecclesiology," p. 220.

tradition without relinquishing some of the fundamental insights of Barth's reworking of the doctrine, Part II begins by asking us to investigate afresh aspects of the scriptural contours of election. This issues in three scriptural guiding principles, and an approach to election through the representational dynamic noted above.

This way of thinking about the nature of election points towards a more radical participation of the elect community in the outworking of God's purposes of blessing than the doctrine of election usually implies. In Chapter 5 I begin to explore what I have called "election to representation" specifically in relation to the church. To do so, I enter into dialogue with Stanley Grenz and Miroslav Volf, probing the use they make of the concept of "perichoretic" personhood in relation to the ecclesial imaging of God within the context of human being-in-relation as the universal *imago dei*. With regard to contemporary theology, as well as to contemporary biblical scholarship, the drawing together of reflection on election and the image proves mutually illuminating.

Part III opens with the recognition that the account of election I develop here raises some sharp questions. In Chapter 6, I consider some of these, firstly concerning the church's role in election in relation to the once-for-all work of Christ and his continuing high-priestly ministry, and secondly with regard to the relationship between the elect community of the church and the rest of humanity. Assistance in responding to the latter comes through a brief exploration of one of the most extreme tests of the way in which we understand human being-in-relation. In the situation of dementia we find a "parable" which, for all its dangers and limitations, draws together, illuminates, and enriches the representational dynamic of election that I am developing here.

This leads to a fuller description of the Spirit's role, and some suggestions concerning the eschatological consummation of election at the parousia. With this I turn again to the "pneumatological problem," and the way in which election to representation seeks to maintain a scripturally and trinitarianly robust election pneumatology comparable to that of the historic Reformed tradition alongside central insights from Barth's reinterpretation of the doctrine.

In the final chapter, I bring my understanding of election and the scriptural guiding principles upon which it is based into direct engagement with Owen and Barth, with some final thoughts on election and eschatology, this time drawing out the implications of my approach to election for the question of the extent of salvation in Christ.

The Epilogue seeks less to summarize that which has gone before than to look ahead, suggesting possibilities for dialogue, and some directions in which election to representation as I outline it here might be further developed. From all of this, my hope is that the wider church might find positive ways to reappropriate this central but so often divisive and damaging doctrine.

PART I

Posing a Pneumatological Problem

CHAPTER 1

Election, the Image, and the Spirit: John Owen

Rediscovering the "Forgotten Man"
of English Theology

Even in a period that produced an abundance of extraordinary and fascinating individuals, John Owen cut a notable figure at the heart of theological and political life in one of the most turbulent periods of British history.[1] Summoned to preach to the House of Commons on the day following the execution of Charles I, he later became one of Cromwell's chaplains, until his forthright objections to Cromwell's inclination to take the crown ruptured the close relationship between them.[2]

Having been at the center of political and theological life during the Commonwealth and Protectorate, Owen remained unwavering in his adherence to dissenting Congregationalism throughout the persecutions that followed the Restoration. Noting Owen's extensive contacts and powerful intellect at the service of the non-conformist cause, the French Ambassa-

---

1. The standard biography of Owen is Peter Toon, *God's Statesman: The Life and Work of John Owen* (Exeter: Paternoster Press, 1971). See also Andrew Thompson, "The Life of Dr Owen," in Owen, *Works*, vol. 1, pp. xvix-cxxii. There is also a brief biographical sketch in Sinclair B. Ferguson, *John Owen on the Christian Life* (Edinburgh: Banner of Truth Trust, 1987), pp. 1-19, and an opening biographical chapter in Carl R. Trueman, *John Owen: Reformed Catholic Renaissance Man* (Aldershot: Ashgate, 2007).

2. Neatly encapsulating much about the decades of the mid-seventeenth century, Owen was also Dean of Christ Church and Vice Chancellor of Oxford University during the 1650s, having left Queen's College before completing his BD as a result of the increasingly rigorous application of the statutes of the then-Chancellor and Archbishop of Canterbury, William Laud.

dor wrote to Louis XIV that Owen had as much religious and political influence in London as its Bishop.[3]

Recognized as among the most erudite theologians of his generation, Owen was also a deep admirer and strong supporter of John Bunyan. Constantly engaged in detailed doctrinal controversies, he also demonstrates deep pastoral concern. In surveying Owen's life as well as his theological corpus, we are left with the inescapable impression of the breadth of his compass.

Until recently, however, in spite of his intellectual stature and political prominence during his lifetime, Owen has provoked relatively little interest either from theologians or from historians. In his seminal study of Owen's theology, Carl Trueman suggests that Owen has been the "forgotten man" of English theology, and the neglect of Owen has likewise been noted from the perspective of historians of the period.[4] Nevertheless, in recent decades there has been a resurgence in Owen studies, from reappraisals of his theological method in its historical context to suggestions for the positive reappropriation of elements of his thought for contemporary theology.[5] Here, aspects of Owen's account of election, the image, and the Spirit will set out some of the key questions for a Reformed approach to election that will occupy the remainder of Part I, and will provide some central themes and concepts for the attempt to rearticulate the doctrine in Parts II and III.

---

3. Quoted in John Carswell, *The Porcupine: The Life of Algernon Sidney* (London: John Murray, 1989), p. 181.

4. Carl R. Trueman, *The Claims of Truth: John Owen's Trinitarian Theology* (Carlisle: Paternoster, 1998), p. 1. See pp. 1-7 for some suggested reasons for this neglect. For the need to give more attention to the role of Owen and the other chaplains to Oliver Cromwell in the historical study of the period, see J. C. Davis, "Cromwell's Religion," in *Oliver Cromwell and the English Revolution*, ed. John Morrill (Essex: Longman, 1990), pp. 181-208, esp. p. 205.

5. Accounts of Owen's theological method and the contours of his theology include Ferguson, *Christian Life*; Trueman, *Claims of Truth*; Sebastian Rehnman, *Divine Discourse: The Theological Methodology of John Owen* (Grand Rapids: Baker Academic, 2002); and Kelly M. Kapic, *Communion with God: The Divine and the Human in the Theology of John Owen* (Grand Rapids: Baker Academic, 2007). Explorations of particular doctrinal loci include Alan Spence, *Incarnation and Inspiration: John Owen and the Coherence of Christology* (London: T. & T. Clark, 2007); Randall C. Gleason, *John Calvin and John Owen on Mortification: A Comparative Study in Reformed Spirituality* (New York: Peter Lang, 1995); Colin Gunton's considerations of Owen's ecclesiology and pneumatology in "Election and Ecclesiology in the Post-Constantinian Church," *SJT* 53 (2000): 212-27; and Jon D. Payne, *John Owen on the Lord's Supper* (Edinburgh: Banner of Truth Trust, 2004).

Election, the Image, and the Spirit in Context: The Shape of Owen's Theology

While much of Owen's life and work has been left in relative obscurity, one aspect of his thought has been more widely and consistently recognized. Without doubt, he is one of the strongest champions of what might be termed the classical Reformed orthodox position on the doctrine of election. Owen's *The Death of Death in the Death of Christ* (1647) is an exhaustive scriptural and theological defense of the efficacy of Christ's death for salvation, and therefore of individual double predestination and "limited atonement."[6] It is among the best-known works in his extensive corpus, and stands with Perkins's *A Golden Chaine* as one of the most famous (or notorious) English presentations of the strictest Reformed interpretation of the doctrine of election.[7]

Moreover, *The Death of Death* is not the only place in which Owen demonstrates his interest in the doctrine; his first published work is the anti-Arminian *A Display of Arminianism* (1642).[8] Throughout his life Owen's theological priorities are shaped by an abiding concern to combat what he considers to be the two greatest contemporary threats to the integrity of the gospel: Arminian and Socinian thought. As a result Owen repeatedly seeks to state and defend a fundamental core of intimately related doctrines, the distortion of which he considers to lie at the root of all falsification of Christian thinking and living. These are, above all, the Trinitarian being of God, the Chalcedonian understanding of Christ's person, and the way in which both of these considerations must inform our understanding of the decrees of God and their outworking. While one or other of these may at times receive greater emphasis, each implies the other two.

Owen's theology, then, might best be described as spiraling round these three ellipses, rather than as a "systematic" enterprise unfolding from a single first principle. In particular, Trueman's detailed and persuasive analysis puts to rest any notion that Owen's theology is a system shaped by

---

6. It is to be found in Owen, *Works*, vol. 10, pp. 139-428.

7. Perkins's *Armilla Aurea* (first published in 1590, revised in 1592) is perhaps best known, like Beza's *Tabula praedestinationis,* for its chart setting out the causes of salvation and damnation. It can be found in *The Workes of . . . William Perkins,* 3 vols. (Cambridge, 1609), vol. 1, pp. 11-117.

8. Owen, *Works*, vol. 10, pp. 1-137.

the inexorable unfolding of Aristotelian teleology, with an abstract double decree at its head.[9]

If the shape of Owen's thinking is not "systematic" in this sense, neither is the nature of his corpus. He offers nothing comparable to his near contemporary Francis Turretin's *Institutio theologia elencticae* or even to Calvin's *Institutio*.[10] Instead, his extensive output largely comprises theological and pastoral treatises on key loci, often in response to contemporary controversies, and a magisterial seven-volume commentary on the Epistle to the Hebrews.

The limitations of such an approach for another of the concerns in this chapter — Owen's account of the *imago dei* — are self evident, in that Owen nowhere presents us with a treatise devoted to the image of God. Instead, he provides occasional discussions of aspects of the doctrine in the

---

9. The account of Owen's theology in Trueman's *Claims of Truth* is greatly to be welcomed, both for its analysis of Owen's thought and its concern to place Owen within his contemporary context. While it is not a direct concern here, and cannot be pursued in detail, it is hardly surprising that Owen studies have been drawn into the so-called "Calvin against the Calvinists" debate. Trueman's work responds throughout to Alan Clifford's account of Owen in his *Atonement and Justification: English Evangelical Theology 1640-1790* (Oxford: Clarendon Press, 1990), which in turn reflects the way in which, e.g., J. B. Torrance points to Owen as an example of the most pernicious kind of Reformed "scholasticism" ("The Incarnation and 'Limited Atonement,'" *Evangelical Quarterly* 55, no. 2 [1982]: 83-94). The first chapter of Gleason's *Mortification* ("Calvin and Calvinism: The Debate") likewise sets his work in this context. For the wider contours of the debate concerning the relationship of Reformed orthodoxy to Calvin, see on the one hand, e.g., Basil Hall, "Calvin against the Calvinists," in *John Calvin*, Courtenay Studies in Reformation Theology No. 1, ed. G. E. Duffield (Abingdon, UK: Sutton Courtenay Press, 1966), pp. 19-37; R. T. Kendall, *Calvin and English Calvinism to 1649* (Oxford: Oxford University Press, 1979); and on the other, e.g., Paul Helm, *Calvin and the Calvinists* (Edinburgh: Banner of Truth, 1982); Richard Muller, *Christ and the Decree: Christology and Predestination in Reformed Theology from Calvin to Perkins* (Durham, NC: Labyrinth Press, 1986) and his articles, "Calvin and the 'Calvinists': Assessing Continuities and Discontinuities between the Reformation and Orthodoxy," *Calvin Theological Journal* 30, no. 2 (1995): 345-75 and 31, no. 1 (1996): 125-60; and *The Unaccommodated Calvin: Studies in the Foundation of a Theological Tradition* (Oxford: Oxford University Press, 2000). For a brief overview and analysis of the debate as a whole, see Stephen R. Holmes, "Calvin against the Calvinists?" in his *Listening to the Past: The Place of Tradition in Theology* (Carlisle: Paternoster, 2002), pp. 68-85.

10. As Trueman points out (*Claims of Truth*, p. 48), only one of Owen's works — his *Theologoumena Pantodapa* (1661), in Owen, *Works*, vol. 17, pp. 1-488 — offers a form of theological "summa." In a study of Owen that in many ways complements Trueman's, Rehnman (*Divine Discourse*) makes *Theologoumena Pantodapa* his principal text for analyzing Owen's theological method.

context of wider concerns. The image, in common with his presentation of many other doctrinal loci, is discussed and clarified less for its own sake than as part of broader arguments centered upon expounding and defending the scriptural and theological validity, as well as the practical consequences for Christian living, of the three ellipses mentioned earlier.

Nevertheless, Owen offers a sufficiently wide-ranging presentation of the image for a consistent picture to emerge with considerable detail and clarity.[11] The contours of Owen's understanding of the image can be drawn from his *Pneumatologia* (1674) and his *Christologia* (1679).[12] Since both of these works also present the core of Owen's doctrine of election, and both go to considerable lengths to spell out the scripturally shaped, soteriologically decisive pneumatological dynamic that binds the doctrines of election and the image of God together, they will form the primary sources for the following account.

If Owen is most widely known for his upholding of individual double predestination and limited atonement, and if his distinctive understanding of the *imago dei* has as yet received little attention, perhaps the most widely appreciated legacy of his theology is his particularly rich pneumatology.[13] As we shall seek to show, this is inseparable from his account of election, which is in turn inseparable from his understanding of the person and work of the Spirit in the triune life of God, and therefore from his approach to the relationship between the Spirit and the incarnate life of the

11. Since my particular concern is with the role of the Spirit, and the relationship between the image and election, a full account and analysis of Owen's understanding of the image of God cannot be offered here. See Kapic's *Communion with God,* chap. 2 for a broader account of Owen on the image, in the context of his insightful account of Owen's "anthroposensitive" theology, and also my "The Pneumatology of the 'Lost' Image in John Owen," *Westminster Theological Journal* 71, no. 2 (Fall 2009): 323-35.

12. *Pneumatologia, or A Discourse Concerning the Holy Spirit,* vols. 3 and 4 of *Works.* Since the issues of particular concern in the present work are treated in Books I-V, and these are found in the third volume, all page references to *Pneumatologia* refer to volume 3 of *Works; Christologia, or A Declaration of the Glorious Mystery of the Person of Christ — God and Man,* in *Works,* vol. 1, pp. 1-272, hereafter cited as *Christologia.* The consistency of Owen's approach to the *imago dei* is such that the remainder of his corpus, including the sermons and the Hebrews commentary, repeats or expands the primary points made in these two works.

13. In addition to Trueman's work, and to the significance accorded to Owen's pneumatology in Gunton's appeal for a renewed ecclesiology in "Election and Ecclesiology," extended reflection on Owen's pneumatology is to be found in, e.g., Ferguson, *Christian Life;* Alan Spence's *Incarnation and Inspiration;* and Gleason's *Mortification,* chap. 3, "John Owen's Doctrine of Mortification," *passim.*

Son. Owen's pneumatology is anchored firmly in and related rigorously to the New Testament presentation of the Spirit's work towards Christ and towards us, and is the lynchpin of the relationship that Owen perceives between the doctrines of election and the image of God. There are few who could set out more clearly and cogently than Owen the nexus of concerns that will occupy the remainder of this work.

The Spirit, Election, and the Trinitarian Being of God

It is axiomatic for the whole of Owen's theology that the economic acts of God express the being of God, or in his own terms, that "the order of the dispensation of the divine persons towards us ariseth from the order of their own subsistence."[14] Inner-Trinitarian relations are a touchstone for the right understanding of all doctrines. Thus, the nature of the Spirit's role in election is understood at once as the reflection of the implications of the New Testament witness, in which the Spirit is the agent of the new creation in Christ, and also as the expression of a principle that is close to the heart of Owen's theology as a whole: the *filioque*-shaped Trinitarian consistency of all of God's dealings with the created order.

Owen is firmly conventional in his adherence to the Western theological tradition's understanding that in the New Testament witness to Christ as the bearer and bestower of the Spirit, and to the inseparability of the Spirit's work from that of Christ, lie both the warrant for and expression of the dual procession.[15] That which sets Owen apart from many is the rigor with which he allows this to inform every aspect of his theology. This is particularly notable in his strongly Trinitarian approach to the electing decree of God and its unfolding in time. Trueman rightly observes that for Owen, the intra-divine covenant of redemption and its outworking in the economy as the covenant of grace are "a specifically functional and soteriological application of the *filioque*."[16]

Thus, in a clear reflection of the inner-Trinitarian order of being, we find that it is the Father and the Son who together determine the extent

14. *Pneumatologia*, p. 61.

15. In addition, of course, this constitutes a powerful argument for the divinity of Christ. The sending of the Spirit by the Son as well as the Father is, not surprisingly, of considerable significance in Owen's defense of a Chalcedonian christology; e.g., *Pneumatologia*, pp. 60-64.

16. Trueman, *Claims of Truth*, p. 146.

and nature of the redeeming work to be undertaken by the Son in our humanity. Owen speaks of God's delight in his determinations, and "Especially . . . these counsels of the Father and the Son, as to the redemption and salvation of the church, wherein they delight and mutually rejoice in each other. . . ."[17]

It is a major aspect of this mutual delight that it is both *in and with* the Son that the Father determines the salvation of the elect, and *in and by* the Son that this is to be accomplished. God "delighteth in these his eternal counsels in Christ . . . [and] because they were all laid in him and with him, therefore [Christ] is said to be his 'delight continually before the world was.'" Owen writes also that it is the "ineffable delight" of God that "whereas in all other effects of his goodness he gives of *his own,* herein he *gave himself,* in taking our nature upon him. . . ."[18]

In turn, as the full expression of the *filioque* dynamic, it is the particular task of the Holy Spirit to ensure the fulfillment in the economy of that which has been determined by the Father and the Son. As the Spirit owes his being to the Father and the Son, so the Spirit's task in the unfolding of election "is not an original but a perfecting work." It is therefore

> the peculiar work of the Holy Spirit to make those things of the Father and the Son effectual unto . . . the elect . . . [so that] in the work of the new creation, God . . . intends the especial revelation of *each person of the whole Trinity* distinctly. . . .[19]

17. *Christologia*, p. 58. See chapter IV, "The Person of Christ the Foundation of all the Counsels of God," pp. 54-64, *passim,* for an extended discussion of the Father and the Son in relation to the decree of election and, through his eternal determination as *incarnandus,* of the eternally elected person of Christ.

18. *Christologia*, p. 59, Owen's italics. For Christ himself as the primary elect of God, and the one in whose election the elect share, see in particular p. 60, in which Owen makes clear that it is first Christ who is the delight and object of God's electing, and not the elect themselves, "in that *in* him were all these counsels [of election] laid, and *through* him were they all to be accomplished" (Owen's italics). See chapter IV, *passim,* for his detailed exposition of Christ as the eternal object and foundation of the electing decree. In other words, to borrow Barth's idiom, Christ is both Electing God, as co-author of the decree, and Elect Man as the one in whose election the elect participate. Muller's painstaking work points us to similar conclusions with regard to earlier expressions of Reformed orthodoxy, such that it can no longer be said without serious qualification that an unsearchable first principle displaces a fully Trinitarian and Christ-shaped understanding of election and predestination, or that the work of Christ is simply subordinated to a causal structure (*Christ and the Decree, passim*).

19. *Pneumatologia*, pp. 189-90, Owen's italics. It is typical of Owen's pneumatological

Thus, while the Spirit's work has its source in and depends upon that of Father and Son, theirs depends upon the Spirit to be brought to its fulfillment. After the eternal counsel of the Father and the Son, and the mediation of the Son,

> There yet remains *the actual application* . . . that [we] may be partakers in the mediation of the Son; and herein is the Holy Spirit to be manifested and glorified, that he also, together with the Father and the Son, may be known, adored, worshipped. . . .[20]

In all of this, we see the outworking for election of a general axiom that operates throughout Owen's theology. Since the Spirit is the logically sequential "third" in the Trinity, so it is the Spirit's task to bring to fulfillment the determinations of the triune God in the economy. For this reason, Owen remarks that in every work of God, "the *concluding, completing, perfecting acts* are ascribed to the Holy Ghost," and the Spirit is therefore the only way in which God chooses to act directly in the created order.[21] It is the Spirit's primary overall function for Owen to be the "immediate . . . efficient cause of all external divine operations."[22]

In turn, the Spirit's role in election clearly corresponds to the notion of the Spirit as the *vinculum amoris* who both expresses and completes the mutual love of Father and Son in the Trinity. His person and work mean that he particularly is the one who conveys the love of God to humanity and enables the human response of love to God in return. Hence, "As the *descending* of God towards us in love and grace issues or ends in the work of the Spirit in us and on us, so all our *ascending* towards him begins therein."[23]

---

care and Trinitarian thoroughness to ensure that we do not consider the Spirit as a "stranger" to the counsels of the Father and the Son, as if he were simply the agent of a decree established without his involvement. Rather, since he proceeds from both the Father and the Son, "he is equally participant of their counsels," and has an infinite knowledge of them (p. 196). Likewise, Owen has also firmly established (pp. 116ff.) that the work of the Spirit in election is not only the outcome of his being sent by the Father and the Son, but is also his own free determination and undertaking. In this, says Owen, we see the nature of his eternal being, in that the Spirit's role in election demonstrates both his dependence for his subsistence on the Father and the Son, and that his work is "his own personal voluntary acting" (p. 117).

20. *Pneumatologia*, p. 190, Owen's italics.

21. *Pneumatologia*, p. 94, Owen's italics. As we shall see below, this exerts an important influence on Owen's christology.

22. *Pneumatologia*, p. 161.

23. *Pneumatologia*, p. 200, Owen's italics; see also, e.g., p. 157, where Owen reminds us

The Spirit's work is therefore decisive in the unfolding of election in the economy, and following the New Testament witness, the concept of being "in Christ" by the Spirit, and so of union with Christ effected by the Spirit, lies at the heart of Owen's understanding of election and the Christian life. The New Testament indicates that it is the Spirit who brings the completed work of Christ to bear upon us and in us, as the agent of union with Christ and new creation in Christ. More will be said later on the role of the Spirit in the New Testament in designating those who belong to the new covenant community in Christ. For the moment, Owen rightly discerns that election is inseparable from the nexus of themes drawn together around the notion of union with Christ, and in turn, that everything about our being found to be "in Christ" presupposes and entails the work of the Spirit in us. Thus, in a characteristic summary, Owen states that "[w]hatever is wrought in believers by the *Spirit of Christ*, it is in their *union* to the person of Christ, and by virtue thereof," such that the Spirit's task in election can be summed up straightforwardly as "to unite us to Christ; and . . . to communicate all grace unto us from Christ, by virtue of that union."[24] Our election is both grounded in and might be summed up by the concept of being "in Christ by the Spirit."

It must be made clear that this does not signify that one only "becomes" elect through the work of the Spirit in the economy. The elect are eternally elect in Christ before the foundation of the world. It is simply that for Owen and the historic Reformed tradition the Trinitarian nature of the decree and its unfolding in time means that there can finally be no participating in Christ's election that does not also include the work of the Spirit. It is this which makes the decree a fully Trinitarian determination and action.

With this in mind, in addition to acknowledging the determinative

---

that no grace or mercy comes to us from God except by the Spirit, and neither is there any return of faith or love by us to God "but what is effectively wrought in us . . . by him alone."

24. *Pneumatologia*, p. 516, Owen's italics. See also, e.g., *Meditations and Discourses on the Glory of Christ in his Person, Office and Grace . . .* in *Works*, vol. 1, pp. 365-67, where Owen reflects upon Christ's giving of the Spirit to the elect, upon which "follows an ineffable union between him and them" (p. 365). The shaping influence of the concept of union with Christ by the Spirit for Owen, as for Calvin, is a major aspect of Gleason's argument that differences in methodology and discourse between the two theologians do not create major differences of theological substance. See, e.g., *Mortification*, pp. 85-95, 147-48. For a brief discussion of the importance of union with Christ in Owen's theology see Kapic, *Communion with God*, pp. 139-42.

role of the Spirit towards us, it is also imperative to recognize the full significance of the Spirit's role in the decree in relation to the Godhead. As the one person of the Godhead who acts directly in the created order, and as the one through whom the terms of the covenant are therefore accomplished in the economy, the Spirit is the guarantor of the unity of God's determination *ad intra* and *ad extra* in the electing decree. Only if we grasp the centrality of this are we able to appreciate that what is at stake in the Spirit's role in election is not simply logical consistency, nor even an attempt to ensure that full account is taken of the New Testament presentation of the Spirit's work, but also the integrity of the being-and-act of God.

At the fulcrum of the relationship between the unfolding of the decree in time and the integrity of the Godhead is the mutual binding of the Spirit's work and that of the ascended Christ. Just as the Son's work is both his own, and the fulfillment of the Father's will, so the Spirit's work is both his own and is the unfolding of the Son's accomplished and continuing work. As we have noted, the Spirit's work in election depends upon Christ's act of bestowal, in accordance with his procession from the Son as well as the Father, and in turn, the fulfillment of Christ's work depends upon the work of the Spirit.

Hence, it is as the Spirit brings about the efficacious application of the work of Christ, on the basis of his mediation, that there is a basic unity in the *Son's* own role in the eternal decree of election and its execution in time, and between the inner-Trinitarian relations that constitute the being of God, the electing decree of God, and the saving acts of God in human history. As co-author of the electing decree with the Father, the Son determines with the Father those who will be saved and the manner in which that salvation will be wrought. As the incarnate Son and primary object of God's electing will, the Son in his atoning work accomplishes through the Spirit all that is needful for that salvation. In his ascended mediation, the elect receive the gift of the Spirit and so are brought to participate in the salvation determined for them in Christ before the foundation of the world.

Here, then, are the theological contours that lead to Owen's upholding of individual double predestination and its strict corollary of "limited atonement." Whatever we make of this interpretation of God's electing decision — and we will have cause to question aspects of it in due course — it cannot be emphasized too strongly that to dismiss it merely as the logical outcome of an abstract system is to avoid the crucial questions that it poses. Instead, we must recognize it as the *theological* consequence of

Owen's total and rigorous commitment to the unity of the person and work of the Son, and in particular, in the present context, to the integrity of the person and work of the Spirit. This in turn is reflected in an election pneumatology that is rooted in the New Testament witness to the Spirit as the gift of the ascended Christ to his people, and its identification of the elect people of God as those who are "in Christ" by the Spirit.

These are issues to be taken up both in analyzing Barth's election pneumatology and in the reexamination of the scriptural contours of election in Part II. For the moment, however, it is Owen's attempt to be faithful to the New Testament understanding of the Spirit — whose particular role is to create the community of the church, through the new birth of union with Christ and the continuing new creation of transformation in Christlikeness — that leads us to examine the intimate relationship between election and the image in his thought.

The Spirit, the Image, and Election

To consider Owen's understanding of the image of God in the light of his pneumatology is to recognize that the same basic principles hold sway: in adherence to the implications of *filioque* and the New Testament witness, the Spirit is both the one through whom God acts in the created order and the only possibility of a life lived in love towards God. In addition, we must note that Owen considers our only access to understanding the image as created is through the lens of the image as it is restored, first in the person of Christ and second in those united to him. Owen remarks that since the image has been

> lost from our nature, it [is] utterly impossible we should have a just comprehension of it . . . until it was renewed and exemplified in the human nature of Christ . . . nor is the Holy Spirit . . . given unto us for any other end but to unite us unto him, and make us like him.[25]

Since it is only in the work of new creation that we can understand the original nature of the image, and since the New Testament makes clear that the Spirit is the agent of that new creation, it is part of the integrity of the Spirit's person and work for Owen that he must also be integral to the im-

---

25. *Christologia*, pp. 171-72.

13

age as first created. In the New Testament account of the restoration of the image in us

> it is plainly asserted that the Holy Ghost is the immediate operator. . . . And he doth thereby restore his own work . . . the Holy Spirit renews in us the image of God, the original implantation whereof was his peculiar work. And thus Adam may be said to have had the Spirit of God in his innocency.[26]

Owen identifies the image in unfallen Adam with a mind able rightly to discern the will of God, a will wholly in accord with God and the "compliance of our affections" in order that we may do God's will and refrain from all sin. He goes on to say that "all these things were the peculiar effects of the immediate operation of the Holy Ghost."[27] This is so in unfallen Adam, and also, in a point to which we shall return, in the person of Christ. Since the natural faculties, even in their sinless perfection, are "not enough to enable any rational creature to live to God," the wholly Godward life which is the Son's imaging of God in his humanity "was wrought in Christ by the Holy Spirit."[28] What at first might appear to be Owen's somewhat speculative account of the role of the Holy Spirit towards unfallen Adam is therefore intimately bound to an understanding of the integrity of the person and work of the Spirit in relation to Christ and to us, as this may be inferred from the New Testament witness.

Even in its first created perfection, Owen is therefore adamant that the image of God is not to be understood as an innate feature of humanness. It "did not flow naturally from the principles of the rational soul," nor was this capacity to live unto God "inlaid" in those natural faculties, but only a Spirit-enabled possibility.[29] For this reason, while the image is to be distinguished but not separated from the natural faculties in unfallen Adam, it is emphatically to be both distinguished and separated from them as a consequence of sin. The very best that can be said of our intellectual faculties, for example, is that they may be spiritually "quickened and saved": since they were once the subject of original righteousness, and therefore, when rightly ordered, were able to give expression to the image of God, so they are "meet to receive again the renovation of the image of God in Jesus

26. *Pneumatologia*, p. 102.
27. *Pneumatologia*, p. 102.
28. *Pneumatologia*, pp. 168-69. See also, e.g., p. 330.
29. *Pneumatologia*, pp. 284-85; see also, e.g., *Christologia*, p. 183.

Christ" when those who are otherwise wholly spiritually dead are brought to spiritual life in an act of new creation by the Holy Spirit.[30]

As this suggests, Owen is reluctant to allow much room for a facultative understanding of the image, preferring the concept of the image as rooted in right relationship with God over the stronger concessions to human rational faculties as the vestige of the image (albeit distorted and soteriologically irrelevant) that we find elsewhere in Reformed orthodoxy. There are examples of the latter in Owen, but they are few indeed in relation to his emphasis on the loss of the image through sin.[31]

A brief examination of Owen and Francis Turretin, and in particular, the way in which both employ the notion of "concreation," brings out the contrast between Owen and the more usual approach of Reformed orthodoxy. Both theologians maintain that the rectitude and integrity of unfallen humanity is "concreated" — created with, but distinguishable and separable from, intrinsic human faculties and abilities.[32] For Turretin, the image in Adam is located primarily in the "substance of the soul," secondly, in "concreated" rectitude and integrity, and finally in the dominion over the rest of creation and immortality that derive from the first two.[33] He therefore defines the image as partly lost and partly corrupt, while making clear that when speaking soteriologically, it refers strictly to original righteousness and can thus be spoken of as lost.[34]

---

30. *Pneumatologia*, p. 296 (see pp. 295-96). Chapter IV, pp. 282-97, gives an account of our spiritual death apart from the Spirit's gift of new life in Christ.

31. Several examples occur in the polemical context of his anti-Socinian tract against John Biddle, *Vindiciae Evangelicae* (*Works*, vol. 12), in response to his opponent's use of the doctrine. Two less polemically oriented examples occur in *Pneumatologia*: one in which he acknowledges that the image has been "defaced" by sin, and that restoration of the image in us is one of the primary reasons for the coming of Christ (p. 629), and the other in which, while discussing human dominion over the rest of creation, he remarks in passing that "notwithstanding some feeble relics of this image yet abiding with us" we are closer to the beasts than we are to God (p. 580). See also *Christologia*, p. 191. Owen refers once in passing to fallen reason as a "spark" of the image in *A Display of Arminianism* (*Works*, vol. 10, p. 78). Nevertheless, such concessions to a vitiated remnant of the image are few indeed in a corpus of twenty-four volumes. For further discussion of Owen's emphasis on the loss of the image through sin, see my "The Pneumatology of the 'Lost' Image in John Owen."

32. For Owen, see esp. *Pneumatologia*, pp. 102, 284-85. For Turretin on the image, see Francis Turretin, *Institutes of Elenctic Theology*, ed. James T. Dennison, trans. George Musgrave Giger, 3 vols. (Phillipsburg, NJ: Presbyterian & Reformed Publishing, 1992-1997), vol. 1, pp. 464-73, 611-13.

33. Turretin, *Institutes of Elenctic Theology*, pp. 466-70.

34. Turretin, *Institutes of Elenctic Theology*, pp. 466, 611-13.

For Owen, however, the Godward orientation of the whole person *is* the *imago dei*.[35] Owen is therefore quite clear that it is *the image of God* itself that is "concreated" with Adam's rational and other natural faculties:

> This in Adam was the image of God, or an habitual conformity unto God, his mind and will, wherein the holiness and righteousness of God himself was represented. . . . In this image he was created, or it was concreated with him . . . it was the rectitude of all the faculties of his soul with respect unto his supernatural end. . . .[36]

Almost without exception across his corpus, Owen identifies the image with the right ordering of our faculties in this way.[37] The overwhelming emphasis for Owen is that the image is not partly lost or partly corrupt; instead, one is either in the image of God or one is not. Tellingly, if unpalatably, the difference between Owen and Turretin may be summed up in that while the latter remarks that it is possible for a person to be both in the image of God (through the possession of a rational soul) and in the image of the Devil (as unregenerate), for Owen one is either in the image of God or in the image of Satan.[38] He goes so far as to claim that to deny the loss of the image through sin and its restoration only through union with Christ by the Spirit is to "renounce the whole gospel."[39]

Owen is therefore unhesitating and blunt in binding the image and election. With explicit and implicit reference to Romans 8:29 — "For those whom [God] foreknew he also predestined to be conformed to the image of his Son, that he might be the first born within a large family"[40] — Owen consistently describes the image as that to which the elect are predestined.[41]

---

35. So in addition to the references already given, see, e.g., *Pneumatologia*, p. 101, in which the image refers to the "moral condition and principle of obedience unto God," which consists in a "universal rectitude of nature" in which all the faculties are rightly ordered to their goal of living towards God. See also p. 222, where the image is "the uprightness, rectitude and ability of his whole soul, his mind, will and affections . . . for the obedience that God required of him."

36. *Pneumatologia*, p. 285.

37. See n. 31 above.

38. Turretin, *Institutes of Elenctic Theology*, p. 466; Owen, *Christologia*, pp. 37, 184.

39. *Pneumatologia*, pp. 287-88.

40. All scripture citations are taken from the NRSV unless included within a quotation from Owen's text.

41. So, e.g., *Christologia*, pp. 36, 170-71, 191; *Pneumatologia*, pp. 509ff., 526-27; *Meditations*, pp. 334, 362ff.

The elect are to be distinguished from the rest of humanity precisely in that the image is restored in them, whereas it remains lost to unbelievers.[42]

Owen's almost unrelieved emphasis upon the loss of the image through sin is without doubt somewhat problematic. While the scriptural implications for the connection between election and the image are strong — and as Part II will indicate, these encompass aspects of the Old Testament as well as the New Testament witness — a scripturally based theological anthropology will always struggle to sustain the argument that the image of God is exclusively confined to the elect. It is not surprising to find Owen dealing only rarely and awkwardly with Genesis 9:6 ("Whoever sheds the blood of a human, by a human shall that person's blood be shed, for in his own image God made humankind") and James 3:9 ("With [our tongue] we bless the Lord and Father, and with it we curse those who are made in the likeness of God").[43]

It is as well to note that Owen's battles against Socinian rationalism and attempts to identify the image of God with the practice of moral virtue undoubtedly influence both the position that he adopts and the uncompromising rigor with which he maintains it.[44] We must be clear, however, that it is not simply the pressure of polemics that leads Owen to the emphatic identification of election and the image, but his desire to offer a scripturally and trinitarianly consistent account of the person and work of the Spirit.

It is here that a brief comparison with Calvin is instructive. Calvin likewise has no hesitation in binding the restoration of the image to the Spirit's role in the outworking of individual double predestination. The image is so corrupted by sin that "in some part it is now manifest in the

---

42. The inability of human beings, deprived of the image, to be in any sense acceptable to God is a commonplace throughout his theology; for an extended discussion of this and other consequences of the loss of the image see *Christologia*, pp. 185-96.

43. The latter is cited only twice in Owen's entire corpus, both times in *Vindicae Evangelicae,* in close association with Genesis 9:5-6, to deny that the concept of the image implies corporeality in God (pp. 100-101) and then (pp. 161-62) to make the exegetically dubious claim that in neither text does it refer to human beings as they are, but only as originally created. He is nevertheless forced two paragraphs later into a rare and reluctant concession that while the image is indeed "utterly lost" there may be "footsteps" of it as a disincentive to mutual wrong and violence. Apart from using Genesis 9:6 as a supporting text to maintain a Trinitarian interpretation of Genesis 1:26, in his only other use of this verse (*Theologoumena Pantodapa,* p. 161), he finishes his citation at 6a, thereby avoiding the question of the image altogether!

44. See further pp. 22-24 below.

elect, in so far as they have been reborn in the [S]pirit; but it will attain its full splendor in heaven."[45] Nevertheless, as is often remarked, Calvin also offers considerable reflection on the indelible and facultative aspects of the image, distorted and soteriologically irrelevant though these might be.

While there are scattered examples of Owen's (often reluctant) concessions to a continuing vestige of the image in us, we search in vain for a level of ambivalence in Owen comparable to that debated in Calvin studies.[46] Very possibly, as T. F. Torrance points out, had Calvin drawn out the full implications of his doctrine of election for his doctrine of the *imago dei*, he would have found no room for equivocation on such matters either.[47] A significant reason for the difference in overall emphasis between Calvin and Owen, however, is not so much that Owen delineates a more grimly rigorous interconnection between the image and election by allowing deductions from the latter to shape the former, but that Owen gives more consistent attention to pneumatological concerns.

Richard Prins points us to the issues in question by remarking that the apparently intractable difficulties in Calvin's account of the *imago dei* have their source at least in part in a relatively underdeveloped pneumatology in this area of his theology.[48] He suggests that in order for Calvin to be pneumatologically consistent in upholding the Spirit as source and sustainer of all that enables human beings to image God, there must either be a recognition that neither reason nor any other faculty can in any sense be considered as the locus of the *imago dei* or an admission that the image has been wholly lost through sin.[49] This, as we have seen, is essentially Owen's pneumatological point in his presentation of the image as created, lost through sin, and restored in the elect.

Prins likewise points out the related pneumatological flaw prevent-

---

45. John Calvin, *Institutes of the Christian Religion*, ed. John T. McNeill, trans. Ford Lewis Battles (Philadelphia: Westminster Press, 1960), I, xv, 4, p. 190 (see pp. 189-90).

46. Significant texts include T. F. Torrance, *Calvin's Doctrine of Man* (Grand Rapids: Eerdmans, 1957); Mary Potter Engel, *John Calvin's Perspectival Anthropology* (Atlanta: Scholars Press, 1988); and Susan Schreiner, *The Theater of His Glory: Nature and the Natural Order in the Thought of John Calvin* (Durham, NC: Labyrinth Press, 1991).

47. Torrance, *Calvin's Doctrine of Man*, p. 93.

48. Richard Prins, "The Image of God in Adam and the Restoration of Man in Jesus Christ: A Study in Calvin," *SJT* 25 (1972): 32-44. We might also add to this critical assessment the positive suggestion that Calvin is content to express, rather than to resolve, the scriptural indications both that the image is in some way shared by the whole of sinful humanity, while also being expressed supremely in the person of Christ and particularly in his people.

49. Prins, "A Study in Calvin," pp. 37-38.

ing a clearer relationship in Calvin between the image in unfallen Adam and its restoration in Christ. While Calvin claims that our understanding of the created image is derived from its restoration in Christ, the Spirit is given no role in this regard towards unfallen Adam. For Calvin, it is the work of the Spirit in Christ and in believers that *distinguishes* the renewed image from its original in Adam, making the former superior to the latter.[50]

For Owen it is on the basis of precisely this principle — that the created image can only be understood in the light of its restoration in Christ — and also of the unity of the person and work of the Spirit *ad intra* and *ad extra,* that he emphatically maintains a pneumatological *unity* between the image as created and as restored. We will shortly see that the difference between the image as created and restored for Owen, and the superiority of the latter over the former, is rooted instead in the hypostatic union.

It might well be argued that Calvin is considerably more successful in safeguarding the decisiveness of the Spirit's role while maintaining a corrupt vestige of the *imago dei* in human reason than Prins is prepared to accept, and that he has a more subtle understanding of the relationship between the image in unfallen Adam, Christ, and us than emerges in Prins's necessarily brief account. Nevertheless, in both the pneumatological inconsistencies that he highlights and the solutions he suggests, we see the theological priorities and contours of Owen's more radically pneumatological account of the image. It is his particular care to present a coherent and consistent understanding of the Spirit's role, as much as any polemical concern, that issues in the uncompromising binding of the image and election.

Once again, therefore, taking Owen's pneumatological rigor seriously raises questions to which we will repeatedly return. In this instance, these relate particularly to how we might retain Owen's concern to do full justice to the scriptural and Trinitarian implications for the Spirit's role in our imaging of God (and the significance of election in and union with Christ in this regard) without downplaying the scriptural and theological claim

---

50. Prins, "A Study in Calvin," p. 43. See, e.g., John Calvin, *The First Epistle of Paul the Apostle to the Corinthians,* trans. John W. Farmer, ed. David W. Torrance and Thomas F. Torrance (Edinburgh: Oliver & Boyd, 1960), pp. 338-40, in which he indicates that it is the pouring out of the Spirit firstly upon Christ, and then through him upon others that distinguishes Christ from Adam, and the regenerate from all other human beings: "the condition which we acquire through Christ is far better than the situation of the first man, because a living soul was given to Adam for himself and for his posterity, but Christ . . . has brought us the Spirit who is Life" (p. 339).

that to be human is to be created in, and to continue to exist in some way as, the image of God.

With regard to Owen himself, however, it is hardly surprising that he is able to express the shape of God's election precisely through the concept of the image, such that we might redescribe Owen's entire understanding of the covenantal engagement of God with humanity in terms of the *imago dei*.

To be created as, and to grow into the fullness of, the image of God is the fundamental gift of God to humanity at creation, which for Owen is bestowed on the basis of the covenant of works, and so is capable of being lost by disobedience.[51]

The purpose of the Father and the Son in the inner-Trinitarian covenant of redemption is the reestablishing of the right relationship with God expressed in the original creation of humanity in the image of God. The image having been separated from human nature in all save Christ, it is therefore for the very purpose of revealing and restoring the lost image of God that the eternal Son and essential image of the Father takes our nature as the Mediator of the outworking of the covenant of redemption in the covenant of grace for those elect in him.[52]

The incarnate Son is enabled by the Spirit perfectly to embody the image of God in his human nature, such that the stability of that image, and so of right-relatedness to God, is eternally secured in him. Owen therefore locates the infinitely greater worth of the restored over the created image not in any difference in its nature or content, but in the hypostatic union, and the fact that insofar as we are united to Christ by the Spirit, we are given to share in *his* imaging of God, such that it can never again be lost. This superiority of the restored over the created image is the superiority of the covenant of grace over the covenant of works, such that, however glorious the relation between God and man at creation, it therefore had "no beauty or glory in comparison of this."[53]

The restoration of the image is therefore founded upon both the person of Christ and the mediation of Christ, at whose behest the Spirit is bestowed. Since the intention of Christ's mediation is the restoration of the image in us, it is therefore to enable us to partake in that image once again

---

51. *Pneumatologia*, p. 102.

52. *Christologia*, chapter V, "The Person of Christ the great Representative of God and of His Will," *passim*.

53. *Christologia*, p. 48; see also, e.g., *Pneumatologia*, p. 102.

through union with Christ that the Spirit is given.[54] Given that the Spirit is bestowed at the mediation of the ascended Christ on the basis of the eternal decree, the restoration of the *imago dei* is therefore both the present content and ultimate eschatological goal of election, and the two are so inextricably bound that for Owen, without the restoration of the image by the Spirit in the elect, "no one end of Christ's mediation [can be] fully accomplished."[55]

The Spirit, the Image, and Representation

As this indicates, if there is a unifying concept that embraces Owen's understanding of the image as created and restored, it is to be found in his identification of the image with the all-encompassing category of the *purposes of God* for humanity. Central to this is the overarching notion of "representation." There are three facets by which Owen expresses at one and the same time our creation in the image of God and God's purpose in creating humanity. First, human beings are created to represent the righteousness, holiness, and love of God in and to the world. Second, we are also to be the means through which the rest of creation renders glory to God. And finally, we are created for the goal of eternal enjoyment of God as the eschatological consummation of a life of loving obedience.[56]

The representational role is primary in that the other two aspects of our imaging derive straightforwardly from it. It is only as human beings embody the righteousness, holiness, and love of God that they are able to fulfill their role towards God in the created order.[57] In turn, it is only as we

54. So, e.g., *Pneumatologia*, pp. 172f.

55. *Pneumatologia*, pp. 628-29.

56. These three are presented and discussed at length in *Christologia*, pp. 182-97. Like Calvin (e.g., *Institutes*, pp. 189, 270, 807), Owen considers that which is primary in the restored image — righteousness, holiness, and true knowledge of God (Col. 3:10; Eph. 4:23-24) — to be indicative of the primary characteristics of the image in unfallen humanity.

57. Owen insists that the right to "dominion" over the created order, like every other aspect of the image, has been lost through sin. Any authority that fallen humanity claims over the natural world is usurped apart from the restoration of the image in Christ (e.g., *Pneumatologia*, pp. 579-80; *Christologia*, p. 182). The priority Owen accords to the concept of representing the holiness and righteousness of God in his account of the created image has its counterpart in his emphasis when speaking of its loss. More significant than the loss of our own enjoyment of God, now and eternally, it results in God's holiness and righteousness no longer being represented in the world, and no glory redounding to God from the rest of

are enabled by the Spirit to grow in holiness, righteousness, and love that we will attain to the eschatological fulfillment of both the image of God in humanity and the purpose of God for humanity. The Spirit constitutes and shapes the image of God in us, which is "the power to live unto God in obedience, that we might come to the enjoyment of him in glory."[58]

With his customary thoroughness, Owen ensures that we note the continuing centrality of the concept of representation in the restoration of the image in Christ and in the elect. Not surprisingly, it constitutes a significant element of his christological argument against those who would deny the divinity of Christ. As the one who is *homoousios* with the Father, Christ uniquely represents God to us, and indeed on no other terms is it possible to say that he does represent God to us. As Owen points out, "Were [Christ] not the essential image of the Father in his own divine person, he could not be the representative image of God unto us as he is incarnate."[59] That in the person of Jesus Christ we see God represented to us requires nothing less for Owen than the acknowledgment of Christ's full divinity.[60]

In turn, such an acknowledgment requires the gift and work of the Spirit in the transformation and renewal of our minds, which forms part of the restoration of the image in us. Since reason alone cannot recognize Christ the image of God in his two natures, and so the one who truly represents God to us, unaided reason cannot itself constitute the image of God in us. Only as the Spirit removes the veil over our minds and enables the vision of faith can the glory of God be seen in the face of Jesus Christ.[61]

Nevertheless, Owen is equally insistent that a mere "rational" acquiescence to the two natures doctrine is as utterly irrelevant as a "rational" denial of it. Propositional knowledge is of no account without union with

---

creation (*Christologia*, pp. 184ff.). Although Owen himself does not pursue the category of "representation" to speak directly of our *representing* the creation *to God*, this is the implication both of the second facet of our creation in the image and the way in which Owen interprets its loss.

58. *Christologia*, p. 183.

59. *Christologia*, p. 78.

60. For an extended treatment of Christ the one true image of God and the concept of representation in relation to this, see *Christologia*, chapter V, "The Person of Christ the Great Representative of God and His Will," pp. 65-79.

61. For representative discussions of the relationship between reason, revelation, and faith with regard to recognizing Christ as the image of God and therefore our transformation into his image by the Spirit as we behold the glory of God in the face of Christ, see, e.g., *Christologia*, pp. 74-79 and *Pneumatologia*, book III, chapter III, "Corruption and Depravation of the Mind by Sin," pp. 242-82.

Christ by the Spirit.[62] It is the love that flows from this union with Christ, firstly towards Christ in his divinity and humanity and then towards others, that constitutes our imaging. This love is the "vital principle" worked in us by the Spirit such that without it, "whatever there may be besides, there is nothing of the image of God."[63]

With this we confront Owen's rejection not only of reason *per se* as the locus of the image in us, but also of any attempt to identify gospel holiness and the image of God in us with mere "moral reformation."[64] Attempts to live "virtuously," or even to imitate Christ, apart from faith and love are meaningless in this regard. In a typically biting comment, he remarks that to "labour after conformity unto God by outward actions only is to make an image of the living God, hewed out of the stock of a dead tree."[65] Instead, the restoration of the image involves the growth in Christ-likeness, which is nothing less than the total transformation of our entire being by the power of the Spirit through union with Christ.[66]

Owen closes his extended treatment of the Spirit's work in sanctification in *Pneumatologia* with a fierce flourish of rhetorical questions, binding together election, the image of God, and the work of the Holy Spirit against any reduction of the image to moral virtue. Is mere moral virtue, he asks,

> that which God hath predestined or chosen us unto before the foundation of the world? Is it that which he worketh in us in the pursuit of his electing love. . . ? Is [this] the principle of spiritual life . . . enabling us to live to God . . . by the effectual operation of the Holy Ghost. . . ? . . . Is it the image of God in us, and doth our conformity to Christ consist therein?[67]

---

62. E.g., *Christologia*, p. 81: "professors of the truth, if separated from Christ as unto real union, are withered branches. . . ." See also, e.g., *Pneumatologia*, p. 260.

63. *Christologia*, pp. 155, 164.

64. For a summary of Owen's objections to equating the restoration of the lost image with moral reformation, see *Pneumatologia*, pp. 217-24.

65. *Christologia*, p. 155.

66. The theme is pervasive. So, e.g., it is in the gradual process of sanctification, in the "universal renovation of our natures by the Holy Spirit" (*Pneumatologia*, p. 386), that the restoration of the image of God in us consists. The entirety of book IV of *Pneumatologia* (some 300 pages) is an extensive treatment of the Spirit's work in sanctification. Not surprisingly, the theme of the restoration of the image in the elect through their union with Christ is never far from the surface.

67. *Pneumatologia*, pp. 526-27.

For Owen the response is unequivocal. Just as reason, exercised without the Spirit's gift of faith, cannot be considered as the image of God, so to identify the holiness in which the image consists with the practice of moral virtue apart from faith in and love towards Christ is "absolutely opposite unto and destructive of the grace of our Lord Jesus Christ."[68] We might also add that it is destructive of the integrity of the person and work of the Spirit.

This is a reminder once again that for Owen the image of God consists in being those creatures specifically called *to represent the holiness, righteousness, and love of God in the world.* In this regard, the significance of the category of representation — and the rigorous thoroughness with which Owen pursues it — is pressed yet further in his description of the restoration of the image in the elect, specifically in terms of a call to "*represent Christ* in all their ways and walkings."[69] This notion that the elect image God by representing Christ in and to the world leads to one of the most distinctive aspects of his account, highlighting at once the consistency with which Owen develops his themes and the problematic outcomes to which this sometimes leads.

It concerns what we might call the "ethics" of the image. This is the one area in which Reformed orthodoxy, following Calvin, generally nods in the direction of a universal vestige of the image, however distorted and soteriologically irrelevant. On the basis of Genesis 9:6 and James 3:9, this becomes the foundation for just and loving dealings with all human beings.

We have noted Owen's wariness of these texts, and that he is distinctive, even within his own tradition, for his extreme reluctance to speak of any vestige of the image outside the elect. While it is the pressure of these texts that forces a rare concession from him — that some "footsteps" of the image in all should restrain us from mutual wrong and violence[70] — what we also find is that through the category of representation and the image, Owen turns the usual Reformed approach on its head. The elect are exhorted to deal lovingly with all people, *not* because of any notion of a vestige of the image of God in humanity as a whole, but because as those in whom the image of God is restored by the Spirit, they are to *represent God* to all other human beings. So, says Owen, when believers "make self and its

---

68. *Pneumatologia,* p. 527.
69. *Meditations,* p. 304, my italics. See also, e.g., *Pneumatologia,* pp. 583-84.
70. *Vindicae Evangelicae,* p. 162; see n. 43 above.

concernments the end of their lives . . . they do very little *either represent or glorify God in the world.*" Instead, in our dealings with all, and most particularly "our enemies and persecutors, the worst of them . . . towards all mankind as we have opportunity, [we must] labor after conformity unto God, *and to express our likeness unto him*" in our readiness to forgive, help, and relieve.[71]

The internal consistency of Owen's position here is irrefutable, and the notion that the elect are called to a representational role is one that will be taken up and developed at some length. Nevertheless, we are left to wonder whether all of the elements that Owen puts together in his account of the image — a strong and consistent pneumatology, a thorough working out of the category of representation for a discussion of the image, an attempt to take with full seriousness the implications of the New Testament witness that it is those who are elect "in Christ" who share by the Spirit in his imaging of God — must necessarily issue in all of the conclusions to which he is drawn.

For the moment, however, we turn to one final facet of Owen's theology which is fundamental to his treatment of the Spirit's role in election and the image: the paradigmatic significance of the relationship between the Spirit and Christ for the Spirit's role towards us.

The Spirit and Christ

The depth of Owen's account of the Spirit's role in the life of the Christian, which has only been hinted at here, is directly related to the rightly acknowledged richness of his presentation of the intimate and intricate unity-in-distinction between the person and work of the Spirit and the incarnate Son.[72] This is predicated in turn upon his profound concern to reflect the integrity of the relationship between the Spirit and the eternal Son in every aspect of his theology. In order fully to appreciate the shape of Owen's doctrines of election and the image, we must therefore sketch

---

71. *Pneumatologia*, pp. 587-88, my italics; see also pp. 582-84.

72. As has been noted, Gunton seizes upon this aspect of his theology in his quest for a fresh understanding of election and ecclesiology, and Spence's *Incarnation and Inspiration* offers a strongly appreciative study of Owen's rich and distinctive christology in this regard. For a summary of Owen's position, which relates it to the wider Trinitarian patterns of his thinking and to Christ's prophetic office, see Trueman, *Claims of Truth*, pp. 169-79, in particular pp. 177-79.

Owen's account of the Spirit's role in the life of Christ, in whose election and imaging we are given to share.

To do so, however, is also to be confronted immediately with the *dissimilarity* between Christ and ourselves. Owen opens his presentation of the Spirit's role in the life of Christ with a forthright statement of the problem: that a thoroughgoing two natures doctrine appears to render the Spirit's role in the life of Christ redundant. As he puts it, "there doth not seem to be any need, nor indeed room, for any . . . operations of the Spirit; for could not the Son of God himself . . . perform all things requisite . . . ?"[73]

There is an elegance and simplicity to his central thesis in response: the Son assumes to himself the humanity prepared for him by the Spirit in the act of the hypostatic union, but having done so, the eternal Son no longer acts directly upon his humanity. Instead, all other actions of the eternal Son upon his human nature are mediated through the Spirit.[74] In Owen's words,

> [t]he only singular immediate act of the person of the Son on the human nature was the assumption of it into subsistence with himself . . . [and] the only *necessary consequent* [sic] of this assumption of the human nature . . . [is the] inseparable subsistence of the *assumed nature* in the person of the Son . . . all other actings of God in the *person of the Son* towards the human nature were *voluntary*, and did not necessarily ensue on the union mentioned.[75]

As he goes on to remark, "all the voluntary communications of the divine nature unto the human were . . . by the Holy Spirit."[76]

---

73. *Pneumatologia*, p. 160. For Owen's detailed account of the role of the Spirit towards the incarnate Son see *Pneumatologia*, book II, chapters III and IV, the former dealing with the work of the Spirit in relation to the hypostatic union and the conception and birth of Christ, and the latter with the unfolding life of Christ.

74. Owen's account of the relationship between the Spirit and the Son brings to our attention his adherence to the *extra calvinisticum*. As he remarks in *Christologia*, p. 46, the eternal Word takes our flesh not by ceasing to be what he was, but by also becoming what he was not. For Owen's description of the Spirit as the one whose creating act forms the humanity assumed by the Son — and his care to affirm the anhypostatic principle — see *Pneumatologia*, pp. 163-66.

75. *Pneumatologia*, p. 160, Owen's italics.

76. *Pneumatologia*, p. 175. In other words, as Trueman points out (*Claims of Truth*, p. 177), the Spirit is the agent of the *communicatio idiomatum*. Owen spells this out in

With this we are reminded of the centrality accorded by Owen to the principle of God's *filioque*-shaped self-consistency to his Trinitarian being in his works *ad extra*. Owen makes the connection explicit:

> The Holy Ghost . . . is the *immediate, peculiar* [i.e., particular] *efficient cause* of all external divine operations . . . [and] is the *Spirit of the Son*, no less than the Spirit of the Father. . . . And hence is he the immediate operator of all divine acts of the Son himself, even on his own human nature. Whatever the Son of God wrought in, by, or upon the human nature, he did it by the Holy Ghost, who is his Spirit, as he is the Spirit of the Father.[77]

The Spirit's role towards the incarnate Son therefore reflects Owen's understanding of the primary general function of the Spirit in the economy, as the only way in which God acts directly in the created order. Likewise, as Owen has made particularly clear here, that the eternal Son mediates the action of his divine upon his human nature through the Spirit is itself the expression of the Spirit's procession from the Son.

Moreover, as the one through whom the purposes of Father and Son are brought to completion, there is a proper dependence of the Son upon the Spirit within the economy, noted earlier in relation to the outworking of the mediation of the ascended Son in Owen's doctrine of election, and explored in his account of the unfolding life of the incarnate Son. Trueman's remark is apt: the richness of Owen's "Spirit christology" arises from the outworking of his adherence to *filioque* with a "specifically incarnational twist."[78]

In turn, it is of enormous significance to Owen, and a vital indicator of the integrity of any account of the Spirit's person and work, that there should be a profound consistency not only between the person and wider work of the Spirit and his role in shaping the personhood of Christ, but also that there should be a harmony and correspondence between the Spirit's work in Christ and the Spirit's work in our election.

Pneumatologia, p. 161, where he insists that "there was no transfusion of the properties of one nature into the other," neither can "divine essential excellencies" be predicated to Christ's humanity by virtue of the hypostatic union. Instead, as Owen stresses repeatedly, all communications of the divine to the human nature are voluntary, and mediated by the Spirit.

77. *Pneumatologia*, pp. 161-62, Owen's italics.
78. Trueman, *Claims of Truth*, p. 178.

In every respect, Jesus Christ is offered to us as the head and the proto-type of the new humanity. Thus, to speak of the work of the Holy Spirit to-wards the elect is to speak firstly of his work in the human nature of Christ. Ours is "a participation [in] those graces whose fullness dwells in him," such that we can have no understanding of the Spirit's role in us except "by an acquaintance with and due consideration of the work of the Spirit of God upon his human nature."[79]

Having safeguarded the divinity of Christ in the act of the hypostatic union, Owen is free to give fullest expression to the work of the Spirit in him as it is suggested to us in the New Testament witness — to the notion of his spiritual development and nescience, and his dependence on the Spirit for his relationship of loving obedience to the Father and for guid-ance, direction, and comfort — in ways that provide the source and para-digm for the role of the Spirit towards the elect.[80]

As Owen puts it: "he who prepared, sanctified, and glorified the hu-man nature . . . of Jesus Christ, the head of the church, hath undertaken to prepare, sanctify, and glorify . . . all the elect given unto him of the Fa-ther."[81] Just as the Spirit's work is decisive as the one who is the very possi-bility of the incarnation, so too he is the only possibility of our new birth through union with Christ. Just as the Spirit is the one through whom Christ himself grows in knowledge, and through whom he lives a life of loving obedience towards the Father, so he is also the one who sanctifies the elect, through the growth in love, knowledge, and holiness that charac-terize our gradual transformation in Christ-likeness.

In this we also see the importance of the relationship between the Spirit and Christ for the *imago dei* in Christ and in us. We have remarked above on the significance of Christ's imaging of God in his divinity, as the one who represents to us the invisible God. This is the unique imaging of God that is proper only to the incarnate Son. We have also noted that his imaging of God in his humanity, by which is expressed for us the perfect Godward life which is the purpose of our creation, is explicitly described as the work of the Holy Spirit in him. Since the Spirit is the only possibility of a life rightly ordered towards God for any human being, Owen is clear

---

79. *Pneumatologia*, p. 188.

80. For Owen's detailed discussion of these and other aspects of the Spirit's role in the life of Christ, see *Pneumatologia*, chapter IV, "Work of the Holy Spirit in and on the human nature of Christ," *passim*.

81. *Pneumatologia*, p. 189.

that Christ too requires the Spirit in order to be a human being in the image of God.[82]

Again, therefore, the Spirit's work in restoring the image through the union of the elect to Christ entails giving us to share in that which he has accomplished first in Christ's own humanity, until finally we are brought to share in the transformed and glorified resurrection humanity, again wrought firstly in him and then in us by the power of the Spirit.[83] In every respect, those who are in Christ by the Spirit are given to share by the same Spirit in that which is firstly Christ's: we are "predestined to be made conformable in all things unto him . . . by the powerful and effectual operation of that Spirit which thus wrought all things in him. . . ."[84]

Conclusion

In Owen we therefore encounter a rich and powerfully integrated understanding of the Spirit's role in election and the image, in Christ and in us. In all of this, he self-consciously seeks to take full account of the implications of the New Testament witness to the Spirit's work and to the relationship between the Spirit and Christ, and to anchor his thinking in the foundational principle that the acts of God *ad extra* express God's Trinitarian life *ad intra.*

By setting out the contours of Owen's presentation of these issues we have also raised major themes and questions to be taken up in all that follows. So, for example, Owen's distinctive emphasis upon the category of representation for the *imago dei* will provide the catalyst for a renewed consideration of the relationship between election and the image in Part II, although the concept will be taken in a somewhat different direction, and within an understanding of the image that is able to accommodate a stronger emphasis upon its continuance in humanity as a whole as well as its particular expression as it is shaped by the Spirit in the community of Christ.

Above all, however, it is with Owen's presentation of the Spirit's role in

82. *Pneumatologia*, pp. 168-69; see p. 14 above.
83. "It was the Holy Spirit that *glorified* the human nature [of Christ], and made it every way meet for its eternal residence at the right hand of God, and a pattern of the glorification of the bodies of them that believe on him." *Pneumatologia*, p. 183, Owen's italics. For Owen's discussion of the role of the Spirit in relation to Christ's resurrection, see pp. 181-83.
84. *Pneumatologia*, p. 183.

election, in intimate relation to the wider integrity of the Spirit's person and work as well as the unity of the work of the Son, that we encounter issues which will recur throughout concerning the pneumatological dynamic of election "in Christ" and the identity and purpose of the elect community. In particular, the scriptural and Trinitarian coherence and consistency of Owen's election pneumatology and the relationship between the work of the Spirit and the Son will provide a challenging touchstone as we turn in the following chapters to the Spirit's role in Barth's two doctrines of election, and the way in which his mature account of the doctrine shapes his understanding of the *imago dei.*

As the preceding account has made clear, this very coherence and consistency in Owen's election pneumatology is inseparably interwoven with an understanding of election in terms of individual double predestination. This makes explicit the pneumatological crux for any Reformed account of election: does a scripturally and trinitarianly robust account of the Spirit's role in election lead us only and inexorably to a version of individual double predestination? Owen's answer is a clear and coherent "Yes." The remainder of Part I will explore the way in which Barth's two doctrines of election respond to the same question, as he wrestles with the historic Reformed expression of the doctrine in the light of his own dogmatic priorities.

CHAPTER 2

Election, the Image, and the Spirit: Karl Barth

Rediscovering a Forgotten Doctrine

In 1921 Karl Barth is appointed to his first university position as Honorary Professor of Reformed Theology at Göttingen. Feeling the pressure both of his relative lack of erudition and of being the sole bearer of the Reformed theological heritage in a Lutheran faculty, the Göttingen years between 1921 and 1925 are extraordinarily intense. His letters throughout this period reveal the constant, desperate scramble to prepare his lectures, and both the frustrations and the excitement of immersing himself at speed, often for the first time, in classical theological texts and in the details of the historic Reformed tradition.[1]

Barth's early years at Göttingen are devoted to an exposition of key Reformed texts and theologians. In 1924, after a fierce battle with the faculty, he then launches into a series of lectures on dogmatics, now published under the editorial title of *The Göttingen Dogmatics*.[2] It is within these lectures that Barth first gives sustained attention to developing an account of the doctrine of election.[3]

---

1. For the unfolding of Barth's life and theology in this period, see Bruce McCormack, *Karl Barth's Critically Realistic Dialectical Theology: Its Genesis and Development 1909-1936* (Oxford: Clarendon, 1995), chapters 7 and 8.

2. See McCormack, *Critically Realistic*, p. 331, for an account of the disputes surrounding Barth's course, and also Hannelotte Reiffen, "Preface," *GD*, pp. ix-x. In his "Translator's Preface," Geoffrey Bromiley gives the reasons for the choice of *The Göttingen Dogmatics* as the English title (*GD*, pp. vii-viii).

3. See McCormack, *Critically Realistic*, pp. 371-74, for a brief discussion of Barth's doctrine of election in *GD*. For a recent exploration of aspects of Barth's work during the

Barth therefore provides us with a unique case study for a Reformed understanding of election by offering us *two* accounts of the doctrine, one in *GD* and the other in *CD* II/2, with each taking a significantly different approach to the Spirit's role. Moreover, given that many major studies of Barth's "doctrine" of election assume that the latter is his first substantial engagement with the subject, the decisive influence of Barth's earlier account on the first two volumes of *CD* cannot be emphasized too strongly.[4] It is the understanding of election set forth in *GD* that shapes the doctrine of the Word of God in *CD*, until the radical alteration prompted by Barth's encounter with the thought of Pierre Maury in 1936 is fully assimilated into his thinking in his presentation of the doctrine of God.[5]

Göttingen period, but devoted largely to his earlier lectures rather than to those that form the *GD*, see John Webster, *Barth's Earlier Theology* (London: T. & T. Clark, 2005). See also Matthias Gockel, *Barth and Schleiermacher on the Doctrine of Election: A Systematic-Theological Comparison* (Oxford: Oxford University Press, 2007), chap. 3, for an account of Barth's doctrine of election in his Romans commentary, and chap. 4 for an account of his doctrine of election in *GD*.

4. For the influence of Barth's *GD* account of election on *CD* I/1 and 2, see my "Barth's 'Other' Doctrine of Election in the *Church Dogmatics*," *IJST* 9 (April 2007): 134-47. Significant earlier studies of Barth's mature doctrine of election include G. Berkouwer's critical reading, *The Triumph of Grace in the Theology of Karl Barth*, trans. H. R. Boer (London: Paternoster, 1956); and the sympathetic studies of Robert Jenson, *Alpha and Omega: A Study in the Theology of Karl Barth* (Edinburgh: Thomas Nelson, 1963); J. D. Bettis, "Is Karl Barth a Universalist?" *SJT* 20 (1967): 423-36; and Colin Gunton, "Karl Barth's Doctrine of Election as Part of His Doctrine of God," *Journal of Theological Studies* 25, no. 2 (1974): 381-92. In turn, a pneumatologically focused comparison with Calvin is offered in Anthony C. Yu, "Karl Barth's Doctrine of Election," *Foundations* 13, no. 3 (1970): 248-61; and Paul Jewett provides a critique particularly on questions of soteriology and exegesis in *Election and Predestination* (Grand Rapids: Eerdmans, 1985), chap. 4. More recent analyses include John E. Colwell, *Actuality and Provisionality: Eternity and Election in the Theology of Karl Barth* (Edinburgh: Rutherford House Books, 1989); Douglas R. Sharp, *The Hermeneutics of Election: The Significance of the Doctrine in Barth's Church Dogmatics* (Lanham, MD: University Press of America, 1990); Katherine Sonderegger, *That Jesus Christ Was Born a Jew: Karl Barth's Doctrine of Israel* (University Park: Pennsylvania State University Press, 1992); Bruce McCormack, "Grace and Being: The Role of God's Gracious Election in Karl Barth's Theological Ontology," in *The Cambridge Companion to Karl Barth*, ed. John Webster (Cambridge: Cambridge University Press, 2000), pp. 92-110; Donna Bowman, *The Divine Decision* (Louisville: WJPK, 2002); and Oliver Crisp, "On Barth's Denial of Universalism," *Themelios* 29, no. 1 (2003): 18-29.

5. Although *CD* I/2 first appeared in 1938, McCormack points out in *Critically Realistic* (pp. 416, 460-61) that the lecture notes upon which it is substantially based date from before his encounter with Maury's views. I/2 remains firmly linked with the election dynamic of *GD*.

What follows is an overview of both accounts of election in Barth, focusing upon the overall dynamic of each doctrine and the way in which the Spirit's role is conceived, along with the relationship between pneumatology and christology. In the case of the earlier doctrine, particular attention is given to those features that are repeated in and central to the foundational presentation of the Spirit's role in *CD* I/1 and I/2. In turn, it is only as we come to recognize the characteristics of Barth's earlier doctrine of election that we are able fully to realize that the dramatic christological reorientation in his thinking on election also entails a much quieter but no less decisive change in his understanding of the Spirit's role.[6]

As with Owen, so with Barth, we will also note the intimate binding of the doctrines of election and the image of God, particularly in the powerful and explicit influence of Barth's mature doctrine of election on his account of human nature and the *imago dei* in his doctrine of creation.

Election and the Spirit in the *Göttingen Dogmatics*

In a structure to be replicated and expanded in the *Church Dogmatics*, the *Göttingen Dogmatics* begins with a consideration of the threefold nature of the Word of God followed by the presentation of the doctrine of God, which concludes with an account of election. Barth is careful to remind us at the outset of his presentation of election that the threefold nature of the Word testifies to the essential hiddenness of God in his self-revelation: the "incognito" of Jesus Christ in his life, and also the way in which preaching and the reading of scripture are received differently by different people, and by the same people at different times.[7] To acknowledge God's self-

---

6. Just as major treatments of Barth on election tend to ignore his earlier doctrine, so treatments of Barth's pneumatology do not take account of this alteration in his thinking. For full-length studies see P. J. Rosato, *The Spirit as Lord: The Pneumatology of Karl Barth* (Edinburgh: T. & T. Clark, 1981); and J. Thompson, *The Holy Spirit in the Theology of Karl Barth* (Allison Park, PA: Pickwick Publications, 1991). Shorter recent accounts include G. Hunsinger, *Disruptive Grace: Studies in the Theology of Karl Barth* (Grand Rapids: Eerdmans, 2000), chap. 7; and, from a more critical angle, Robert Jenson, "You Wonder Where the Spirit Went," *Pro Ecclesia* 28, no. 3 (1993): 296-304; and Eugene F. Rogers, Jr., "The Eclipse of the Spirit in Karl Barth," in *Conversing with Barth,* ed. John C. McDowell and Mike Higton (Aldershot: Ashgate, 2004), pp. 173-90.

7. *GD,* e.g., pp. 442-43, 446-47.

revelation is not an inherent human possibility; God's sovereign freedom as irreducibly Subject rather than universally accessible object in his self-revelation means that God remains veiled to unaided humanity even in his revelation.

This is fundamental to Barth's theology in *GD*, and to his theology as a whole. Here, however, it is explicitly the driving force behind his understanding of election. Bruce McCormack aptly summarizes Barth's approach to election in *GD* as "a necessary consequence arising out of an analysis of the situation of revelation."[8] As Barth's *Leitsatz* makes clear, this understanding of revelation sets us "under a twofold possibility grounded in God himself."[9] Either "nothing special happens," so that, although wholly unaware of it, we remain on the road to eternal perdition, or "something special" does indeed happen, so that we know ourselves as the objects both of the "No" of God's judgment, and the "Yes" of his grace and salvation. "In the first case we are passed by or rejected by God; in the second case we are elected or accepted of God," whose glory triumphs "no matter how the decision goes."

The "something special," which is both the determining factor in the human response to God's self-revelation and at the same time the enacting of God's decision of election or rejection, is the Holy Spirit. The Holy Spirit is "the special thing in the election of grace. His action is . . . the last and proper thing, at which we see God aiming in his rejecting and electing."[10] The gift of the Holy Spirit is thus decisive in the election of God: revelation as event for the individual, the reality of reconciliation, and to be elect to salvation are one. Barth explicitly defines the *massa perditionis* as that section of humanity not constituted by "the efficacious grace of the Holy Spirit."[11]

While rejection has no independent reality except as the corollary of the electing "Yes" which is the purpose of God's self-revelation, God's predestining will is indeed twofold, with rejection functioning as the revelation of God's righteousness, that his mercy in election may also be known.[12] Moreover, while rejection is the result of God's "non-willing, non-awakening, non-effecting," this is still a "planned and purposeful ac-

---

8. McCormack, *Critically Realistic*, p. 371.

9. This and all the following quotations in this paragraph are from the *Leitsatz* to Barth's discussion of election, *GD*, p. 440.

10. *GD*, p. 466.

11. *GD*, p. 458.

12. *GD*, pp. 460-61.

tion of God, a specific holding back, a presence and activity that produces a vacuum on the human side."[13]

Barth therefore stresses that God is not passively neutral or an on-looker in reprobation. Just as the will and decision of God is the only source of faith, so there is no basis for unbelief outside the divine will. We cannot take up an attitude towards God as if he were simply the object of revelation. Rather, "from all eternity this supposed object has . . . decided about you and no matter what attitude you take, you are his either for grace or for perdition."[14] "The choice or decision between the two possibilities does not lie in our hands but in God's."[15] In the face of God's two-fold predestination, we must bow in recognition that "God's will is a Therefore! that brooks no Wherefore?"[16]

Predestination for the Barth of *GD* is therefore emphatically individual, unconditional, and double in accordance with the strictest Reformed ortho-doxy.[17] He upholds the Synod of Dordt as containing all that needs to be said concerning God's relationship to humanity and ours to God, and is later ex-plicit in stating his preference for limited atonement. On his own admission, his only departure from the classical Reformed tradition — his "incisive de-viation" — is his radically "actualist" understanding of the decision of God.[18] Building on a reconceiving of temporality that is as yet not fully de-veloped, he interprets the eternal election of God not as signifying a com-pleted act in the pre-temporal past, but as a "living eternity" and "the eternal act of predestinating" in the moment-by-moment divine deciding for or against an individual in each God-determined possibility of revelation.[19]

Barth therefore rejects, not the notion that election signifies the deter-mination of the destiny of each individual — that is taken as axiomatic — but the notion that humanity has already been divided into two numerically

13. *GD*, pp. 451-52.
14. *GD*, p. 444.
15. *GD*, p. 451.
16. *GD*, p. 445.
17. So, e.g., in the passage cited above concerning the Spirit as the "special thing" at which God aims in election, Barth goes on to spell out that this means we are speaking here of "God who precisely in his revelation shows himself to be the God of eternal, uncondi-tional, twofold predestination" (*GD*, p. 466); see also, e.g., p. 453, where he cites Romans 9–11 as undeniable proof of this way of understanding predestination, and p. 455 with reference to Dordt vs. the Remonstrants.
18. *GD*, p. 443; see also pp. 453ff., although as he points out, his supralapsarianism makes his a minority voice within the Reformed tradition (pp. 466ff.).
19. *GD*, pp. 453-54.

fixed groups of the elect and the rejected. He considers this to be the grave weakness of Reformed orthodoxy, in that it directs our attention to the existence of a "certain people" (the pre-temporally determined number predestined to salvation) rather than to the predestining God, and so mechanizes predestination into a fixed system. Instead, predestination refers not to the individuals who are its object, but to the attitude of God, part of whose freedom is not to be the "prisoner of his own decision for grace or its opposite" but to interact with us as a "living person."[20] For the Barth of GD, Romans 9–11 is the decisive proof, both that predestination is eternal, individual, unconditional, and twofold, and also that God is wholly free to have mercy or to harden as he wills — free, that is, "not only to elect and reject different people, but also to elect or reject a particular individual at different times."[21]

From this it will be clear that, with the exception of Barth's actualism — and his supralapsarianism — he and Owen are substantially at one in their understanding of the contours of God's election. In particular, for our purposes, the lynchpin in the dynamic of election for both is very explicitly the gift and work of the Spirit. As the determining factor in the human response to God's self-revelation, which is at the same time the enacting of God's decision of election or rejection, the gift of the Holy Spirit quite simply *is* the decisive factor in the economic unfolding of God's electing decree. The event of revelation for us is the actualizing of reconciliation, as, through the Spirit's irresistible work, we respond in faith and obedience to the reality of God in his self-revelation.[22]

Barth's actualism might in fact seem to offer an even more significant role for the Spirit than the historic tradition. The Spirit's work is not simply the actualizing of God's "prior" determination, but is itself the decision of eternal election. Nevertheless, a renewed election pneumatology is not to be sought here. Significantly, one of Owen's foremost priorities with regard to the Spirit's work in election — the concept of *union with Christ* — is entirely absent. One of the most problematic features of Barth's early account is that the almost exclusive concentration upon election as the reception of revelation comes at the expense of any proper recognition of what it means to be elect "in Christ."[23]

20. Citations from GD, pp. 454 and 444 respectively.

21. GD, p. 454.

22. GD, p. 450; see also p. 440.

23. McCormack points out that "What is missing in this account, as judged by the standards of Barth's later . . . doctrine of election . . . is any serious reflection on the fact that election is 'in Christ'" (*Critically Realistic*, p. 373). It is missing when judged by the standards of

Barth will later acknowledge, albeit indirectly, that his attempts to circumvent the difficulties raised by his earlier doctrine are unconvincing and inconsistent, through his critique of the view of election presented at the 1936 *Congrès international de théologie calviniste* by his brother, Peter.[24] What Barth omits to mention here, is that not only is the view held by his brother essentially one to which he himself had been deeply committed, but most particularly, it is this view that shapes the opening volumes of the *Church Dogmatics*.

Election and the Spirit in *Church Dogmatics* I/1 and I/2

The essential features of Barth's doctrine of election in the *Göttingen Dogmatics* are repeated in and central to *CD* I/1 and I/2.[25] Much work remains to be done on the way in which this early doctrine of election influences the major theological loci in these volumes, and indeed on the significance of the shift in Barth's understanding of election for the long-recognized tensions between the first two volumes and the remainder of the *Church Dogmatics*.[26] The primary concern, here, however, is to point towards those areas in which the dynamic of election influences Barth's understanding of the relationship between pneumatology and christology in

---

the historic Reformed tradition as well, even if the concept of "in Christ" is worked out somewhat differently. Barth's own concerns with his presentation of the doctrine surround the question of assurance, to which he recognizes that his innovation poses a serious challenge (*GD*, pp. 468-72). This is not helped by inconsistencies within his account. While he wishes to maintain that God's electing purpose has a teleology — that the way "leads fundamentally from rejection to election, not vice versa. . . . God wants to go forward with us, not backward" (p. 461) — more true to the logic of his moment-by-moment dynamic is the statement that to move from election to reprobation is "to be passed from one hand of God to the other," very much including the vice versa — that "he who now receives us could with the same power reject us" in the absolute freedom of his grace (p. 452).

24. *CD* II/2, pp. 188-94, where, for example, in tacit recognition of the contradiction noted in the previous footnote, he remarks that it appears as little more than a "mere game which God plays with man, a game which is completely bewildering . . ." (p. 190). His encounter with the thought of Pierre Maury at this same conference forms the catalyst for his own monumental reworking of the doctrine.

25. See in particular §5, "The Nature of the Word of God," and §6, "The Knowability of the Word of God," where Barth refers to election in the context of his account of revelation in ways that recall, and are in complete accord with, his approach in *GD*.

26. For the way in which this account of election shapes a wider range of *loci* than can be considered here, see my "Barth's 'Other' Doctrine of Election."

election, in order that the pneumatological significance of the shift in Barth's understanding of election might be made more apparent.

In *CD* I/1, as in *GD*, consideration of revelation and of election is inseparable. It remains axiomatic that: 1) since unaided humanity can neither receive nor respond to God's self-revelation, the possibility of this event lies only in the gift of God; and 2) this is to be identified with God's electing or rejecting decision. In a passage that would sit equally comfortably within *GD* on election, Barth characteristically remarks that:

> Whatever attitude [one] may adopt [towards God] it will be done within and on the ground of an attitude that God has adopted to him. If he believes, this will be just a confirmation of the fact that he has God's promise and is claimed, judged and blessed by God. If he does not believe, this again will not be a possibility he can freely choose. He will sin against God's Word. . . . He . . . will be rejected.[27]

While the reality of election is known and actualized in the right hearing of the Word, whether ours is a right or a wrong hearing is not in our hands: as we decide and determine, so we act in accordance with and actualize the "secret judgment of the grace or disfavour of God."[28] This is also determinative for our imaging of God. Identifying the image supremely with *rectitudo* and the capacity for God, Barth insists that as a consequence of sin, the image is not just "destroyed apart from a few relics, it is totally annihilated."[29] It is restored in us only by our reconciliation to God in Christ through the gift of acknowledging the Word.[30]

Barth therefore repeats a familiar theme from *GD* — that the Word has a "twofold possibility of its operation," the "inner ground" of which is God's free decision concerning the individual.[31] On this basis, Barth asks:

27. *CD* I/1, p. 154. For Barth's extended discussion of the relationship between individual self-determination and God's determination of each individual, see "The Word of God and Experience" (pp. 198-227, *passim*).

28. *CD* I/1, p. 201.

29. *CD* I/1, p. 238.

30. *CD* I/1, pp. 238-39. The contrast between this and Barth's later position (see p. 52 below) is as great as — and indeed *is* — the contrast between Barth's two understandings of God's election.

31. *CD* I/1, pp. 160-61. Barth is speaking here of the coming of God's Word to us as the crisis of decision, and again with regard to the relationship between self-determination and God's determination of us, reinforces that "whether my act is faith or unbelief, obedience or disobedience, correct or incorrect hearing" it is also the divine decision about me (p. 160).

> Do we have to know an inner reason for the choice, a vindication of God for the freedom he takes and enjoys, when speaking to man, now to accept and now to reject him . . . to treat one as Peter and the other as Judas? *By way of justification one need say no more than in the case of the general dogma of predestination disclosed here, namely, that the decision taken in the Word is God's decision and therefore it is a just and good decision.*[32]

We might recall at this point Barth's assertion in *GD* that God's eternal decision to save some and to leave the rest without the efficacious work of the Spirit as the *massa perditionis* is a "Therefore!" that brooks no "Wherefore?"

As will be evident from the previous discussion, it is Barth's actualist understanding of election that lies behind one of the most characteristic features of the doctrine of the Word of God in the *Church Dogmatics*: the urgent and repeated emphasis upon revelation as event, and as a moment-by-moment possibility within the gift or withholding of God.[33] While actualism remains a characteristic of Barth's theology as a whole, and will retain its significance, with christological qualification, in Barth's later doctrine of election, at this stage the relationship between the event of God's self-revelation to the individual and the shape of election belongs within the very different dynamic expressed in *GD*. Since the event of revelation for the individual is also the enacting of God's electing or rejecting decision, neither the reception of revelation nor election can be resolved into a static or permanent state. Instead, both election and revelation cast us in utter dependence upon the future coming of the Word as event for us by the gift of the Spirit.[34]

As was the case in *GD* the Spirit's work in revelation, and therefore in

---

32. *CD* I/1, p. 160, my italics.

33. In the light of this, the stress in *CD* I/1 on revelation only as a Spirit-enabled possibility, and that an experience of the Word does not mean that the store of human possibilities has been enriched by a further one, such that it becomes a predicate of our existence (pp. 209-10) needs to be seen not simply as a general principle for the whole of Barth's theology, but also as the expression of the very particular understanding of election at work in his theology at the time. This surreptitious turn to the self, which Barth here calls the "indirect Christian Cartesianism" of the tradition (p. 214) is also, as we have noted, Barth's only criticism of Reformed orthodoxy on election in *GD*, and the source of the "incisive deviation" of his radical actualism.

34. For the locus of our assurance as the future expectation of the coming of the Word, and for the possibility that grace may be replaced by non-grace, acknowledgment of the Word by an incapacity to do so, according to God's determination of us, see *CD* I/1, pp. 224-26.

election, is decisive.[35] As Barth puts it, "The Lord of speech is also the Lord of our hearing. This Lord who gives the Word is also the Lord who gives faith," and this is the Lord the Spirit.[36] This naturally influences the way in which the relationship between christology and pneumatology in election is understood, or in other words, between the "objective" and "subjective" aspects of revelation, since for the early Barth, the subjective reality of objective revelation is also the reality of election. In this regard, we find the same essential dynamic that we have noted in I/1 is also at work in I/2, where Barth gives his more detailed account of the outworking of God's act of revelation in its objective form *for* us and its subjective fulfillment *in* us.[37]

As Barth insists, Jesus Christ, the Word incarnate, is the objective reality of God's self-revelation, regardless of whether he is acknowledged as such or not, and in Christ, the revelation and reconciliation that we receive have already taken place.[38] Our subjective appropriation is not a later addition to objective revelation, but our acknowledgment of its achieved reality.[39]

We must not, however, think of this "subjective" aspect of revelation as in any way subordinate to the "objective," lest we call into question the *homoousia* of the Spirit.[40] The decisiveness of the Spirit's work is expressed negatively in the harsh reality that if the revelation and reconciliation achieved in Christ are not perceived by us, then they stand "to our eternal destruction."[41] Positively he remarks that while "there took place in [Christ] revelation and reconciliation between God and man," it is our apprehension of this by the Spirit that "effects revelation and reconciliation."[42] Again speaking interchangeably of "the act of divine revelation or reconciliation," Barth states that "only through the Holy Spirit can [we] . . . be a recipient of [God's] revelation, the object of the divine reconciliation."[43]

---

35. Since it is the Spirit who guarantees that some will indeed receive God's revelation, Barth says that "we shall have to call this third operation of the Spirit the decisive one" (*CD* I/1, p. 456).

36. *CD* I/1, p. 182.

37. §13, "The Incarnation of the Word," and §16, "The Outpouring of the Holy Spirit" respectively. It must be emphasized that this subjective reality of revelation can in no sense be confused with "subjectivism." It is only in God's gift of himself — the Spirit as God in his Revealedness — that our human response to God is enabled.

38. *CD* I/2, p. 173.

39. See esp. *CD* I/2, pp. 238-39.

40. *CD* I/2, p. 208.

41. *CD* I/2, p. 238.

42. *CD* I/2, p. 214.

43. *CD* I/2, p. 198. In *CD* I/2, Barth continues his practice in I/1 of expressing the rela-

This follows from his earlier account of the subjective event of revelation, in which we are placed with the Son by the Spirit, where Barth states: "Herein consists (our) participation in the atonement effected in Christ. This is what it means to have the Holy Spirit. To have the Holy Spirit is to be set with Christ in that transition from death to life."[44] It is also the only way in which we can become what we otherwise are not and cannot be: children of God.[45] Revelation as reconciling event therefore requires that something else be "added to the givenness of the revelation of the Father in the Son."[46] Barth speaks here of the Spirit as the "special element" in revelation, and as this "special act" that must be added, just as he has spoken in *GD* of the Spirit being the "special thing" in the election of God.[47] Without this fullness of revelation, Barth asserts, we are "certainly lost."[48]

Barth's understanding of the relationship between election and the concept of being "in Christ" sums up the implications of his position at this time in a way that must be borne in mind if we are to appreciate the full extent of the shift in his thinking. In a clear presentation both of the positive definition of what it is to be "in Christ" and its uncompromising negative corollary, Barth insists that to be in Christ is to be made a hearer and doer of the Word in the church. We are "with God" only insofar as we are "in Christ," and to be "in Christ" is not something intrinsic to our human being. Rather, it is a "new thing added to our being" by the Spirit's work of revelation. Once again, Barth does not shy away from the negative corollary: "as long as and to the extent that it is not added to that being as something new, the being itself is excluded from it." "All this," he adds, "is as true as the Word of God itself."[49]

---

tionship between reconciliation and revelation as an event for us in the language of election — see, e.g., his further exploration of self-determination within God's determination of the self in relation to the reception of revelation, in which he remarks that "I in my apparently unrepeatable selfhood apprehend, or do not apprehend, am called or not called, am elected or rejected" (p. 266).

44. *CD* I/1, p. 458.

45. *CD* I/1, p. 457 (see pp. 457-59). This point is reiterated, p. 486.

46. *CD* I/1, p. 449.

47. *CD* I/1, p. 449.

48. *CD* I/1, pp. 450-51.

49. *CD* I/2, p. 258. For further discussion of the relationship between revelation and reconciliation in this context, see my "Barth's 'Other' Doctrine of Election," pp. 140-46.

The Christological Reorientation in *Church Dogmatics* II/2

McCormack characterizes the shift in Barth's doctrine of election — and with it the whole orientation of his thinking — as a move from a "pneumatological" to a "christological" phase. He remarks that while the "theoretical ground" of Barth's early theology was christological, its basic orientation, in its focus upon the event of revelation, remained pneumatological. With Barth's mature doctrine of election comes the "final adjustment" by which his becomes "a Christologically grounded, christocentric theology."[50]

At the opening of his account of election in II/2, however, Barth is also keen to ensure that we recognize the intimate connection between what will follow and what has gone before. The preparation for his dramatic reorientation both of his own previous approach to election and that of the Reformed tradition as a whole is to summarize the guiding principle of all speech about God which he has established from the outset: that only in Jesus Christ can God be known, and it is truly God himself who is made known to us in him. All theology, he reminds us, must begin with Jesus Christ, and not with general principles, and must also end with Jesus Christ, and not "with supposedly self-evident general conclusions."[51] What follows is a rigorous undertaking to apply this insight to the doctrine of election.

The effect is immediate and dramatic, as the focus shifts from Barth's earlier emphasis upon our reception of revelation to the person of the Son and the very being of God. Election has now become the primary ontological category for God himself, belonging in the doctrine of God not as one aspect of his nature among many, or even as the first of his "works," but as the fundamental self-determination by which the triune God is who he is, in his free decision to be God-for-us in Christ.[52]

In the person of the Son who comes to us as God in his love and freedom, God is revealed as the one who chooses to enter into gracious relationship with humanity, and as such elects *himself*. Since this electing God is known only in the Son, there can be no absolutizing of the concept of

50. McCormack, *Critically Realistic*, p. 328, although it should be noted that there is no suggestion in Barth's earlier theology that the Spirit's work can in any way be detached from Christ's.

51. *CD* II/2, p. 4.

52. *CD* II/2, e.g., pp. 76-77; see also "The Place of the Doctrine in Dogmatics," pp. 76-93, *passim;* "Jesus Christ, Electing and Elected" (pp. 94-144) and, for a summary, p. 175.

"election" in itself, nor can the electing freedom of God be considered in the abstract. Election has a shape and a character of which we can be graciously assured: it is "the eternal willing of the man Jesus and of the people represented in Him" for the working out of God's purposes of love.[53]

Barth insists that in Jesus Christ — and in him alone — we see the electing God and the elect man. Moreover it is in him — and in him alone — that we see the full content of the doctrine.[54] Election is indeed eternal, unconditional, and double, but the whole of election is now concentrated in the person of Christ.[55] Jesus Christ is not only the one elect, but also, for Barth, the only truly rejected human being.[56] In the "Yes" of the Son, as subject and object of the eternal divine self-electing and in his obedience as the true covenant partner of God in Jesus Christ, he takes upon and exhausts in himself the "No" consequent upon humanity's rejection of God. Election now has a clear teleology. The Son takes upon himself his election to bear our reprobation, so that the "No" of God is solely for the sake of the "Yes," reprobation for the sake of the consummation of the election of grace. Thus, Jesus Christ *is* the election of God, and election is nothing less than "the sum of the gospel."[57]

The christological focus of Barth's doctrine is not only the unfolding for election of his already established theological method. Barth's radical reorientation of election is also worked out in repudiation of the *Deus nudus absconditus* of Reformed orthodoxy, in which he considers that individual double predestination is the outcome of an insufficiently Christ-centered account of the nature of election. On this understanding, Jesus Christ is seen as the chosen means to bring about the ends of an impersonal absolute decree; he is the catalyst for the inexorable unfolding in time of an unfathomable pre-temporal decision in which the individual destinies of every member of the human race have been arbitrarily determined. While Barth acknowledges the Trinitarian and christological intent of earlier formulations, Reformed scholasticism is seen as tending towards

53. *CD* II/2, p. 25 (see pp. 25-26).

54. Developed particularly in "The Eternal Will of God in the Election of Jesus Christ," *CD* II/2, pp. 145-94.

55. *CD* II/2, pp. 161-62; explored throughout pp. 161-75 in terms of the divine "Yes" and "No" of election.

56. For this theme, see *CD* II/2, e.g., pp. 318-19, 346, 352-53.

57. This phrase opens the *Leitsatz* (*CD* II/2, p. 3), and is taken up and developed, e.g., pp. 10-17 (see p. 14, where election is also described as "the gospel *in nuce*... the very essence of all good news").

an understanding of election as the first principle of a remote, ultimately unknowable deity, rather than looking to the eternal Trinity for the basis of the doctrine and to the incarnate Son for its content.[58]

The preceding chapter has made clear that within Owen's profoundly Trinitarian election dynamic Jesus Christ *is* considered to be both Electing God and Elect Man. Christ is the co-author of the decree, and it is in Christ's election that the elect are given to participate. Barth's crucial re-shaping of the doctrine, however, lies precisely in asserting that Jesus Christ *is* the predestination of God. Election does not consist primarily in predestining individuals.[59]

Barth considers that no variation upon the historic Reformed under-standing can offer anything other than an "instrumental" rather than a truly "foundational" election christology, since it implies that in Jesus Christ we do not see the true nature of God's electing decision, but only a "later and subordinate decision" based on the mysterious prior *decretum absolutum* to save some but not others, a decision that is executed by Christ, but not, for Barth, truly founded in him.[60] Moreover, however "Trinitarian" it may appear, the ultimate basis upon which the triune God decides to make that instrumentality effective to some and not to others remains a fearful mystery. Instead, Barth's concentration of the entirety of election in the representative person of Jesus Christ means that Jesus Christ *replaces* the *decretum absolutum* as himself the electing decree of God.[61]

It therefore cannot be emphasized too strongly that for Barth, the *only* act of election and predestination is God's self-determination to be for us in Christ. God's covenant is not made with "man in general," still less with "a small total of individual men," but with "the one man Jesus Christ and the people represented in Him."[62] This concentration of the

58. For Barth's critique of the historic Reformed and Lutheran traditions see, e.g., *CD* II/2, pp. 45ff., 60-76, 106-17, 149-50, 181ff.

59. While strongly upholding the reality of individual election (so, §35, "The Election of the Individual," *passim*) Barth insists that this can only be rightly understood in relation to the radical concentration of election in Christ, and also to the way in which the election of the community is interpreted. For his hostility to the usual understanding of the election of the individual see, e.g., *CD* II/2, pp. 41ff., 133ff.; and "Jesus Christ, the Promise and Its Recipient" (pp. 306-40, *passim*).

60. For Barth's account of the ways in which Reformed orthodoxy falls short of seeing Christ as truly foundational for election, rather than merely instrumental, see *CD* II/2, e.g., pp. 62-70.

61. *CD* II/2, pp. 100-101.

62. *CD* II/2, p. 8.

whole of election and reprobation in the person of Christ creates a division within humanity not on the basis of a decree whose content is the eternal destiny of each individual, but according as we represent a particular facet of *Christ's* election: either the reprobation that Christ has borne and cancelled, or the destiny of humanity with God in Christ that is the purpose of his election.[63]

This division based upon the manner of our participation in Christ's election is materially and formally decisive for his presentation of the election of the community and of individuals. The community particularly designated "elect," because called into self-conscious covenant relationship with God, is Israel-and-the-Church.[64] This community exists as the "inner circle" of election in Christ, which serves to bear witness to the shape of Christ's election to the rest of humanity — the "outer circle" of election in Christ.[65]

The elect community therefore exists in a twofold form that parallels the nature of Christ's election. Israel is designated the "passing man," whose resistance to its election and whose reprobation Christ takes upon

63. In this regard, we may note Sharp's thesis that election in Barth is primarily "noetic," by which he means that it is seen above all as an aspect of God's self-revelation, intended to give knowledge of the nature of God's self-election in Christ. Hence Sharp interprets the fundamental significance of the election of the community of Israel-and-the-church as "rendering them participants in God's continuing self-disclosure" on the basis of his self-election in Christ (*Hermeneutics,* p. 70), and hence what he considers to be Barth's relative lack of concern about soteriological questions with regard to the election of individuals. The primary point of an individual's participation in Christ's election is to make manifest a particular aspect of his election (see, e.g., pp. 83-84).

64. See *CD* II/2, §34, "The Election of the Community," *passim.*

65. *CD* II/2, pp. 196-97. Schleiermacher also speaks of "inner" and "outer" circles in relation to his doctrines of the church and election (*The Christian Faith,* ed. H. R. Mackintosh and J. S. Stewart [Edinburgh: T. & T. Clark, 1928], §113, §116, §117, *passim,* laying the foundations for his extended account of predestination in §119-§120). The inner circle is "the totality of those who live in a state of sanctification" as the common life of believers within the church, and the outer is "the totality of those on whom preparatory grace is at work" (p. 525). There then remains "the world," in which there is as yet no stirring of grace. For Schleiermacher, all three divisions are bound to the consciousness of the need for redemption. This need is suppressed in the world and known only in an inchoate form by the outer circle, whereas the nature of this need is known in its fullness and its remedy experienced within the fellowship of the church (pp. 527-28). The distinction between the outer and inner circles is also identified with the New Testament distinction between the "called" and the "elect" (e.g., pp. 534, 536). For Schleiermacher, therefore, the term "inner circle" can refer only to the church, and he confines the language of election exclusively to this inner circle of the believing community (p. 534).

himself, precisely in order to overcome it.[66] Israel embodies within the elect community the significance of God's self-election in Christ for all the "rejected" who continue to exist in the "outer circle" of election.[67] The church is the "coming man," existing as those who have responded in faith to the reality of their election in Christ, and so live in the light of and as witnesses to the reality of Christ's election to bear rejection.[68]

This division within the one elect community, which is held together in Christ and embraced by the twofold nature of Christ's election, is replicated in the discussion of the election of the individual. Here, Barth describes the distinction within humanity in terms of belonging either to the "elect" believing community of the church or to the rest of as-yet un-

66. So, e.g., *CD* II/2, pp. 208-10, where Barth speaks of the futility and non-finality of Israel's attempt to resist its election in Christ, since it cannot in fact reverse the objective reality of what God in Christ has done for it and for humanity as a whole. We will see that the same is true for the "rejected" individuals outside the elect community of believers.

67. *CD* II/2, p. 263. Barth's understanding of Israel is one of the most prominent aspects of the contemporary discussion of his doctrine of election. A seminal text for this aspect of Barth's doctrine of election is Sonderegger's sympathetic account and critique, *Born a Jew.* See also, e.g., R. Kendall Soulen's critiques in "Karl Barth and the Future of the God of Israel," *Pro Ecclesia* 6, no. 4 (1997): 413-28 and "YHWH the Triune God," *Modern Theology* 15 (January 1999): 25-54, esp. 40-41; and Eberhard Busch's robust historical and theological defense of Barth's position in "The Covenant of Grace Fulfilled in Christ as the Foundation of the Indissoluble Solidarity of the Church with Israel: Barth's Position on the Jews During the Hitler Era," trans. James Seyler, *SJT* 52 (1999): 476-503. As the title indicates, Eugene F. Rogers, "Supplementing Barth on Jews and Gender: Identifying God by Anagogy and the Spirit," *Modern Theology* 14 (January 1998): 43-81, makes the association between some of the difficulties posed by Barth's doctrines of election and the image and the relative underplaying of the Spirit's role in both. For a sympathetic Jewish response to this aspect of Barth's thought, see Michael Wyschogrod, "A Jewish Perspective on Karl Barth," in *How Karl Barth Changed My Mind*, ed. Donald K. McKim (Grand Rapids: Eerdmans, 1986), pp. 156-61, and his "Why Was and Is the Theology of Karl Barth of Interest to a Jewish Theologian?" in Michael Wyschogrod, *Abraham's Promise: Judaism and Jewish-Christian Relations*, ed. R. Kendall Soulen (Grand Rapids: Eerdmans, 2004), pp. 211-24. For a recent contribution to the debate, see Chris Boesel, *Risking Proclamation, Respecting Difference: Christian Faith, Imperialistic Discourse, and Abraham* (Eugene, OR: Cascade Books, 2008).

68. For Barth's detailed exploration of the correspondence of the two forms of the elect community to the twofold form of Christ's election, see §34, 4, "The Passing and the Coming Man." As a representative summary of Barth's position: "The elected community . . . must correspond to this twofold determination of its Head by existing itself also in a twofold form, in a passing and a coming form. . . . It fulfils its determination grounded in its election by representing . . . and attesting to the world both the death taken away by God from man and also the life bestowed on man by God." The notion of Israel-and-the-church as the two sides of the one elect community will be discussed further in Chapter 7.

believing, and so "rejected" humanity. The contrast between them is relative, however, and the use of the terms does not equate with the way in which "elected" and "rejected" are more conventionally understood.[69] For Barth, the distinction is that between the called and the as-yet uncalled, the believing and the godless, and therefore the elect and "apparently rejected," both of whom are united by and held together within Christ's election.[70]

Once again, the difference between them lies above all in the aspect of Christ's election that each represents, and the function that each fulfills within the all-embracing election of Christ in which both participate. The rejected represent the sin which Christ has borne and the reprobation he has cancelled.[71] While they continue to live *as if* rejected, they too are elect in Christ, the only rejected individual.[72] The elect community consists of those who are given to recognize and live in accordance with the nature of Christ's election, and the particular function for which the elect are set apart is to witness.[73] The vocation of the elect is to proclaim to the rest of humanity that the election of Jesus Christ is their own election.[74]

And the Spirit?

It is with the division of humanity into the elect, believing community, and the rejected who as yet remain outside it that we are led to the issue of pneumatology. It has so far been possible to outline the shape of Barth's mature doctrine of election without reference to the Spirit. This is far from atypical. Key summaries and analyses, from Gunton's discussion of Barth's doctrine of election in relation to his doctrine of God to a recent essay by McCormack, make only passing reference to the Spirit's role.[75] This is in turn a reflection of Barth's own presentation of the doctrine, in which ref-

---

69. *CD* II/2, p. 327; see pp. 327-29. See also pp. 350-54.

70. *CD* II/2, p. 351; see also p. 329. Note the contrast here with Barth's earlier understanding of the human situation, summed up in the statement that one is either "called or not called . . . elected *or rejected*" (*CD* I/2, p. 266, my italics; see fn. 43 above).

71. E.g., *CD* II/2, pp. 352-53; see also, e.g., pp. 316-18.

72. *CD* II/2, p. 352.

73. *CD* II/2, e.g., pp. 342-47,

74. *CD* II/2, pp. 343-45. See also, e.g., p. 318, where the message of the elect to the rejected is that "he, too, is an elect man."

75. Gunton, "Karl Barth's Doctrine of Election"; McCormack, "Grace and Being."

erences to the Spirit are relatively few.[76] Nevertheless, Barth does indeed provide a clear outline of the Spirit's role.

When considering election from the perspective of the triune life of God, Barth's primary emphasis is upon the relationship between Father and Son. Indeed, election is described specifically as "the decision made between Father and Son from all eternity."[77] He does, however, offer a Trinitarian account of the self-electing decision by which God determines his being: as it is the eternal choice of the Father to be gracious towards humanity in offering the Son, and the Son's choice to offer himself up in obedience to the Father, so it is the Holy Spirit's resolve to preserve the unity of the Godhead, such that it "should not be disturbed or rent by this covenant with man, but . . . made the more glorious," in the demonstration and confirmation of God's love and freedom.[78] For Barth, therefore, the Spirit equally with the Father and the Son is the very possibility of God being for us in election.

In turn, the Spirit's primary task in bringing the accomplished work of election in Christ to bear upon humanity is that of calling, realized in the "twofold possibility of proclamation and faith."[79] It is precisely Spirit-empowered proclamation issuing in Spirit-enabled faith that leads to incorporation into the believing community of the elect. Barth is therefore clear that the distinction between the elect and the rejected consists in the presence or absence of the Spirit. It is because they "lack the gift of the Holy Spirit" that the rejected continue to live as if rejected in spite of their election.[80] As will be explored in the following chapter, while the Spirit's work of faith reveals the nature of God's self-election in Christ and brings it to articulation, the whole of humanity is included in Christ's election to bear rejection whether it recognizes the reality of its own situation or not. An objective change in the entire human situation before God has already occurred in Christ apart from the Spirit's work in us.[81]

---

76. Bowman notes that the triune exposition of election in Barth is at times "more confessional than theological . . . [with the] Holy Spirit . . . largely absent from the discussion" (*Divine Decision*, p. 33).

77. *CD* II/2, p. 90.

78. *CD* II/2, p. 101; see also pp. 105-6.

79. *CD* II/2, pp. 345ff. We will turn to elements of the outworking of this in Barth's doctrine of reconciliation in Chapter 7.

80. *CD* II/2, p. 345; see also p. 346: those outside the community of the visibly elect "do not possess the Holy Spirit," and so continue in their ultimately "futile attempt to live the life of one rejected by God."

81. For Christ's election as the eternal presupposition and basis of the reality of the

With this we are starkly confronted with the difference between his mature doctrine of election and that which shapes the opening volumes of *CD,* and the recognition that the crucial differences between them lie in his account of the Spirit's role as much as Christ's. As has been seen, in his earlier work, Barth sets out an account of the human situation before God in which the gift of the Spirit is soteriologically determinative of election or rejection, and in which to be "in Christ" is something "added" to our being by the Spirit. There is no sharing in the reconciliation to be found in the person of Jesus Christ as God's Revelation without the corresponding activity of the Spirit as God's Revealedness. With the concentration of the entirety of election in the person of Christ and participation in his election as the ontological reality for all, the relationship between Christ's work and the Spirit's in election has been decisively altered.

Barth's mature position in this regard, and some of the issues that it raises, will be explored further in the following chapter. For the moment, however, we turn to the influence of this approach to election on his presentation of the *imago dei,* and the drawing together of election and the image in the notion of "true" or "real" humanity of Christ. What follows, then, will not be an exhaustive account of Barth's rich and complex doctrine of the image of God, any more than that which precedes is an exhaustive account of Barth's two doctrines of election. Rather, the focus here is upon how our imaging of God relates to our election in Christ and how christology and pneumatology play out in Barth's account of the image of God in the light of his doctrine of election.

Election and the Image of God

In the first instance, it is necessary to note the broader creational contours within which Barth's account of the human imaging of God is set. Creation as a whole is seen as the external basis of the covenant and the covenant as the internal basis of creation.[82] This covenant is nothing other than the eternal, loving, and self-determining decision of God in his self-

---

whole human situation before God see, e.g., *CD* II/2, p. 321. For the "decisive alteration of the human situation" already brought about by God's self-election in Christ see also, e.g., *CD* IV/1, pp. 310ff.

82. Seen as the hermeneutical keys to Genesis 1 and 2, explored in §41, sections 2 and 3 respectively.

election to be God-for-humanity in the person of Jesus Christ.[83] More widely than the human sphere alone, the creating God, as the covenant God, elects to bear the No of all that threatens to descend into non-being in order that the Yes of God's purpose of blessing might prevail, such that the covenant purpose of God in the person of Christ is therefore the goal of God's creating act.[84]

For Barth, that God chooses to bring anything other than himself into being is the expression of his gracious intentions towards and purpose for it, so that we might say that creation in its entirety is literally loved into being.[85] The very act of creation is grace and blessing, and the very fact of being created is itself "election and acceptance."[86] As a result, whatever any creature may attempt to make of itself, it is elected, accepted, and justified by virtue of God bringing it to be.[87]

Here, then, we see the outworking not only for humanity but for creation as a whole of the all-encompassing self-election of God in Christ. Within this understanding of the wider creation, the image in us consists in the fact that we are created to be the covenant partners of God, as the one creature able to hear and obey God. Summoned and addressed by God, we are God's "counterpart" in creation.[88] Our imaging consists in an *analogia relationis,* central to which is the notion of differentiation and relation in "I-Thou" encounter. This characterizes our existence as the covenant partners of God and our engagement with one another in our cohumanity. In both of these sets of relations, we are imaging the inner being of God, who is himself differentiation-in-relation, in the "I-Thou" relationship of Father and Son.[89]

---

83. So, the inner basis of the covenant itself is "the free love of God, or more precisely the eternal covenant which God has decreed in Himself as the covenant of the Father with His Son," as the one who enters creation in the person of Jesus Christ (*CD* III/1, p. 97). See also, e.g., pp. 229ff.

84. E.g., *CD* III/2, pp. 143-44; *CD* III/1, pp. 330-34.

85. E.g., *CD* III/1, pp. 94ff.

86. E.g., *CD* III/1, p. 331.

87. *CD* III/1, p. 366. The relationship between creation, election, and God's Yes and No is briefly set out at the start of §42, "The Yes of God the Creator" (pp. 330-32), and given full discussion in section 3, "Creation and Justification," *passim.*

88. *CD* III/1, p. 184, introduces the concept (see pp. 183-85). For a recent development of the theme of the image as counterpart, see Robert Jenson, *Systematic Theology,* vol. 2: *The Works of God* (Oxford: Oxford University Press, 1999), chaps. 18 and 20 in particular.

89. So, for example, in humanity as God's created counterpart we see "the divine form of life repeated in the man created by him . . . In God's own being . . . there is a counterpart"

It is in this context that Barth points to our creation as male and female as a central element of the *imago dei*. In turn, the male/female relation points beyond itself, as the paradigmatic representation in the very structure of humanness of the covenant relation towards God in which we all stand, and which is the goal of our creation. This reality is made explicit in the relationship between Yahweh and Israel, and supremely, Christ and the church.[90] So, drawing together the language of election, covenant, and imaging, Barth speaks of "the divine likeness of man as male and female which in the plan and election of God is primarily the relationship between Jesus Christ and His Church, secondarily the relationship between Yahweh and Israel and only finally . . . the relationship between the sexes."[91]

On the basis of the image as the *analogia relationis,* we find the rejection of any particular faculty as the locus of the image in us.[92] Rather, the image refers to our whole personhood as those who exist in differentiated relation towards God and each other. Neither, however, is Barth willing to locate the image in our relationship to God in quite the way that Owen suggests. His focus is not upon the image as our *right-relatedness to God,* but rather the nature of *God's relationship to us,* determined in his self-election in Christ, and therefore in his very being as Trinity, from all eternity.[93]

---

of which, in our imaging, we are the copy and reflection, since this "I-Thou" relationality is "first constitutive for God and then for man created by God" (*CD* III/1, p. 185). See also, e.g., pp. 196-201.

90. As a convenient summary of a pervasive theme, "The fact that he was created man and woman will be the paradigm of everything that is to take place between him and God, and also of everything that is to take place between him and his fellows," and as a type of the history of the covenant and salvation (*CD* III/1, pp. 186-87). For further exploration of the concept of marriage in relation to the covenant between Yahweh and Israel, which in turn points to its supreme realization in Christ and the church, see, e.g., pp. 312-29, and also Barth's continued development of the image as differentiated relation with regard to marriage and our existence as covenant counterparts of God in *CD* III/4, §54, 1, "Man and Woman." Nathan MacDonald offers an account of exegetical criticism of Barth's identification of the image as male/female, but also of the hermeneutical issues at stake, giving a positive assessment of the wider validity of Barth's insight that the image is to be identified primarily with our creation as God's counterpart. See his "The *Imago Dei* and Election: Reading Gen 1:26-28 and Old Testament Scholarship with Karl Barth," *IJST* 10 (July 2008): 303-27.

91. *CD* III/1, p. 322.

92. So, e.g., *CD* III/1, pp. 184ff.

93. *CD* III/1, pp. 190f., 200.

POSING A PNEUMATOLOGICAL PROBLEM

Barth therefore emphatically rejects any suggestion that the image might have been lost. Even in the face of our sin, the image can neither be abrogated nor even partially, let alone completely, destroyed.[94] As he pointedly remarks, "What man does not possess, he can neither bequeath nor forfeit."[95] It is intrinsic to our very being that we are created to be God's counterparts, in indestructible relation to him because God is in irreversible relation to us. To be created in the image of God as God's counterpart is to be created for blessing, in such a way that this cannot be lost or reversed, "even in the face of the total contradiction between it and the being of man."[96] Instead, we await the fullness of its realization in us, as its fullness has been manifested by and achieved for us in Christ.

This understanding of the image clearly reflects and parallels his account of election, in which election signifies in the first instance God's fundamental disposition towards us in Christ, and only secondarily our response to God.[97] Moreover, just as the community particularly termed "elect" exists as those who live in the light of and bear witness to the participation of the whole of humanity in Christ, so Barth draws together the image and election by speaking of the particular election of Israel, Christ, and the church as both the confirmation of the election of humanity as a whole, and also as the demonstration of the universal reality of the image in humanity's special calling as the creature who is addressed and summoned by God.[98] Thus, as our participation in Christ's election is a basic ontological reality for human beings, so too is our existence as the *imago dei*. Through the universal human reality of male/female, pointing beyond itself as a sign of the goal of the covenant in Christ and his people, all human beings participate in that to which they point. This is the case "even before they know Him, even before they believe in Jesus Christ. . . . It does not alter the fact that in all their humanity, willingly or wittingly or not," they share in the strength and certainty of the divine plan for humanity which has Christ as its goal. This is, for Barth, the indestructible blessing

---

94. *CD* III/1, p. 200, where he also rejects the image as *rectitudo*. The stark (but unacknowledged) contrast with his earlier position is evident. See p. 38 above.

95. *CD* III/1, p. 200.

96. *CD* III/1, p. 190.

97. For a brief account of Barth's doctrine of election as determinative for the structure of his theological anthropology see Wolf Krötke, "The Humanity of the Human Person in Karl Barth's Anthropology," trans. Philip G. Ziegler, in *The Cambridge Companion to Karl Barth*, ed. John Webster (Cambridge: Cambridge University Press, 2000), pp. 159-76, 163-66.

98. E.g., *CD* III/2, pp. 149-50.

that is our creation in the image of God.[99] To be created in the image of God is already to be the object of blessing, and the one for whom blessing is ultimately intended.[100]

As this indicates, it is therefore above all to the person and work of Christ that we must look for the source of the intimate relationship between Barth's account of election and the image. Just as in Jesus Christ, Electing God and Elect Man, the entirety of election is concentrated, so in Jesus Christ we see the fullness of the imaging of God, in his existence as the perfect divine and human counterpart.

As we might expect, Barth, like Owen, makes clear that Jesus Christ is uniquely the one true image of God in his divinity by virtue of the *homoousion*.[101] He is also the image of God because in his humanity he is the revelation and fulfillment of the meaning and goal of *Israel's* existence.[102] It is in Israel that we see the concentration of the nature and purpose of the image of God — that human beings are created as God's counterparts and partners in his covenant — in the unfolding of history until the incarnation. So, for Barth, "The image of God, and therefore the divine likeness of [humanity], is revealed in God's dealings with Israel . . . as the goal towards which it moves."[103] In turn, as it is the relationship of Yahweh to Israel that reveals the covenanted "I-Thou" relation that constitutes our imaging of God, so Christ is the image of God in his inseparable differentiation-in-relation with his community in the world, the church.[104] In all of this, Christ is also the perfection of the differentiation-in-relation between human beings, living in perfect "co-humanity" as the one who is utterly "for" God and therefore utterly "for" others.[105]

In a central concept for Barth, Jesus Christ is therefore God's "true" or "real" humanity.[106] It is only by looking to Christ who embodies this for us that we know the nature of humanity as created by God. In him is revealed

---

99. *CD* III/1, p. 191.

100. So, e.g., *CD* III/1, p. 189.

101. See, e.g., *CD* III/1, pp. 201f.

102. *CD* III/1, pp. 201-2.

103. *CD* III/1, p. 200.

104. See esp. *CD* III/1, pp. 203-5, 320ff.

105. Discussed in the context of Christ's true humanity in *CD* III/2 §45, 2, "The Basic Form of Humanity," *passim*. We will return to Barth's conception of Christ as the one uniquely "for" others in Chapter 7.

106. Barth begins to discuss Christ the "true" or "real" human in *CD* III/2 §43, 2, "Man as an Object of Theological Knowledge" (particularly pp. 48ff.), and develops the theme in greater detail in III/2, §44, 3, "Real Man," *passim*.

to us both who God irrevocably and unequivocally is towards humanity and what is basically, ontologically true of all human beings, which sin cannot alter.[107] Jesus is "man as God willed and created him. What constitutes true humanity in us [and therefore our true imaging of God] depends upon what is in Him."[108]

As we participate in Christ's all-embracing election, so we participate in his all-encompassing imaging of God. What humanity is, is determined by the eternal self-election of God in Christ and his life, death, and resurrection which correspond to that election.[109] For the image, as for election, in Jesus, "the first and last word is spoken about us, and the last with all the power of the first." Sin cannot revoke what is decided in Jesus concerning the true nature of human beings, so that while we may corrupt and distort our humanity, "What [we are] is decided elsewhere in such a way that [we] cannot affect the decision."[110] Drawing together election and the image in discussing our "real humanity" in Christ, and so our primary ontological determination as those created to be in the image of God, Barth offers the summary that to be human is to be "with the One who is the true and primary Elect of God" such that humanity "must and may be described as elected along with the man Jesus," and destined to share in his victory.[111]

And the Spirit?

As was the case with election, we have given an account of the contours of Barth's understanding of the image of God without reference to the Spirit. Once again, this is a reflection of much of Barth's presentation. It is not without justification that Gunton points to the binitarian tendencies in Barth's presentation of the image.[112] Duality dominates his account,

---

107. *CD* III/2, p. 43.
108. *CD* III/2, p. 50.
109. *CD* III/2, p. 50; see also, e.g., pp. 142-47.
110. *CD* III/2, p. 50, for both quotations.
111. *CD* III/2, p. 145. See pp. 145-47 for a discussion of the grounding of humanity in the self-election of God in Christ, so that as "the fellow-elect of Jesus," humanity is "predestined to be the victor and not the vanquished in the defence of being against non-being" (p. 147).
112. Colin Gunton, "Trinity, Ontology and Anthropology: Towards a Renewal of the Doctrine of the *Imago Dei*," in *Persons, Divine and Human*, ed. Christoph Schwöbel and Colin E. Gunton (Edinburgh: T. & T. Clark, 1991), pp. 47-61, p. 58. See also, e.g., Rogers, "Supplementing Barth," pp. 68-77, for a critique and suggested pneumatological correctives,

from the inner-divine foundation of the "I-Thou" relation between Father and Son to the fundamental structural division of humanity into male-female and the covenant relations to which this points. While the Spirit's role in each of these does not go entirely unremarked, it is most certainly underweighted.

We have noted that Barth spends only a very little time pointing to the Spirit's role in the inner-Trinitarian dynamic by which God determines his own being in self-election. He spends even less to indicate the Spirit's role in the fundamental "I-Thou" relationship that constitutes the being of God and establishes the shape of our imaging of God. While the "I-Thou" relationship of Father and Son is all-pervasive, the Spirit's place in this relation is noted a bare handful of times in passing. So, for example, Barth suggests a Trinitarian dynamic for the "I-Thou" relationship in God in terms of God who posits himself, is posited by himself, and confirms himself, as the one who loves eternally, is loved eternally, and is eternal love; and that in the "I-Thou" of God, the Father and the Son confront one another as "I-Thou" in the Holy Spirit.[113] While it might be said that the Spirit's role should simply be assumed wherever it is not stated, at the very least his role in this decisive relationship suffers from benign neglect.[114]

When it comes to the imaging of God in the economy, however, the Spirit's role is somewhat more prominent.[115] Again, there are clear paral-

---

and Grenz's account and critique of Barth's use of the "I-Thou" paradigm in *The Social God and the Relational Self: A Trinitarian Theology of the Imago Dei* (Louisville: Westminster/John Knox Press, 2001), pp. 294-303.

113. *CD* III/2, pp. 218-19 and 324 respectively.

114. In this context, we might also note that while his emphasis upon the "I-Thou" relation between Father and Son in the Godhead indicates that Barth has now moved away from his reluctance to use the language of "persons" for the Trinity in I/1, his understanding of the Spirit remains the same. In I/1 he points out that if it is difficult to use the language of "person" for Father and Son, it is impossible with regard to the Spirit (*CD* I/1, p. 469; see pp. 469-70). The functional, rather than in any way "personal" language about the Spirit in his doctrine of creation is extremely pronounced. So, for example, Barth is able to say that the "Spirit in His being *ad extra* is neither a divine nor a created something, but *an action and attitude of the Creator in relation to His creation. We cannot say that the Spirit is, but that He takes place as the divine basis of this relation* and fellowship" (*CD* III/2, p. 356, my italics). Rogers sums up the criticisms of Barth in this regard by remarking that what is needed in his theology more generally is a clearer sense in which the Spirit is an actor together with the Father and the Son, and not merely their act ("Eclipse of the Spirit," p. 184).

115. Although even here, in places where we might most expect to find an emphatic pneumatology, we are confronted with pneumatological silence. So, for example, in an extended treatment of the centrality of hearing and obeying the Word for our imaging of God

lels between the Spirit's role in the human imaging of God and in election. Just as the primary role of the Spirit in the self-election of God relates to his work in the economy, ensuring that the unity of Father and Son is not rent by the incarnation, so in the context of Christ's true humanity and imaging of God Barth speaks of the unique relationship of Christ to the Spirit. The Spirit is the source of Christ's very existence and he lives not only from the Spirit but in the Spirit, as the one to whom the Spirit is given without measure.[116]

Our humanity too has a correspondingly pneumatological nature, and once again this is tightly bound to the notion of our election. In his discussion of Genesis 2, that which marks human beings as elect is the giving of God's breath in personal encounter, by which Adam becomes a "living soul."[117] This is a theme he pursues through the notion that it is by the Spirit that human beings are the souls of their bodies.[118]

Here, we may speak of the twofold nature of the Spirit's role, which once again demonstrates the close interweaving of Barth's understanding of the image with his approach to election. First, we exist because by the Spirit of God we have spirit, such that we are constituted as soul-and-body. This pneumatological principle of our being means that we are constituted and maintained by God and therefore that we literally cannot "be" without God. This is linked both to the image (by this we are inherently constituted as God's counterparts) and to election (we are constituted as the recipients of God's covenant of grace). That by God's gracious determination, through the Spirit, human beings are soul-and-body is therefore the sign

---

(CD III/2, pp. 163ff.), there is no reference to the Spirit as the one through whom alone we can do either.

116. CD III/2, pp. 332-34.

117. Barth's interpretation of Genesis 2 is closely and explicitly interwoven with the theme of election, seeing in every element of this creation story the pre-historical prefiguring of the covenant relationship between Yahweh and Israel, and the shape of election as exaltation and humiliation, pointing in turn to the nature of election in the person of Christ. So, for example, referring specifically to the fashioning of Adam from the dust of the earth and his constitution by the breath of God, Barth remarks that "The whole history of Israel . . . and ultimately the whole history of its fulfilment in Jesus Christ lies behind this brief description" (CD III/1, p. 244). This close binding of our creation, election, and our imaging of God in terms of covenant partnership and "I-Thou" relation is signified in his choice of overarching theme for this section (III/1, §41, 3): the covenant as the internal basis of creation.

118. See CD III/2, §46, 2, "The Spirit as Basis of Soul and Body." That we exist as soul-and-body through the agency of the Spirit is another example of the differentiation-in-relation that characterizes our imaging of God at every level of our being.

and guarantee of the loving purpose of God towards us, and a basic, unalterable ontological fact of all human being.[119]

Second, the Spirit is also the one who sets apart particular individuals — and, in the case of the church, a particular community, as well as individuals within that community — for a unique role in the unfolding of the covenant purposes of God. As Barth indicates, to "have" spirit as the gift of the Spirit in the creational sense is one thing; to receive the Spirit in such a way as to enable us to acknowledge the self-revelation of God in Christ is another.[120] The latter, "revelational" role of the Spirit towards us is not intrinsic to our being, or determinative of our imaging (or, as we have noted, of the reality of our election). The coming of the Spirit for this purpose is the particular gift of God within the overall participation of humanity in Christ's election, and within the imaging of God that takes place by virtue of our being human.

This means that once again we also see repeated in this context the theme that we noted in Barth's account of election and the image: the community particularly designated elect, and set apart for this purpose by the Spirit, exists to demonstrate and witness to the reality in which all share, whether we realize it or not. Thus, "As the elected . . . and to that extent 'new' man lives in the covenant by the fact that God gives him His Spirit, the natural man also lives in the same way" because the Spirit is the principle of his creaturely reality, and the fact that all human beings are soul-and-body, just as human beings exist as male-and-female, points beyond itself to the truth that all exist as the covenant partners of God.[121] To say that the Spirit is the principle of our existence as a unity of soul-and-body is to say nothing less than God is for us and turns to us in grace, and so is to reiterate the reality of our participation in God's self-election for us in Christ.[122]

Conclusion

To discuss Barth's account of the image of God is therefore also in large measure to restate and to draw out some further implications of his mature doctrine of election. In so doing we have seen both the richness and

---

119. *CD* III/2, e.g., pp. 344-47.
120. See, e.g., *CD* III/4, pp. 359-62; *CD* III/2, pp. 355-58.
121. *CD* III/2, p. 359.
122. *CD* III/2, e.g., pp. 344-47, 363.

the coherence of the relationship between the two, and will find that as with some of the key emphases of Owen, many of the insights offered by Barth here will resurface in Part II, in the context of an engagement with contemporary biblical scholarship, to assist in resolving some of the dilemmas raised by their respective doctrines of election.

As we have begun to hint, however, it is when we come to Barth with the pneumatological consequences and implications of his approach in mind that some difficulties are also raised in a particularly acute form. The impact of the shift in Barth's doctrine of election upon his pneumatology is inescapable. While the Spirit clearly remains God's gracious gift of himself whereby human beings, otherwise wholly incapable of apprehending God, are enabled to encounter God in his self-revelation, there is a clear alteration in the significance of the Spirit's role within the dynamic of election and a corresponding alteration of the balance between Christ's work and the Spirit's. While the shortcomings of Barth's earlier, strongly pneumatological account of election are many, it must also be said that at the very least, his mature election christology raises some serious pneumatological questions.

It is to an analysis of some of the pneumatological difficulties raised by Barth's later understanding of election "in Christ" that we turn in the following chapter. Moreover, by exploring these pneumatological concerns in more detail, we will also be in a position to give fuller expression to *the* pneumatological problem for a Reformed doctrine of election, posed at the end of the previous chapter.

CHAPTER 3

Election "in Christ" in Barth: Some Pneumatological Queries

We have seen that in his earlier account of election, Barth focuses so intensively upon the relationship between election and the Spirit-enabled reception of revelation that in *GD* in particular, the notion that election is "in Christ" is all but lost. Although to be "in Christ" by the Spirit receives somewhat more attention in the early volumes of *CD*, the nature of revelation remains the primary lens through which the Spirit's work in relation to election is understood.

That election is radically "in Christ" is the claim at the very heart of Barth's reorientation of the doctrine. As has been suggested, however, it is almost invariably overlooked that his highly distinctive approach to the "in Christ" of election has decisive implications for the way in which it is also considered to be "by the Spirit." The concern of this chapter is to seek to assess the implications of Barth's monumental christological reworking of the doctrine for his presentation of the Spirit's role.

In so doing, it rapidly becomes apparent that difficulties and inconsistencies surrounding the Spirit's role are at the heart of many of those aspects of the doctrine that are usually identified as particularly problematic. Moreover, the outcome of his mature doctrine of election for the relationship between Christ's work and the Spirit's is such as to suggest that, however exhilarating in conception, the scriptural and Trinitarian adequacy — as well as the internal coherence — of Barth's account of election "in Christ" must be seriously questioned.

Participating in Christ's Election

As the previous chapter has made clear, that election is radically "in Christ" signifies for Barth that Christ is not simply the co-author of the decree, nor is it only the case that those who are elect are so in that they are given to participate in his election. It means above all that in Christ we see the whole predestination of God, such that Jesus Christ alone *is* the election of God. Election is "in Christ" because there is for Barth only the one predestining act: God's self-election to be God-for-us in the person of Jesus Christ. There is no separate and separable election of particular individuals. Instead, we are told that Christ has taken on the rejection of "all those that are elected 'in Him.'"[1]

Once we turn from the concept of election itself being "in Christ" to the question of our participation in Christ's election, however, we find that Barth's choice of terms to describe those who share in that election is by no means easy to reconcile. They are variously denoted as the "people called and united by Him";[2] "the many (from whom none is excluded)";[3] the rejected "in himself and as such who in and with the election of . . . Jesus is loved from all eternity and elected . . .";[4] the godless, whose choice of godlessness is rendered void, "eternally denied and annulled in Jesus Christ";[5] and those who believe in Christ, who are therefore "in Him" and "the object of the divine election of grace."[6]

It is helpful to clarify that Barth is effectively operating with a twofold understanding of the term "elect" with regard to our sharing in the primary election of Christ. To be elect in Christ is both a description of those whose reprobation Christ has representatively borne (and therefore includes the apparently "rejected"), and it is also the "peculiar determination for the service of God" that characterizes the believing community of the church.[7]

Within this twofold understanding, we might summarize by stating that the elect community of the church is to be distinguished *functionally but not ontologically*, and *pneumatologically but not christologically*, from

1. *CD* II/2, p. 123.
2. *CD* II/2, p. 43.
3. *CD* II/2, p. 195.
4. *CD* II/2, p. 123. Barth goes on to speak of Christ accomplishing all that is necessary "for all who are elected in Him, for man in himself and as such."
5. *CD* II/2, p. 317 (see pp. 316-17).
6. *CD* II/2, p. 127 (see pp. 126-27).
7. *CD* II/2, p. 343; see also p. 196.

the rest of humanity. As we noted in the previous chapter, like Israel and the church, the believing elect and the unbelieving rejected are united in and held together by the twofold determination of Christ's election. They are distinguished by the aspect of Christ's all-embracing election that they represent and the role that they fulfill.[8]

In this, the Spirit is determinative. As those "without the Spirit," the rejected continue to live in futile rebellion against their election.[9] Through the gift of the Spirit, the elect are set apart as those who know, live by, and proclaim the foundational reality that the whole of history is the unfolding of God's self-election for humanity,[10] and that the only truly rejected one is the Son.[11] The *Leitsatz* at the head of Barth's account of the election of the individual sums up the witness of the elect to the rejected: that their rejection has been borne and cancelled by Jesus Christ, so that they are therefore "not rejected, but elected by God in Jesus Christ."[12]

In the christologically determined ontology of election, Barth is able to speak categorically of Christ as the one who takes from the apparently rejected "the right and possibility *of his own independent being and gives him His own being.*"[13] The gap that needs to be bridged is therefore between the reality of the *being* of the rejected, which is nevertheless that of election in Christ, and the *lived acknowledgment* of that ontological reality. Hence, Barth asserts that "[i]t is *not for his being but for his life* as elect that he needs to hear and believe the promise."[14] In this way, that which is real

8. See Chapter 2, pp. 45-47.
9. *CD* II/2, p. 346.
10. *CD* II/2, pp. 185-86.
11. *CD* II/2, p. 319; see also pp. 346-47, 349, 352-53.
12. *CD* II/2, p. 306.
13. *CD* II/2, p. 453, my italics. Barth precedes this statement with the definition of the divinely imposed limit to the threat of rejection, which is that "the rejected man exists in the person of Jesus Christ only in such a way that he is *assumed into His being* as the elect and beloved of God" (p. 453, my italics). Thus, Barth continues by insisting that there can be no independent existence of the rejected *as* rejected, but that they exist only as those for whom Christ elected irreversibly to bear rejection.
14. *CD* II/2, p. 453, my italics. This encapsulates the distinction in Barth's mature doctrine of election between what we may describe as the "ontological" (the christological determination of our being) and the "ontic" (whether or not we are brought into lived correspondence with this ontological reality), and the division of these aspects into the christological and pneumatological respectively. See, e.g., Thompson's summary of Barth's position: "We, by putting on Christ [by the Spirit], experience a renewal of our being — a change noetically corresponding to that wrought in our humanity ontologically by the union of God and humanity in Jesus Christ" (J. Thompson, *The Holy Spirit in the Theology*

objectively for the rejected ("his election in Jesus Christ") will become "real subjectively."[15]

The Spirit's activity for the believing elect is therefore both noetic and ontic; the two are inseparable for Barth, since knowledge of God always entails transformation. To be "in Christ," however, is a christologically achieved ontological reality not just for the circle of believers to whom the Spirit has been given, but for all, even if they never come to live in accordance with their election.[16] In other words, those who live "without the Spirit" are nevertheless "in Christ."

This is one reason for Barth's refusal to allow our response of faith or unbelief to have any bearing on the reality of our election in Christ. The historic Reformed tradition itself sought to eschew simple deductions concerning election or rejection on the basis of apparent faith or lack of it. As Barth rightly points out, the judgment of charity in the tradition means that all must be regarded as potentially of the elect, and therefore as those who may come to faith at God's chosen time.[17] Through the concentration

---

of *Karl Barth* [Allison Park, PA: Pickwick Publications, 1991], p. 9; see also P. J. Rosato, *The Spirit as Lord: The Pneumatology of Karl Barth* [Edinburgh: T. & T. Clark, 1981], e.g., p. 124). This point must be borne in mind, for example, in relation to Barth's use of "ontological" language concerning the Spirit's role in sanctification. This does indeed make a real "alteration" in our being (so, e.g., *CD* IV/2, p. 259), but it does not affect or alter the christological ontology that defines the existence of each and every person.

15. *CD* II/2, p. 322. Our being as elect in Christ is paralleled by Barth's discussion of the conversion of humanity and the world to God in Christ. This event of conversion takes place, and its universal reality is established, in the event of the cross (summarized in *CD* IV/1, p. 296, but a central theme of the preceding section, "The Judge Judged in Our Place"), so that our conversion to faith by the Spirit is our noetic and ontic participation in the christologically achieved ontological reality of this prior conversion in Christ. In Barth's account of "The Being of Man in Christ," this christological/pneumatological, ontological/ontic distinction is clear. Speaking of unbelievers (and so, of the "rejected"), he remarks that "It is not that they lack Jesus Christ and in Him the being of man reconciled to God. What they lack is obedience to His Holy Spirit . . . experience and knowledge of the conversion of man to God which took place in Him" (*CD* IV/1, p. 93).

16. *CD* II/2, p. 321. As we have noted, Barth makes similar points in the context of our sharing in Christ's "true" or "real" humanity, remarking, e.g., that as we are with Jesus and so with God, we are "elected in the divine election of grace," such that humanity "may and must be described as elected along with the man Jesus" (*CD* III/2, p. 145). Colwell rightly states that for Barth, the ontological definition of humanity is "that of man [*sic*] as reconciled to God in Jesus Christ" (John E. Colwell, *Actuality and Provisionality: Eternity and Election in the Theology of Karl Barth* [Edinburgh: Rutherford House Books, 1989], p. 261).

17. *CD* II/2, pp. 327-28.

of the whole of election in the person of Christ, however, Barth is able to press beyond the tradition to speak of all as elect in Christ *whether or not* the subjective response is of faith or unbelief. The vocation of the believing elect is to bear witness to the rest of humanity the reality of its own participation in Christ's election: its proclamation to the rejected is that "[i]n Jesus Christ thou . . . art not rejected but elected."[18]

Any discussion of the significance or otherwise of faith or unbelief is immediately a discussion of the significance of the Spirit's role, since for Barth it remains the case that only through the Spirit as God's Revealedness are we enabled to acknowledge the self-revelation of God.[19] Just as a response to historical factors is inextricably woven with dogmatic priorities in the development of Barth's election christology, so also the rejection of tendencies within the tradition influences his treatment of the Spirit.

Rosato in particular stresses the link between Barth's intense christological focus and his diagnosis of the decline of pneumatology into human subjectivity and its increasing detachment from the person and work of Christ in Schleiermacher and neo-Protestantism.[20] From the synergistic tendencies of the practical syllogism to the absorption of pneumatology into anthropology via Schleiermacher and "Christian existentialism," Rosato rightly points out that an overriding concern for Barth is to distance himself from the merest suggestion that election might be in some way identified with human subjectivity.[21]

---

18. *CD* II/2, p. 322.

19. This central tenet of his earlier theology remains prominent in *CD* II/2. See, e.g., pp. 126, 238-39, 320, 326-29, 345-46, 348, 458, in which Barth makes clear that it is only the work of God by the Spirit through faith that anyone can know the electing God, their own election, and that God's self-election is for all.

20. Rosato opens *Spirit as Lord* with a detailed discussion of this issue (Chap. 1, "The Haunting Ambiguity of Pneumatology"), and it is a recurring theme throughout his exposition of Barth's pneumatology, which he sees as a "tireless effort to redeem the valid insights and excise the dangerous errors of Schleiermacher" (p. 3). Rosato considers that 1947 is a seminal year for Barth's pneumatology in this regard, but this must be qualified by recognizing the watershed in Barth's thinking on the Spirit's role a decade earlier, as a result of the shift in his understanding of the nature of election. For a brief recent account of the role played by Schleiermacher's thought in the development of Barth's pneumatology see Eugene F. Rogers, Jr., "The Eclipse of the Spirit in Karl Barth," in *Conversing with Barth*, ed. John C. McDowell and Mike Higton (Aldershot: Ashgate, 2004), pp. 173-90, esp. pp. 176-78. His opening remark aptly summarizes his overall contention: "Karl Barth allows the Son to eclipse the Spirit when he allows his fear of Schleiermacher to overshadow his admiration for Athanasius" (p. 173).

21. Rosato, *Spirit as Lord,* esp. pp. 1-22, and with particular regard to election, pp. 83ff. See also, e.g., Colin Gunton, "Karl Barth's Doctrine of Election as Part of His Doctrine of

To what extent, however, is this a new concern in Barth's mature doctrine of election, and to what extent does Barth's distinctive election christology in particular contribute to safeguarding it? Barth has already established the Spirit as the one who preserves the objectivity of the Christ event in its subjective application. Where the Spirit is held to be God himself in his Revealedness, and where only the gift of the Spirit enables the human response of faith and obedience, no form of "subjectivism" is possible.

George Hunsinger's categories of "soteriological objectivism" and "soteriological existentialism" bring the issues into sharp focus.[22] He rightly describes Barth's understanding of "in Christ" in terms of a "soteriological objectivism" in which salvation is entirely constituted, complete, and effective for all apart from our response or lack of response.[23] Any form of "soteriological existentialism," in which our subjective appropriation can be thought of as decisive for or constitutive of salvation, cannot be countenanced.[24]

Since existential appropriation is the work of the Spirit in us, the presentation of our response as non-determinative of, and non-constitutive for, soteriology and our election "in Christ" is also a description of the relative marginalizing of the Spirit's work in these spheres. Moreover, while Christ's work is indeed identified as the "objective" element in the divine act of salvation, it is altogether less clear that our *subjective* response nevertheless remains the *objective* work of the Spirit in us. It is not surprising that in his mature doctrine of election (and in its continued outworking in his theology) Barth has been seen as unnecessarily ceding the pneumatological ground to his opponents, by implicitly colluding with the tendency to identify pneumatology and anthropology.[25]

God," *Journal of Theological Studies* 25, no. 2 (1974): 381-92, pp. 382-83. For Barth's anxieties about the dangers of experiential criteria in election — whether our response of faith, or the "works" that are the fruits of faith, all of which are, of course, the work of the Spirit in us — see *CD* II/2, e.g., pp. 38-44, 333-39.

22. George Hunsinger, *How to Read Karl Barth: The Shape of His Theology* (Oxford: Oxford University Press, 1991), chap. 5, "Truth as Mediated: Salvation," *passim.*

23. Hunsinger, *How to Read Karl Barth,* p. 114.

24. Hunsinger, *How to Read Karl Barth,* p. 113.

25. With characteristic pungency, Jenson remarks: "It appears that, for Barth, an act of the Spirit would not transcend the subjectivity of our hearing." Robert Jenson, *Systematic Theology,* vol. 1: *The Triune God* (Oxford: Oxford University Press, 1997), p. 154; see also Robert Jenson, "You Wonder Where the Spirit Went," *Pro Ecclesia* 28, no. 3 (1993): 296-304, p. 298, and Rogers, "The Eclipse of the Spirit," p. 177, for the suggestion that Barth effectively cedes too much pneumatological ground to Schleiermacher.

Behind these ambiguities relating to the Spirit's role and the diminished importance of subjective appropriation, however, lies more than a dissatisfaction with the historical trajectory of pneumatology. As we have indicated, a decisive shift has occurred in Barth's own understanding of the Spirit's role *within CD*. This alteration concerns not so much the *nature* of the Spirit's role, as its *significance,* and is inextricably bound to the alteration in his understanding of election. As we have seen, in *CD* I/1 and I/2 the necessity of the Spirit's work for the reality of our election and reconciliation is axiomatic, and it is bound to a version of individual double predestination. Barth's christologically grounded rejection of this way of understanding election exerts its own influence on the struggle to accommodate a robust pneumatology within his mature understanding of the nature of election "in Christ."

This aspect of the tension between christology and pneumatology in Barth's mature doctrine of election will be explored further below. For the moment, we must note that Barth's christological reorientation of election issues in a twofold diminution in the Spirit's role in relation to that of Christ: the tendency either to allow christology to subsume key functions more generally attributed to the Spirit, or to reduce the significance of those tasks left to the Spirit in relation to the work of Christ.[26]

Hence, as we have already noted, our being elect "in Christ" is a christological reality for all apart from the Spirit's work in us, paralleled in Barth's later account of the overarching reality of conversion, in which, even though not all receive the gift of the Spirit such that they hear and are obedient, in and by Christ himself, the conversion of all to God has taken place.[27] Thus, our Spirit-enabled response of faith has shifted from an earlier understanding in which it is co-determinative with the work of Christ

---

26. See Rogers for a recent account and diagnosis of this area of concern, even if his assertion that christological statements render pneumatological ones largely superfluous in much of *CD* between I/1 and IV/4 ("The Eclipse of the Spirit," *passim,* esp. pp. 173-75, 180-84) is somewhat exaggerated! Rogers is of particular interest here because, while he stresses the need to offer a more substantial pneumatology within Barth's mature doctrine of election and comments throughout upon the potential of Barth's presentation of the Spirit's role in I/1, he makes no connection between the relative strength of this earlier pneumatology and the earlier doctrine of election. To Rogers's puzzled question as to why Barth does not pursue the possibilities of I/1 on the Spirit (p. 182) we might respond that, for Barth, the robust pneumatology of I/1 is inseparable from a form of individual double predestination. As it stands, and as we shall explore further below, the strong pneumatology that Rogers rightly comments upon in I/1 is actually incompatible with the nature and intention of Barth's mature election christology.

27. E.g., *CD* IV/1, pp. 250-51. See n. 15 above.

in the reality of election to being a functional distinction between those who represent different sides of Christ's election. For Barth, our response or lack of it is taken up and included in the election of Christ, and serves to illustrate one or another aspect of Christ's election: either the rejection of our election, which Christ has rendered void, or the recognition of our election, and with that, the realization that Christ is the only rejected one, and all are elected in him. As a reflection of this, Barth will later state that central aspects of the Spirit's work in the New Testament stand in a merely *de facto* relationship to the *de jure* of what has already been achieved by Christ for all, apart from the Spirit's work: "The sanctification of man, his conversion to God, is, like his justification . . . a new determination which has taken place *de jure* for the world and therefore for all men. *De facto*, however . . . (it is grasped) only by those who are awakened to faith."[28]

Some of the Trinitarian issues raised by Barth's account will be explored towards the close of the chapter. For the moment, Barth's presentation of the relationship between the Spirit's work and Christ's sets him on a collision course with the overwhelming thrust of the New Testament's presentation of the Spirit's role towards us. Barth rightly remarks that the mystery of the Spirit's work in salvation means that while theology must ask the "how" questions, it cannot ultimately answer them.[29] The problem is that the New Testament gives us some highly significant contours for speaking of the Spirit's role in our being "in Christ" to which Barth struggles to do full justice.

Elect "in Christ": Some New Testament Difficulties

The next chapter will endeavor to sketch some wider scriptural contours for a doctrine of election. Here, the focus is specifically upon the way in which the New Testament conceives of the Spirit's role with regard to how we are found to be "in Christ," and undisputed main lines can be stated very briefly.[30]

---

28. *CD* IV/2, p. 511; see also, e.g., IV/3/1, pp. 278-79. Hunsinger admits that the soteriological significance of the Spirit's role in regeneration is "underdeveloped and excessively diminished" (G. Hunsinger, *Disruptive Grace: Studies in the Theology of Karl Barth* [Grand Rapids: Eerdmans, 2000], pp. 166-67, n. 23).

29. *CD* IV/1, pp. 648-49. See also Hunsinger, *How to Read Karl Barth*, pp. 111-12.

30. In addition to N. T. Wright, whose interest in the nature of election will be of considerable importance in my later engagement with New Testament scholarship, the principal

Major accounts of Paul's pneumatology remind us that to speak of being found "in Christ" is to refer to one of the primary spheres of the Spirit's activity.[31] It is the Spirit's work that makes "the decisive difference," effecting the "crucial transition" to being "in Christ."[32] The Spirit effects the new relationship to God in Christ, which is also the new status of covenant righteousness within the people of God.[33] To be "in covenant" is to be "in Christ," and this is inseparable from the work of the Spirit through the gift of faith. As such, the Spirit is described as the new "boundary marker" of the people of God, in that it is the Christ-focused presence and activity of the Spirit which defines the community of the new covenant.[34]

The contrast between Barth's approach in his mature doctrine of election and this understanding of the Spirit's role is inescapable.[35] The con-

---

sources upon which I shall draw here are J. D. G. Dunn's account of the role of the Spirit in Paul, especially in his *The Theology of Paul the Apostle* (Edinburgh: T. & T. Clark, 1998), and Gordon D. Fee, *God's Empowering Presence: The Holy Spirit in the Letters of Paul* (Peabody, MA: Hendrickson Publishers, 1994), in particular chap. 14, "The Soteriological Spirit," and chap. 15, "The Spirit and the People of God."

31. So, e.g., Dunn, *Theology*, §16, *passim*.

32. Dunn stresses the centrality and decisiveness of this aspect of the Spirit's work for Paul throughout *Theology*, §16. These examples cited are from pp. 423 and 414 respectively. See likewise Fee, *God's Empowering Presence*, e.g., pp. 854-55, for the "absolutely crucial" role of the Spirit in this regard.

33. Dunn, *Theology*, e.g., p. 435f. This is also a significant sub-theme for N. T. Wright in *The Climax of the Covenant: Christ and the Law in Pauline Theology* (Edinburgh: T. & T. Clark, 1991), particularly chaps. 8, 9, and 10. It is interesting to note that for all the criticism leveled by the "New Perspective" on Paul at other aspects of Reformation-inspired exegesis, its conclusions concerning the nature and significance of the Spirit's role in the Pauline corpus are in strong accord with the thrust of Reformed orthodoxy on the subject.

34. This is closely related to the leading ideas behind the "New Perspective" on Paul, in which faith in Christ through the gift and work of the Spirit replaces the ethnically distinctive "works of the law" as the distinguishing feature of the covenant people. Wright speaks representatively for this view in describing the community of the new covenant as those "whose boundary-marker is Christ and the Spirit and not Torah" (*Climax*, pp. 196-97; see also Dunn, *Theology*, p. 424), and in emphasizing that it is the Spirit who brings about membership of the covenant people in Christ (e.g., Wright, *Climax*, pp. 204-5). See also Fee, *God's Empowering Presence*, p. 855, where he remarks that since it is the Spirit who brings us to participate in the salvation wrought by God in Christ, it is now "the Spirit alone who identifies God's people," and again (p. 871) that Christ and the gift of the Spirit together mark "the new way by which God's people are constituted."

35. Although we are reminded of Barth's earlier approach, where to be "in Christ" is to be a hearer and doer of the Word, so that to be "in Christ" is a reality that must be "added" to our being by the work of the Spirit (*CD* I/2, p. 258; see Chapter 2, p. 41 above).

cept of the Spirit and faith as the boundary markers of those who are "in Christ" captures the essence of the Pauline approach, and its significance must not be minimized. It does *not* imply that the Spirit's task in creating the church is to form "a community whose existence . . . corresponds to the divine election of all men in Jesus Christ," bringing about in some the conscious sharing in that which is already objectively and ontologically the case for all.[36]

Rather, in James Dunn's utterly withering and exegetically accurate remark, for Paul, there can be absolutely no suggestion of "all men and women as willy-nilly 'in Christ' whether they want to be or not, whether they know or not."[37] Instead, it is the presence and activity of the eschatological Spirit that categorically delineates those who are "in Christ" and therefore belong to the new covenant people, and those who are not, and so do not.[38] The succinct negative summary of Romans 8:9 spells out the significance of the Pauline view: "Anyone who does not have the Spirit of Christ does not belong to him."[39]

It is, of course, precisely the notion of election "in Christ before the foundation of the world" (Eph. 1:4) that does allow us to speak of a being "in Christ" that precedes the Spirit's work in us in time. The problem being highlighted here is that in his understanding of election "in Christ" Barth allows the separation of that which the New Testament demands we hold together. The New Testament suggests that there is no way of conceiving of being elect "in Christ" that does not involve and entail the Spirit's work as well as Christ's.[40]

---

36. Rosato, *Spirit as Lord*, pp. 67-68; see also Thompson, *Holy Spirit*, p. 89. Nor can it be described in terms of a shift from a "virtual and unresponsive" mode of participation in salvation to one that is "active and alive" (Hunsinger, *How to Read Karl Barth*, p. 113). This neatly captures Barth's position, but once again demonstrates the tension between Barth's approach and the implications of the New Testament witness.

37. Dunn, *Theology*, p. 323.

38. For the Spirit's work in this regard, setting out the Pauline division within humanity as a whole, no longer between Jew and Gentile but between those who are in Christ by Spirit and those who are not, see Fee, *God's Empowering Presence*, p. 855.

39. We might note that the context here forbids us to interpret this "having" the Spirit of Christ with the universal work of the Spirit that Barth describes in relation to the constitution of human beings as soul-and-body (see Chapter 2, pp. 56-57 above).

40. In Trinitarian terms, too, we might say not simply that the unity of the triune divine act *may* have, but that it *requires* both its christological and its pneumatological movements. In this regard, Gunton's summary of election in Barth as a universal act with "possibly particular" appropriation is both apt and telling ("Salvation," in *The Cambridge*

Thus, while the Spirit's work cannot be separated from, and is dependent upon, that which God has accomplished in Christ, neither can Christ's work be separated from the Spirit's.[41] Dunn captures both the subordinate and yet indispensable and decisive nature of the Spirit's role when he remarks that the Christ-focused nature of the Spirit's work is a "soteriological lynchpin" of Paul's theology.[42]

It is because of this inseparable unity-in-distinction between the work of Christ and of the Spirit, and because it is the gift of the Spirit which delineates those who are "in Christ," that by a retrospective reflex it becomes possible to speak, in the way that Ephesians 1:4 does, of *the "we" of the believing community* as those who are elect "in Christ before the foundation of the world." What the implications of the New Testament understanding of the Spirit's work cannot readily be made to accommodate is the construction of a doctrine of election in which it is possible to say that those who are "without the Spirit" are nevertheless elect "in Christ" (still less that those who may never receive the gift of the Spirit may still be elect "in Christ"). Nor can we speak of being "in Christ" in ways that suggest this can be considered (and achieved) christologically, apart from the Spirit's work in us. Instead, the New Testament asks us to take with full seriousness the notion that to be "in Christ" can only be a pneumatological as well as a christological reality.[43]

Companion to Karl Barth, ed. John Webster [Cambridge: Cambridge University Press, 2000], pp. 143-58, p. 149).

41. See, e.g., Fee, *God's Empowering Presence,* p. 854, for the inseparability of the "objective" aspect of that which God has achieved in Christ and its "absolutely crucial" correlate in the work of the Spirit by which this is appropriated. As a summary of Paul's position, he quotes Swete: "Without the mission of the Spirit, the mission of the Son would have been fruitless; without the mission of the Son the Spirit could not have been sent" (p. 854, n. 9). We are reminded of Calvin's remark that without the Spirit's work within us "Christ, so to speak, lies idle" (John Calvin, *Institutes of the Christian Religion,* ed. John T. McNeill, trans. Ford Lewis Battles [Philadelphia: Westminster Press, 1960], III, i, p. 541).

42. James Dunn, *The Epistle to the Galatians* (Peabody, MA: Hendrickson, 1993), p. 220. On this, as the first two chapters have indicated, Owen and the earlier Barth are agreed. Fee's position echoes that of Dunn, summarizing the Pauline understanding of salvation in Christ in terms of Christ effecting "eschatological salvation for the people of God through his death and resurrection" and the "effectual realization and appropriation" of this as the work of the Spirit, such that "there is no salvation in Christ which is not made effective . . . by the . . . coming of the Spirit" (*God's Empowering Presence,* p. 898).

43. Again, Fee's remarks are apt: "election has now taken place in Christ, and people are elect by virtue of *their association with Christ through the Spirit*" (*God's Empowering Presence,* p. 870, my italics). One is elect in Christ "as one has been incorporated into, and thus belongs to, the chosen people of God" (pp. 870-71, n. 3).

Elect "in Christ" — or Not? God's Self-Election for Us

Although difficult to reconcile with the thrust of the New Testament witness, it is wholly consistent with the internal logic of Barth's election christology to maintain that the Spirit's work relates to the *functional* setting apart of the witnessing community, but not to the *ontological* inclusion of humanity as a whole in the election of Christ. It is important to note, however, that this is not the only way that the Spirit's role is presented in *CD* II/2. With this we encounter serious pneumatological problems *within* Barth's mature doctrine of election that take us to the root of wider questions concerning the coherence of his account.[44]

It is with this that we turn to the vexed question of *apokatastasis* in Barth's doctrine.[45] As is frequently rehearsed, Barth is able to assert both that the godless still live under the threat of actual rejection, and face eternal condemnation, and also that the godless cannot in fact annul the reality of their election, since that threat is "rendered powerless by Jesus Christ" who has borne the rejection of the apparently rejected.[46] The overwhelming thrust of Barth's account of God's single act of election in the person of Jesus Christ is that Christ takes humanity's rejection of God and conse-

---

44. In delineating some of the internal problems raised by the role of the Spirit in Barth's doctrine of election, Hunsinger's warning is well taken: we should be wary of elevating coherence and consistency to the status of supreme theological virtues. He reminds us that, for Barth, a scriptural consistency that results in theological paradox is always to be preferred to a theological coherence that collapses mysteries into false dogmatic certainties (*How to Read Karl Barth*, pp. 107, 110-12). Nevertheless, in addition to the scriptural questions already raised, pneumatological inconsistencies within Barth's account of the doctrine result not so much in paradoxes as in outright contradictions that bring it to the point of collapse.

45. The *locus classicus* for setting out the issues concerning Barth's refusal to affirm or deny *apokatastasis*, and whether or not this is the logical outcome of his doctrine of election, remains J. D. Bettis, "Is Karl Barth a Universalist?" *SJT* 20 (1967): 423-36, who sets his own defense of Barth's position in the context of the criticisms offered by G. Berkouwer, *The Triumph of Grace in the Theology of Karl Barth*, trans. H. R. Boer (London: Paternoster, 1956) and by Brunner. The debate has been revived recently in Oliver Crisp, "On Barth's Denial of Universalism," *Themelios* 29, no. 1 (2003): 18-29, where he strongly upholds the view that *apokatastasis* flows of logical necessity from Barth's doctrine. It is notable, however, that the issue has almost never been placed in a properly pneumatological as well as christological context. Rogers ("The Eclipse of the Spirit") and in particular Colwell (*Actuality*) offer a rare and welcome recognition that Barth's understanding of the Spirit's role in election lies at the very heart of the issues at stake.

46. *CD* II/2, p. 321, see pp. 321-22, and also, e.g., pp. 318-19, 346.

quent rejection *by* God into himself, exhausting it in his own person, so that "[w]ith Jesus Christ the rejected can only *have been* rejected. He cannot *be* rejected any more."[47] Through the exchange that took place on Golgotha,

> Rejection cannot again become the portion or affair of man. . . . For this reason faith in the divine predestination . . . means faith in the non-rejection of man . . . it is God Himself who is rejected in His Son . . . that we might not be rejected. Predestination means . . . the non-rejection of man.[48]

That Barth wishes to retain the ultimate possibility of rejection, and therefore steadfastly refuses to maintain or to deny *apokatastasis,* is consistently based upon his desire to preserve God's freedom.[49] Thus, "Just as the gracious God does not need to elect or call any single man, so He does not need to elect or call all mankind."[50] Here is God's radical freedom to choose between the whole gamut of alternatives posed by the concept of election: he may elect all, none, or any number in between. But this is to treat election, and the freedom of God, in abstraction. Barth's election christology insists that God is *not* radically free in relation to the world.[51]

---

47. *CD* II/2, p. 453, Barth's italics.

48. *CD* II/2, pp. 166-67. In a reminder of the issues raised in relation to creation and the image in the previous chapter, we might refer again to his extended discussion of the "No" and "Yes" of God in relation to the justification of creation (*CD* III/1, pp. 366-88) in which, while we (and God) must indwell the contradiction of the "No" and the "Yes" without seeking a too-ready resolution, nevertheless the self-revelation of God in Christ as the one who bears the "No" for the sake of the "Yes" reveals God's intention to overcome the "No" of sin and nothingness. More succinctly, he insists that "as the fellow-elect of Jesus, man as the creature of God is predestined to be the victor and not the vanquished in the defence of our being against non-being" (*CD* III/2, p. 147; see pp. 146-47).

49. So, e.g., *CD* II/2, pp. 422-23, where Barth insists upon God's "free will . . . in relation to the world" as the basis upon which some may be rejected. Salvation can only ever be an "unexpected grace," since "Even though theological consistency might seem to lead [towards *apokatastasis*], we must not arrogate to ourselves that which can be given and received only as a free gift" (*CD* IV/3, p. 477). Hunsinger's summary is apt: for Barth, universal salvation can neither be deduced nor excluded as a possibility, since "Neither the logical deduction nor the definite exclusion would properly respect the concrete freedom of God" (*Disruptive Grace,* p. 245).

50. *CD* II/2, p. 417.

51. Part of the problem lies in the slippages in Barth's use of the term "freedom" in relation to God, particularly between freedom as self-determination and freedom as choice. See, e.g., G. S. Hendry, "The Freedom of God in the Theology of Karl Barth," *SJT* 31 (1978): 229-44, for a critique of the fluidity with which Barth uses the term.

Instead, God has constituted his very being in free self-determination to be one who elects to take humanity's rejection upon himself in the person of the incarnate Son.[52]

It is important to recognize, however, that the difficulties raised by Barth's denial of *apokatastasis* have their source not only in the counter-claims of God's freedom and human logic, but in the consequences of an overweighted election christology at the expense of pneumatology, and in a generally inconsistent account of the relationship between the two.

Thus, while it is wholly consistent to the logic of his election christology that the Spirit's work relates to the functional election of the witnessing community, but not to the ontological inclusion of humanity as a whole in the election of Christ, this is not the only way in which the Spirit's role is understood in II/2. Berkouwer asks rhetorically what right Barth can possibly have to reject *apokatastasis*.[53] The answer, although he does not recognize it, is in fact a pneumatological one. If it is the case that the Son's assumption of our reprobation to himself may ultimately apply only to some but not to others, and if this is not to be the exercise of an arbitrary freedom that Barth insists is foreign to God, then it requires an election pneumatology in which, after all, the Spirit's role is decisive in delineating those who are elect "in Christ" and those who are not.

Since the bestowal of the Spirit is the unconditional gift of God, such a pneumatology entails nothing less than an implicit return to the dynamic of individual double predestination, which Barth's entire election christology sets out to combat. And this is precisely what is implied when we turn to elements of Barth's account of our election of God.[54]

Elect "in Christ" — or Not? Our Election of God

On the one hand, in the *Leitsatz* at the head of his discussion of the election of the individual, Barth insists that the choice of the godless is in fact "void," since "he belongs eternally to Jesus Christ." The rejection he deserves is borne and cancelled by Christ so that he is not in fact rejected but

---

52. It is the refusal to follow through this *a posteriori* necessity that Colwell rightly identifies as Berkouwer's "devastating" argument against Barth (*Actuality*, p. 271; see also the extended discussion of *a priori/a posteriori* necessity in Barth, pp. 221ff.).

53. Berkouwer, *Triumph of Grace*, p. 116.

54. For Barth's understanding of our election of God as taking place within, and as the purpose of, God's self-election in Christ, see *CD* II/2, p. 177.

elected by God in Christ.[55] On this basis, as we have noted, the Spirit's work in enabling our response is significant for the way in which we live now — either in recognition of our election, or in ignorance and opposition to it — but is in no way determinative of the reality of our election.

Nevertheless, there are occasions when Barth also appears to insist that the Spirit's work *is* necessary, not simply for the apprehension of our election in Christ, but for its reality. If such passages are to be accepted at face value, then it would seem that, after all, only those in the inner circle of believers are *the* elect — the ones who are eternally reconciled to God in Christ.

Thus, Barth insists that "in faith in [Christ] it is decided . . . who belongs to the fullness" of God's people in Christ.[56] As Barth acknowledges, the New Testament unequivocally identifies election with faith, and so with the work of the Spirit: "Election means faith. And since those who believe are the Church, election means to be in the Church. We have here a closed circle. . . . There is no election of an individual . . . on the basis of which he is not led by the Word into faith . . . and therefore into the Church."[57] The people of Jesus Christ are "all who believe in Him, and are therefore the object of divine election."[58]

Similar difficulties therefore arise from the point of view of our election of God as from the perspective of God's self-election in Christ. We have noted that although God's election of reprobation for himself in Christ means that reprobation can no longer be a human possibility, nevertheless, in God's "freedom" ultimate rejection remains a genuine threat. So also, although we are repeatedly told that while the rejection of our election in Christ is in fact subsumed within and overridden by Christ's election, nevertheless, if there is to be ultimate rejection, this will be as a result of the perverse obstinacy of human choice against God in the face of God's choice for us.

Hence, the rejected is the one who "isolates himself from God by re-

55. *CD* II/2, p. 306. Barth again emphasizes that "In the negative act of this void choice of nothing . . . [the godless] is vanquished and overtaken even before he begins by that which God has eternally decreed for him and done for him in the election of Jesus Christ" (p. 316), and cannot "reverse or change the eternal decision of God . . . he can accomplish nothing which abolishes the choice of God" (p. 317). We are again reminded of similar statements in the previous chapter, in the context of our sharing in Christ's true humanity.

56. *CD* II/2, p. 300.

57. *CD* II/2, p. 427; see pp. 426-28.

58. *CD* II/2, p. 430; see also p. 127.

sisting his election as it has taken place in Jesus Christ," and who "maliciously and perilously transgresses" against the love of God.[59] The rejected are those from whom God has turned away because they have turned their backs upon God.[60] Later in his corpus, Barth goes so far as to state that "[t]o the man who persistently tries to change the truth into untruth, God does not owe eternal patience and . . . deliverance."[61]

If the significance of Barth's election christology holds — if those who are "without the Spirit" and so are "abandoned to eternal perdition" are also those whose "futile attempt to live the life of one rejected by God" cannot alter the reality that in Jesus Christ, the only Rejected One, this threat is averted[62] — then the ambiguity of Barth's stress upon our choice is not of ultimate significance.[63] If final reprobation is after all a genuine possibility as a result of our decision to reject our election in Christ, then it is clear that Barth's emphasis upon choice is highly problematic, to say the least.[64] Berkouwer stresses Barth's desire to maintain the "open situation" of the gospel proclamation as the source of the contradiction in this aspect of his doctrine.[65] In fact, the crux of the issue is that in a very significant sense, the gospel proclamation is *not* open. We need to be reminded once again that

59. *CD* II/2, pp. 449 and 451 respectively.

60. *CD* II/2, p. 455.

61. *CD* IV/3/1, p. 477. He goes on to remark that while we cannot count on the withdrawal of this final threat, because we have no claim on God, we may pray for it and hope for it (pp. 477-78). While we may have no claim on God, once again, we must ask whether Barth has taken sufficient account of the claim made upon the being and act of God by God's own free self-determination as he has described it.

62. *CD* II/2, p. 346.

63. So, e.g., our assurance is to be located in the will of God for salvation, expressed in his self-election, which is "unconditional in its certainty, preceding all self-determination and outlasting any change in self-determination on the part of the creature" (*CD* II/2, p. 31).

64. Sung Wook Chung refers to this as a tension between "Calvinistic" and "Arminian" tendencies in Barth's doctrine, but rightly points out that Barth would resist any accusation of Arminianism. Sung Wook Chung, "A Bold Innovator: Barth on God and Election," in *Karl Barth and Evangelical Theology: Convergences and Divergences*, ed. Sung Wook Chung (Milton Keynes: Paternoster; Grand Rapids: Baker Academic, 2006), pp. 60-76, p. 74, n. 32. In fact, given Barth's understanding of the Spirit's role, the tension is not so much between Calvinistic and Arminian tendencies as between the only two "logical" possibilities for a fully Reformed understanding of God's sovereign election of grace — universalism or individual double predestination. For a clear presentation of these as the two possibilities within an Augustinian-Reformed theological framework, see Oliver D. Crisp, "Augustinian Universalism," *International Journal for Philosophy of Religion* 53 (June 2003): 127-45.

65. Berkouwer, *Triumph of Grace*, pp. 116, 122.

those who reject their election remain deaf to the proclamation and unable to live in accordance with the reality of their election in Christ *because they have not received the gift of the Spirit.* Once again, it must be said that Barth's fundamental account of the Spirit as God in his Revealedness remains unchanged: there is no possibility of recognizing and accepting God's self-revelation apart from the Spirit's specific enabling.[66]

Barth's assertion that the rejected exist in the sphere of God's "non-willing" must therefore be balanced against a pneumatology which dictates that this "non-willing" of God is also the expression of God's decision to withhold the Spirit.[67] While we may indeed continue to resist our participation in Christ's election, our only possibility of freely choosing to share in it lies in God's own decision to bestow the Spirit to this purpose. If God chooses to grant this gift efficaciously to some and not to others, and if a negative response contains the real threat of ultimate exclusion from the reality of participation in election in Christ, then for all Barth's rhetoric to the contrary, there are aspects of his mature doctrine of election that tacitly remain within the dynamic of individual double predestination.[68]

The Son and the Spirit: Some Trinitarian Considerations

The focus of this chapter so far has been upon the relationship between christology and pneumatology in the economy with regard to our election. In this regard, it is clear that the "relative underweighting of the pneumatological in the appropriation of salvation" consequent upon the reorienta-

66. It is the failure to reckon with this that undermines Colwell's appeal to Barth's temporality as part of his defense of the logic of Barth's rejection of *apokatastasis*. The question of temporality is not strictly relevant here. The issue at stake is not *when* our election takes place — whether in the "pre-temporal past" or on the basis of Barth's complex interweaving of divine and human time — but *whether* the gift of the Spirit is necessary or not.

67. See *CD* II/2, e.g., pp. 27, 450, 458 for rejection as the "non-willing" of God.

68. A failure to acknowledge the pneumatological issues raised by Barth's mature doctrine of election seriously mars Bettis's claim that Barth avoids the universalism/*apokatastasis*/individual double predestination impasse. Thompson also sidesteps the major issues in question when, after citing Barth's remark that those who reject their election "will not yield their own spirits and wills" to the Spirit (*CD* IV/3, p. 354), he summarizes Barth's position as: "to reject the Spirit is to turn one's back on God. There is no inadequacy in its presence and power but only in us" (*Holy Spirit*, pp. 181-82). Unlike Bettis, however, Thompson acknowledges that Barth's account of those who persist in unbelief is not entirely satisfactory (p. 184).

tion in Barth's thinking on election creates difficulties at many levels.[69] These pneumatological considerations must also be placed within the wider Trinitarian context of the relationship between the Son and Spirit in the immanent Trinity and in the incarnation, and indeed, the whole life of the incarnate Son, although this can only be touched upon here.[70]

To clarify some of the issues at stake, we will turn firstly to the question of the implications of *filioque* for the Spirit's role in election in both Owen and Barth.[71] Each is as committed as the other to the dual procession of the Spirit, and as the opening chapter has made clear, Owen is as insistent as Barth that the works of God *ad extra* point us to and are the reflection of the shape of the Trinitarian life *ad intra*.[72]

Looking firstly to Barth's description of the inner-Trinitarian decision of election, we noted in the previous chapter that this is specifically "the decision made between Father and Son from all eternity."[73] Barth then goes on to describe the three electing choices in the Godhead. It is the Father's choice to establish a covenant with humanity by giving the Son, and the Son chooses to offer himself up that this might be accomplished; the Spirit's choice is to ensure that the unity of Father and Son should not be rent, but made more glorious, in the Son's assumption of our flesh.[74]

This is clearly entirely in keeping with Barth's adherence to *filioque* as the fundamental dynamic of inner-Trinitarian being-in-relation. The

69. The phrase cited is Gunton's ("Salvation," p. 152), although he does not relate this pneumatological underweighting to the *shift* in Barth's thinking on election. It must be noted that this criticism hardly applies to the Barth of I/1 and 2, for whom the Spirit's role in this regard is decisive. As this suggests, great care must be taken in attempting to speak in generalized terms of Barth's "pneumatology" without recognizing the significance of the alteration in his thinking on election.

70. It should also be noted that only specifically pneumatologically related matters will be dealt with here, although the wider Trinitarian issues raised by Barth's formulation of the doctrine are of far-reaching significance, such as the debate concerning the relationship between election and God's triunity initially sparked by the positions in Bruce McCormack, "Grace and Being: The Role of God's Gracious Election in Karl Barth's Theological Ontology," in *The Cambridge Companion to Karl Barth*, ed. John Webster (Cambridge: Cambridge University Press, 2000), pp. 101-2; and Paul Molnar, *Divine Freedom and the Doctrine of the Immanent Trinity* (London: T. & T. Clark, 2002), pp. 61-64, and his "The Trinity, Election and God's Ontological Freedom: A Response to Kevin W. Hector," *IJST* 8 (July 2006): 294-304.

71. For Barth's defense of *filioque* see *CD* I/1, pp. 473-87.

72. See Chapter 1, pp. 8ff. above.

73. *CD* II/2, p. 90; see Chapter 2, p. 48 above.

74. *CD* II/2, p. 101.

Spirit is not in any way the source of the being of Father and Son; rather his being is dependent upon the logically prior relationship between Father and Son. The Spirit is therefore not to be seen as in any way the "source" of the electing decision by which God determines his being; rather his work arises from and brings to completion the logically prior decision of Father and Son.

As such, for all the differences in the way that they understand the content of election, Barth's account of God's electing decision demonstrates the same basic Trinitarian pattern as that upheld by Owen. For Owen too, and for the same reason, the decision concerning the nature of election and the representative work of Christ is attributed to the Father and the Son, while the Spirit's task is to bring this to effect in the economy.[75] Nevertheless, these two essentially identical accounts of the dynamic of the inner-Trinitarian decision of election issue in two very different approaches to the relationship between christology and pneumatology in our participation in Christ's election.

For Owen, as we have seen, the implications of *filioque* result in the decisive nature of the Spirit's activity in the economy of election, as that upon which the Father and Son depend for the enacting of their own work. The gift and work of the Spirit are the lynchpin of election's Trinitarian dynamic: while it is the Father and Son who have together determined those whose election is to be accomplished in Christ, it is the bestowal of the Spirit at the mediation of the ascended Christ that brings about the fulfillment of this eternal decision of election.

There is therefore a delicately poised relationship between Christ's work and the Spirit's. On the one hand, there is a clear asymmetry: there is no "independent" work of the Spirit, which is entirely Christ-focused and Christ-shaped. On the other, Christ's work cannot be separated from the Spirit's role in bringing this to bear upon us and within us.[76] Owen and the

---

75. Trueman's assessment of Owen's doctrine of election bears repeating here: that it is a specifically functional and soteriological application of *filioque* (see Chapter 1, pp. 8-13 above). Carl R. Trueman, *The Claims of Truth: John Owen's Trinitarian Theology* (Carlisle: Paternoster, 1998), p. 146.

76. Bringing Owen into dialogue with Rogers's comparison between Athanasius and Barth is instructive here. Owen offers us precisely that which Rogers laments is lacking in Barth: an "Athanasian" balance between the person and work of the Son and of the Spirit, a Trinitarian "interval" of time between the work of the Son and the Spirit, a clear sense of the personal "otherness" of the Spirit, and the "gift dynamic" in which the Spirit is the "gift bidden by the Son and granted by the Father" who also adds his own contribution to the work of

earlier Reformed tradition maintain that there can ultimately be no "in Christ" apart from the Spirit's work, and that the Spirit ultimately delineates not simply whether or not one *recognizes* that one is elect in Christ, but whether one is elect in Christ or not. As noted above in relation to the New Testament and in Chapter 1 in relation to Owen, this does not signify that one only "becomes" elect through the work of the Spirit in the economy. It is simply that the Trinitarian nature of the decree and its unfolding in time mean that there can finally be no union with Christ, no election in Christ, no participation in his saving work, apart from the Spirit.

Barth's radical concentration of the whole of election in Christ means that the outworking of *filioque* for his later doctrine effectively issues in a *subordination* of pneumatology to christology that is foreign to the careful scriptural and Trinitarian balance of the earlier tradition. The pattern of the dual procession still holds: the Spirit remains the one who brings the electing decision of the Father and the Son to bear in the economy. Nevertheless, the significance of the Spirit's role has been radically relativized. Election as it relates to humanity is less clearly a triune act, in which the Spirit's work is co-determinative with that of the Father and the Son; rather, it is a reality that has already been accomplished in God's self-election in Christ, which may or may not be made known to individuals by the Spirit.[77] As we have seen, Barth is clear that the participation of all in Christ's election need not include the Spirit's work; this simply delineates one manner of that participation but not the other.

In the context of Barth's emphasis upon the all-embracing nature of

---

Father and Son ("The Eclipse of the Spirit," p. 179; see pp. 178-79). Anticipating the full expression of the pneumatological problem for a Reformed doctrine of election at the close of this chapter, the account of the Spirit's role that Rogers requires of Barth, and that Owen provides, seemingly cannot help but direct us back towards individual double predestination.

77. Here we note again (see n. 40 above) Gunton's comment that election for Barth is a universal act with "possibly particular" appropriation ("Salvation," p. 149). He also remarks on the need to find room for a fuller sense of the Spirit as the personal divine other who himself elects us into communion with the Father through the Son if election is to be considered a fully Trinitarian action. Colin Gunton, *The Promise of Trinitarian Theology* (Edinburgh: T. & T. Clark, 1991), p. 134. The point is well taken in the context of strongly upholding the *unity*-in-distinction of the actions of the Spirit and the Son in election, as in all things. See also Robert Jenson, "The Holy Spirit," in *Christian Dogmatics*, vol. 2, ed. Carl E. Braaten and Robert W. Jenson (Philadelphia: Fortress Press, 1984), pp. 101-78, 134-39. Here, in discussing the role of the Spirit in predestination, Jenson urges a much clearer account than Barth is able to give of the Spirit, as well as Christ, as the "electing God," and therefore of the doctrine's eschatological future as well as its pre-temporal past.

Christ's election, consistency to the implications of *filioque* therefore provides a theological framework for the scriptural imbalance that we have already noted: christology is allowed to subsume within itself key activities more generally attributed to the Spirit in the understanding of the Trinitarian activity *ad extra,* and those tasks left to the Spirit are subordinated to that which has already been realized in Christ. We might well wonder if the earlier Barth would have found this sufficient grounds to call into question the *homoousia* of the Spirit.[78]

In fact, the only work of the Spirit that is unequivocally determinative of the reality of election in Barth's mature account of the doctrine is not directed towards us but towards the Son. It will be recalled that it is the particular choice of the Spirit in the inner-Trinitarian decision of election to ensure the relationship between Father and Son is not sundered by the incarnation. This leads us to a further aspect of Trinitarian relations that has a particular bearing on how we are to think of the Spirit's role in election: the union of the two natures in the person of Christ. As Owen helps us recognize, with due regard for that which is absolutely *dissimilar* between the incarnate Son and ourselves, the Spirit's role in the hypostatic union is also paradigmatic for the way in which we conceive of the Spirit's role with regard to our union with Christ, and so for the pneumatological dynamic of election.[79]

---

78. *CD* I/2, pp. 238-39; see Chapter 2, p. 40 above. We might also wonder whether Jenson's conclusion concerning the root of the oft-noted symptoms of a relative pneumatological deficiency in Barth's theology needs to be nuanced somewhat. He considers the heart of the problem to be Barth's radically thoroughgoing application of the *filioque*-shaped dynamic of inner-Trinitarian relations to the works of God in the economy ("You Wonder," pp. 299-301). While he rightly points to the centrality of Barth's mature doctrine of election for the way in which the Spirit's role *ad intra* and *ad extra* is understood (p. 310), Barth's unique election christology, far more than the tendencies of Western Trinitarianism *per se,* is at the heart of the pneumatological problems he diagnoses in the later Barth, most notably the apparent christological "takeover" of key aspects of the Spirit's work *ad extra.* While Jenson might still regard the Spirit's role in Reformed orthodoxy, and indeed in the early Barth, as insufficient in both these instances, a rigorous commitment to *filioque* does provide room for something approximating to the "salvation-historical initiative" of the Spirit that he seeks, without compromising the close binding of the Spirit's work and Christ's.

79. See "The Spirit and Christ," in Chapter 1, pp. 25ff. above. As Owen likewise reminds us, the role of the Spirit in the unfolding life of Christ is also of paradigmatic significance. In this regard, although it cannot be discussed in detail here, we might note that, while Barth is clear about the Spirit's role as the "mediator of communion" (Hunsinger's term, forming the title of his chapter on Barth's pneumatology in *Disruptive Grace*) between the incarnate Son and the Father, as he is between us and God, Gunton's analysis is significant. He remarks that

In both *CD* I/1 and I/2, Barth, like Owen, ensures that we note this correspondence between the miracle of the hypostatic union, enabled by the Spirit, and the miracle of our being found in Christ, likewise by the Spirit. In both instances, this union is an otherwise impossible relationship of complete dissimilarity. "The very possibility of human nature's being adopted into union with the Son of God is the Holy Ghost" is a description of the reality and possibility of the incarnation; it is also a truism for the reality and possibility of our being "in Christ."[80] The same preparation of our humanity for God by God that takes place in the incarnation takes place for us, as by the Spirit we become "a recipient of [God's] revelation, the object of the divine reconciliation."[81]

A proper distinction must be maintained: in our union with Christ by faith ours is a separate existence brought into communion with God, whereas in the incarnate Word, humanity is the predicate of his divinity.[82] Nevertheless,

> What is ascribed to the Holy Spirit in the birth of Christ is the assumption of human existence . . . into unity with God in the mode of being of the Logos. That this is possible, that this other, . . . this flesh, is there for God, for fellowship and even unity with God . . . is the work of the Holy Spirit. . . . This work . . . is prototypal of the work of the Spirit in the coming into being of the children of God.[83]

For the Barth of I/1 and I/2, as for Owen, there is a clear consistency between an account of the Spirit's role in the hypostatic union and in our election. Just as the Spirit is the ground and possibility of the Son's assumption of our humanity, so the Spirit is the ground and possibility of our union with Christ.[84]

---

the Spirit's role in the humanity and ministry of Jesus is nevertheless downplayed in Barth, with a tendency to see the humanity of Jesus as "too much a function of his direct relationship to the Father." He links the immediacy of Christ's relationship to the Father directly to the corresponding tendency, so prominent in his mature doctrine of election, to stress the "miraculous transference" of Christ's work to us in such a way as to downplay the significance of the Spirit as the one who himself actually mediates that to us ("Salvation," p. 152; see pp. 152-57).

80. *CD* I/2, p. 199.
81. *CD* I/2, p. 198; see pp. 198-200.
82. *CD* I/2, p. 162.
83. *CD* I/1, p. 486.
84. This is so whether we have a "personal" understanding of union with Christ or, as

Hunsinger's account of Barth's pneumatology helps to point towards the difficulties raised in this regard in Barth's mature doctrine of election. Hunsinger describes the Spirit as the one who bridges the divine/human ontological divide, pointing specifically both to the coherence of Barth's approach with the scriptural witness to the Spirit's work in Christ and in us, and to the Spirit's role in the hypostatic union.[85] The Spirit is the only source of our union with Christ, and therefore of our participation in the communion of the Trinity, so that "through our union with Christ effected by the Spirit" we are given to share in the self-knowledge of God which is also fellowship with God.[86]

While this is unequivocally true of Barth under the influence of his earlier election dynamic, it becomes difficult to say quite the same thing in quite the same way after the christological reorientation in his thinking on election. The outcome of Barth's mature election christology is that while the Spirit's work remains noetic (our only access to true knowledge of God) and ontic (the Spirit's work is always transformative), the Spirit can no longer straightforwardly be described as the one who bridges the *onto-logical* gap between us in our humanity and the divine-human person of Christ, such that he is source or effectual agent of our union with Christ.[87]

McCormack prefers, an "ethical" view of it as union of wills. Bruce L. McCormack, "What's at Stake in Current Debates over Justification? The Crisis of Protestantism in the West," in *Justification: What's at Stake in the Current Debates,* ed. Mark Husbands and Daniel J. Treier (Downers Grove, IL: InterVarsity Press, 2004), pp. 81-117. The point here is twofold. First, Trinitarian (and, as we have noted above, scriptural) consistency with regard to the Spirit's role suggests that no matter how "union with Christ" is understood, the work of the Spirit is integral to and constitutive of it. Second, in making these connections between the Spirit's role towards the Son and towards us, neither Barth nor Owen jeopardizes the uniqueness of the incarnation. Both are able to maintain necessary and absolute distinctions between the hypostatic union and our union with Christ, while at the same time asserting a proper con-tinuity between the Spirit's role in constituting the being of the incarnate Son and constitut-ing our being "in Christ."

85. See Hunsinger, *Disruptive Grace*, pp. 160, 162, 168-69.

86. Hunsinger, *Disruptive Grace*, pp. 170-71.

87. It is interesting that when he has no need to describe the Spirit's role in this regard (and when he is drawing on the later Barth) Hunsinger himself speaks of the *christologically achieved* "ontological connection" that establishes the being of all people in Christ *apart from* the Spirit's work (*How to Read Karl Barth,* e.g., pp. 129, 136). We must also note at this point that, when speaking specifically of the Christian's union with Christ and being "in Christ" as part of the goal of vocation, Barth is rightly clear that this is indeed the work of the Spirit in us (*CD* IV/3/2, pp. 545-54). Nevertheless, this must be set in the context of his account of "The Being of Man in Jesus Christ," *CD* IV/1, esp. pp. 92-93. While we do indeed

Rather, as we have noted, the union of all humanity with Christ *has been achieved christologically* in the Son's assumption of our human nature.[88]

Barth's role for the Spirit towards the Son in the self-election of God, however, remains exactly as it was in the account of the Spirit's role in the incarnation in the earlier volumes. The Spirit is the only possibility by which the eternal Son can assume our humanity. What has been lost is the theological coherence and scriptural consistency with regard to the Spirit's role in the hypostatic union and our election in Christ, in which *both* that the Son can assume flesh, *and* that we can be found "in Christ" are possible *only* through the activity of the Spirit. There can be no suggestion that the Son brings about union with himself apart from the Spirit, any more than the Son can assume humanity in the incarnation apart from the Spirit. The work of the Spirit is required to accomplish both. In another layer of pneumatological inconsistency, Barth's primary understanding of the Spirit's role towards us in his mature doctrine of election therefore stands in profound tension with his understanding of the Spirit's primary role in the inner-divine electing self-determination.

Conclusion: The Pneumatological Problem

Barth's mature doctrine of election leaves us with the inescapable sense of two essentially irreconcilable views of the dynamic of election sitting uneasily side by side, and that the crux of the dilemma is pneumatological. If Barth makes Paul's clarion call in Romans 8:1 his own — "there is no con-

---

say that Christians are "in Christ" as the particular determination of their being, we can and must say that "the same being in Jesus Christ" is granted also to those not yet aware of its reality (p. 92). That which can be said of Christians, but cannot be said of others, is that in Christians the reality of being "in Christ" is known and reflected. Thus, as was cited above (n. 15), non-believers do not lack Christ, or their being as reconciled to God in him; they lack the Spirit's work of obedience and knowledge. "For that reason," says Barth, "the being of man reconciled to God in Jesus Christ is not — yet — reflected in them" (p. 93).

88. The same problem is also in evidence in the analyses of Rosato and Thompson. Each appeals to the early Barth in order strongly to affirm the centrality of the analogy between the Spirit's role as the only possibility of the hypostatic union and our union with Christ (e.g., Rosato, *Spirit as Lord*, pp. 20, 60, 63-64, 68-69; Thompson, *Holy Spirit*, chap. 3) while also maintaining a noetic/transformative pneumatology and ontological christology in which, to use Thompson's summary, "The Lord as servant . . . has altered the whole situation between himself and humanity [and] exalted us into permanent union with himself" (*Holy Spirit*, p. 183).

demnation — literally none — for those that are in Christ Jesus"[89] — he is less than clear with regard to the implications of the claim that "[a]nyone who does not have the Spirit of Christ does not belong to him" from Romans 8:9.

Instead, Barth's later doctrine of election oscillates between two conceptions of the Spirit's role. On the one hand, he develops an account of the Spirit that is compatible with his election christology, but is far from a robustly pneumatological account of what it means to be found "in Christ," and in which the implications of the Spirit's choice in the Trinitarian self-election stand in tension with the primary thrust of the Spirit's role in our election. On the other, he sometimes suggests a pneumatology which is closer to the balance between Christ's work and the Spirit's suggested by the New Testament, but which effectively neutralizes the implications of his concentration of the whole of election in the person of Christ. His desire to avoid the universalist implications of his election christology leads to a lurch back towards individual double predestination through what is effectively an appeal to the gift and work of the Spirit, such that the tension between his election christology and pneumatology leave his doctrine in danger of imploding.

With this in mind, we are now in a position to pose the central pneumatological question of election in its fullest form. The first side of that question was articulated at the close of the opening chapter. Owen presents us with a scripturally and trinitarianly robust account of the Spirit's role in election, which is also utterly and inextricably bound up with the doctrine of individual double predestination. In Barth's earlier doctrine of election we likewise find that the Spirit's role is decisive, and that it shapes and is shaped by a version of individual double predestination. Barth's christological reorientation of the doctrine self-consciously sets out to refute any such notion of the electing decision of God, but can do so only at the expense of the scriptural and Trinitarian consistency of the Spirit's role, and at the constant risk of a pneumatologically led return to the older election dynamic.

An analysis of election, the image, and the Spirit in Owen and Barth therefore leads us to ask: Does a due weighting of the "by the Spirit" of election as well as the "in Christ" of election lead only and inexorably to individual double predestination within a Reformed theological framework? Each in his own way, both Owen and Barth, give us little choice but

---

89. *CD* II/2, p. 166.

to answer "Yes." What follows in Parts II and III is an attempt to rearticulate the doctrine of election in such a way as to be able to offer at least a tentative "No" to a question that effectively asks us to choose between a decisive election christology and a decisive election pneumatology.

The very fact that we are confronted by two such weighty and apparently incompatible alternatives suggests that we would be well advised to take several steps back, and to ask whether some false turnings at other points in the theological journey have led to this particular impasse. Part II begins by asking us to reconsider the scriptural witness, both with regard to election and to the image of God, in order to lay some foundations for a renewed approach to election, in which the rich and coherent pneumatology of Reformed orthodoxy might be restored, while still retaining seminal insights from Barth's reworking of the doctrine, and while still upholding the inseparability of the Spirit's work from the person and work of Christ.

PART II

Re-Presenting the Image; Re-Imaging Election

CHAPTER 4

Sketching Some Scriptural Contours

It is in stepping back to look afresh at the scriptural witness that we will begin to find a way beyond the apparent pneumatological impasse to which Owen and Barth have led us. In so doing, however, we also find that one of the central theological insights taken up in different ways by each offers a clue to the direction that this might take. The Reformed tradition forges strong connections between the doctrines of election and the *imago dei,* and both Owen and Barth demonstrate the theological consistency of this close association. Tracing some of the conceptual continuities between the image and election in the light of recent biblical scholarship will be a central aim of this chapter. Thus, the task ahead is not so much to offer a detailed exegesis of key passages as to sketch some scriptural contours for a renewed approach to election, drawing upon some of the insights offered to us by a convergence of key themes within Old Testament and New Testament studies.

In this undertaking, one of Owen's categories for thinking about the image of God points to a fruitful way forward. The first chapter indicated that one of Owen's contributions to Reformed orthodoxy's account of the image is his use of the notion of representation as a motif throughout. As we will see, the concept of representation in fact provides a vital link that unites significant strands of Old Testament and New Testament biblical scholarship on the image and election. Exploring the relationship between election, the image, and representation, and teasing out some of the facets of representation beyond those offered by Owen, will lead to the formulation of some scriptural guidelines for a theological reappraisal of the nature and purpose of election. It will also prepare the way for the following chapter's continuation of the dogmatic links between election and the image, when we will begin to reformulate the doctrine of election in conversation with recent theological considerations of the ecclesial *imago dei*.

Re-Presenting the Image: A Scriptural Overview

Turning firstly to the Old Testament, and with Genesis 1:26-27 particularly in mind, it would seem that Owen's understanding of representation vis-à-vis the image of God is well founded. While later interpretation of Genesis 1:26-27 may be less keen to use Ephesians and Colossians to specify the image as humanity's role to represent the righteousness, holiness, and love of God in the world, the category itself is still considered to be highly significant. So, even though Brueggemann declines to offer any extended consideration of the image because of the paucity of direct Old Testament reflection on the subject, he nevertheless includes representation prominently among the few key elements of the image that may be derived from the Old Testament material.[1] He suggests that a primary aspect of the creation of humanity in the image of God consists in the task of representing God in and to creation as the "regent who represents the sovereign in the midst of all other subjects where the sovereign is not directly and personally present."[2] Grenz's survey of biblical scholarship on Genesis 1:26-27 comes to a similar conclusion. Drawing on the royal ideology generally considered to be a significant aspect of the ancient background to the concept — where we find that for the writer of Genesis 1 it is no longer kings alone but human beings as a whole who are made in the image of God — and also on the understanding that something of the presence of the one of whom an image has been made is mediated through the image itself, human beings are seen as those through whom God has chosen to make something of himself manifest in the created order, and through whom he mediates his presence.[3] Thus, Grenz concludes that "representational belief is likely to have formed the heart of the concept" of the image of God for the author.[4]

---

1. In addition to Genesis 1:26-27, only Genesis 5:1-3, 9:5-6, and Psalm 8 provide direct Old Testament reference points for the concept of humanity as made in the image of God. See Walter Brueggemann, *Theology of the Old Testament: Testimony, Dispute, Advocacy* (Minneapolis: Fortress, 1991), pp. 451-54, for his discussion of the concept.

2. Brueggemann, *Old Testament*, p. 452.

3. Stanley Grenz, *The Social God and the Relational Self: A Trinitarian Theology of the Imago Dei* (Louisville: Westminster/John Knox Press, 2001), pp. 198-99.

4. Grenz, *Social God*, p. 200. See pp. 184-203 for a helpful discussion of approaches to

In turning to the New Testament, again, direct references to the image are few, but generally carry considerable theological weight.[5] A minority usage continues the Old Testament theme of the universal presence of the image.[6] Nevertheless, the primary focus has shifted from the image in relation to humanity as a whole supremely to the person of Christ. The central texts in this regard are 2 Corinthians 4:4-6, Colossians 1:15, and, although the language of image/likeness is not directly used, Hebrews 1:3. Jesus Christ is seen as *the* image of the invisible God, the one in whose face we behold God's glory, the one who is the reflection and the impress of the nature and glory of God. The theme of representation, not surprisingly, is never far from the surface: Jesus Christ uniquely and definitively images God and so is able uniquely and definitively to represent God to us, because he may be said to participate in the reality of that which he images in a way that has taken us some distance from the Genesis conception of the image as created in humanity as a whole. Christ is now the one true image of God because, in Barrett's terms, in Christ we see the *Göttlichkeit* of God in human form.[7]

As Christ himself is now seen as the one true image of the invisible God, so, derivatively and secondarily, those who are in Christ are transformed into his image by the Holy Spirit. While the New Testament does not deny the universality of the image, the primary thrust of the New Testament witness is that it must be considered supremely in the context of, and as pertaining above all to, the new humanity in Christ. In Grenz's words, the New Testament sees the *imago dei* as "the glorious destiny of the believing community"; it is the eschatological goal of the new humanity that has been brought to share in Christ's "true" humanity.[8] The notion of

---

Genesis 1:26-27, including some dissenting voices with regard to the concept of representation, most notably that of Claus Westermann.

5. While the exegetical details of all of the central "image" texts in the New Testament are much disputed, these generally do not affect the limited aims here: to establish the validity of the concept of "representation" as one key category for discussing the image, to trace the ways in which it may be understood, and to indicate the close binding of election, the image, and the work of the Spirit.

6. Strictly speaking, the only example of this is James 3:9. Here, the term *homoiosis* (likeness/*demut*) is used, not *eikon* (image/*selem*), but the reference to Genesis is clear. 1 Corinthians 11:7 appears to confine the image of God only to men. On this verse see Gordon Fee, *The First Epistle to the Corinthians,* New International Commentary on the New Testament (Grand Rapids: Eerdmans, 1987), p. 515.

7. Grenz, *Social God,* p. 212.

8. Grenz, *Social God,* p. 224.

participating in and being transformed more fully into the image is identified with every aspect of the believing community's life, making for an intimate binding of the image, election, and the work of the Spirit.

Thus, towards the close of Romans 8, after an account of the Spirit's role in uniting believers to Christ, shaping their present and their eschatological future, we learn that those who become members of the family of Christ through the Spirit of adoption have been predestined from all eternity to be transformed into the image of the Son (Rom. 8:29).

The ongoing transformation in Christ-likeness wrought by the Spirit is none other than the believing community being transformed more and more into the image of Christ the image and glory of God (2 Cor. 3:12-18; 2 Cor. 4:4-6). The pattern of the community's social and ethical life is intimately related to its calling to live as the new creation, re-created in the image of God in Christ (Eph. 4:22-24; Col. 3:9-11). Finally, to share in the image of Christ, rather than the image of Adam, is the ultimate destiny of those who are in Christ (1 Cor. 15:49). As we have summarized Owen's view, so we might also sum up the New Testament witness: the image is the present content and eschatological goal of election, and a pneumatological dynamic holds both together and draws them to their consummation.

The Twofold Dynamic of Representation

That the believing community is now the primary locus of the image within the created order is the inescapable conclusion to be drawn from the New Testament witness, and also forms the basis of Grenz's constructive proposal.[9] In this regard, although he does not speak directly of the connection between the image and election outside his discussion of Romans 8, we should note how closely he intertwines the language of the church as image and the church as elect community: to image God is the "divinely mandated calling" — in other words, the *election* — which is the basis of the church's existence.[10]

The culmination of his account of a Trinitarian, relational conception of the image of God is his description of the *imago dei* as the "ecclesial self" — a personhood that is constituted in Christ by the Spirit in the community of the church. The church exists in the world as the proleptic embodi-

9. Grenz, *Social God*, pp. 312-36.
10. Grenz, *Social God*, p. 336.

ment of the eschatological fulfillment of the image, and serves above all as a sign to the rest of humanity.[11] As the new humanity, reconciled to the Father in Christ by the Spirit, the church is to be the manifestation in and to the world of the triune life of love.[12] In other words, the image is once again defined particularly in terms of representation. The church is the ecclesial image of God because in "the Spirit-fostered mutuality of unifying love — the perichoretic life — within the ecclesial community [we see] a visual, human coming-to-representation of the mutual indwelling of the persons of the Trinity."[13] The church is called to represent God to the world.

If we are to take our bearings for an account of the image of God from Christ, however, then we must also acknowledge that while the centrality of the concept of representation is beyond dispute, the usual way in which theology and exegesis has spoken of the image and representation reveals a singular one-sidedness. In Grenz's description of the ecclesial self, as in Owen's thoroughgoing account of the representational imaging of God, and in Old Testament and New Testament scholarship alike, the imaging of God is presented supremely in terms *representing God to others.* On the basis of the Genesis account, human beings may be thought to represent God *to the created order;* discussion of Christ the one true image of God focuses on the way in which Christ represents God *to us;* Grenz and Owen are typical in reflecting on the ways in which the church represents God in Christ *to others.* Yet if Christ the one true image of God represents to us the fullness of who God is, and if his imaging is the touchstone for our own, then we must also include the notion of *representing others to God.*[14] Christ the image of God not only represents God to us; Christ most fully *represents who God is to us* by *representing us to God.*

Later in this chapter, I will note something of what this might mean in

11. Grenz, *Social God,* e.g., pp. 321, 331.

12. So, for example, ideally, in the character and quality of the relations within the church, the world may see reflected — however imperfectly — a model of the "fullness of the love present within the dynamic of the Triune God" (Grenz, *Social God,* p. 335).

13. Grenz, *Social God,* p. 336. The potential — and problems — of the use of "perichoretic" language in this way will be discussed in Chapter 5.

14. There is also at least a possibility of making a connection with the Genesis creation narratives in this respect, in the episode of the naming of the animals (Gen. 2:18-20). This is usually related to the account of humanity's creation in the image of God as an example of representing God *to* the created order, as an expression of "dominion." Even so, might there not also be scope to consider the naming of the animals in terms of representing — and indeed, re-presenting — the animals *to God?*

terms of Christ and Israel. What this might mean for *our* imaging of God — and indeed for the nature of our election — must wait until the following chapters. For the moment, however, it is to the concept of election that we turn, to discover that the themes and issues raised by a discussion of representation and the image resurface in and are interwoven with the dynamic of election in the Old Testament and the New.

Re-Imaging Israel's Election

The strong New Testament connection between the image and election has already been noted. What, if anything, may be said of the relationship between the image and election in the Old Testament? Brueggemann's caution concerning the reticence of the Old Testament on the theme of the image of God is well taken. If we turn, however, to intertestamental and rabbinic writing on related questions, we discover a theme we have noted in relation to New Testament reflection on the image: the question of the locus of God's "true humanity." For the New Testament, this resides first in Jesus Christ and then in those who are united to him by the Spirit. Thus the emphasis is upon Christ and then the church as the locus of the image, and God's "true humanity" and not humanity as a whole. Intertestamental reflection on the concept of God's true humanity is focused upon Adam, and as Wright has pointed out, rabbinic and intertestamental reflection on Adam does *not* refer to humanity in general, but to Israel in particular. That which was given to Adam and the purposes that God intended to fulfill through humanity in general are transferred to God's chosen people. Israel itself becomes, or will become, God's true humanity, the eschatological second Adam, in and through whom God's original intentions for humanity as a whole will be accomplished.[15]

This trajectory of thought begins to draw the image into the sphere of the long-recognized shape of the narrative relationship between the earlier and later chapters of Genesis. Here we see the narrowing of the horizon of the history of humanity's interaction with God to focus upon the setting apart of God's chosen people, Israel. While explicit mention of the *imago dei* is confined to the earlier chapters of Genesis — and Genesis 9:5-6 insists that the image remains a universal human concept — there are never-

---

15. E.g., N. T. Wright in *The Climax of the Covenant: Christ and the Law in Pauline Theology* (Edinburgh: T. & T. Clark, 1991), chap. 2, "Adam, Israel and the Messiah," esp. pp. 18-26.

theless significant and largely unremarked conceptual continuities between the notion of the image in Adam and that which Israel, brought into being by its election, is created to be and to do.[16]

One element of this continuity can be found in the notion of representation. As Old Testament scholarship is generally agreed that the image includes humanity's role to represent God in the world in a unique way, so it will be seen that the recent convergence of opinion on the nature and function of Israel's election might be summed up in terms of an "election to representation." The function first given to humanity as a whole, and jeopardized by human rebellion and sin, devolves particularly upon the elect people of God.

In this regard, it is intriguing to note that as Brueggemann singles out the notion of representing God as one of the few legitimate Old Testament categories for thinking about the image, so, although he does not make the connection explicit, his description of Israel as the elect community might be summed up in precisely this way. Indeed, his account of the purpose of Israel's election brings us very close to Owen's definition of the image as the representation of God's righteousness, holiness, and love. Insofar as Israel lives in obedience, Brueggemann suggests that Israel fulfills the purpose of its election by revealing the character of God in the world, most particularly by manifesting the love and justice of God, and in "hosting the holiness" of God.[17] Thus, Israel uniquely demonstrates — indeed, uniquely *represents*, although Brueggemann does not use the term — in and to the world the being of God in his holiness and the loving justice of God in his actions towards the world.

While this dynamic of representation (or, we might equally say, this imaging of God) largely occurs within and is focused upon Israel's common life as the elect community, the significance of that which Israel is and does reaches beyond itself to the world. Thus, two questions become one: How are we to describe the contours of the relationship between elect Israel and the non-elect nations; and how does Israel's representational role

---

16. As yet, Old Testament scholarship has paid little attention to what this might signify. Nathan MacDonald offers a brief but highly suggestive word-study, noting the way in which key terms in Genesis 1:26-28 are applied elsewhere to Israel. Nathan MacDonald, "The *Imago Dei* and Election: Reading Genesis 1:26-28 and Old Testament Scholarship with Karl Barth," *IJST* 10 (July 2008): 303-27, esp. pp. 321-26.

17. For the former, see Brueggemann, *Old Testament*, pp. 421ff., and the latter, p. 428 (see pp. 425ff.). Israel's role in reflecting the being and action of God is summarized in pp. 428-29.

express and enact the purposes of God in the wider world? With questions such as these we enter into one of the significant areas of concern in recent English-speaking Old Testament scholarship on the issue of Israel's election: the nature and significance of "mission."[18]

Election, "Mission," and God's Purpose of Blessing

The last major English attempt to delineate the scriptural sweep of the doctrine, Rowley's *The Biblical Doctrine of Election*, summed up the scholarship of its time in the central claim that election is above all for "service," and that the primary category by which Israel's election is to be understood is active mission to the nations. It is the failure of God's chosen people to act upon, and indeed fully to recognize, their vocation to mission, so defined, that leads Israel to forfeit its election to the church.[19]

Recent responses to Rowley's position range from polite dismissal to indignant protest.[20] The straightforward imposition of the New Testament concept of missionary evangelism as the chief category for, and criterion by which to judge, Israel's election gravely distorts any attempt to give an account of Israel's self-understanding as the elect people of God. While the foundational promise of Genesis 12:2-3 suggests that Israel's election will

---

18. Recent works of biblical scholarship devoted to the subject of Israel's election include Jon D. Levenson's *The Death and Resurrection of the Beloved Son: The Transformation of Child Sacrifice in Judaism and Christianity* (New Haven: Yale University Press, 1993), and his "The Universal Horizon of Biblical Particularism," in *Ethnicity and the Bible*, ed. M. G. Brett (Leiden: Brill, 1996), pp. 143-69; see also the work of two Jewish theologians, David Novak, *The Election of Israel: The Idea of the Chosen People* (Cambridge: Cambridge University Press, 1995), and Michael Wyschogrod, *The Body of Faith: God in the People Israel*, 2nd ed. (Northville, NJ: Jason Aronson Inc., 1996); and further biblical studies from Joel S. Kaminsky, "The Concept of Election and Second Isaiah: Recent Literature," *Biblical Theology Bulletin* 31, no. 4 (2001): 135-44, and most recently, his *Yet I Loved Jacob: Reclaiming the Biblical Concept of Election* (Nashville: Abingdon Press, 2007); Christopher Seitz, *Figured Out: Typology and Providence in Christian Scripture* (Louisville: Westminster/John Knox Press, 2001), chap. 11, "The Old Testament, Mission and Christian Scripture," pp. 145-57; and Nathan MacDonald, *Deuteronomy and the Meaning of "Monotheism"* (Tübingen: Mohr Siebeck, 2003), chap. 5, "Hear O Israel: 'Monotheism' and Election," pp. 151-81 (see also pp. 213-15). The theme is also significant in Richard Bauckham's *The Bible and Mission: Christian Witness in a Postmodern World* (Carlisle: Paternoster, 2003).

19. H. H. Rowley, *The Biblical Doctrine of Election* (London: Lutterworth Press, 1950).

20. So, respectively, Brueggemann, *Old Testament*, p. 146, and Kaminsky, "Concept of Election," *passim*.

result in blessing for the nations, it is far from self-evident that this entails any concept of active mission. Moreover, the existence of several diverging strands of thought concerning the theological significance of Israel for the nations prevents any simple account of the relationship between God's purposes for his chosen people and his ultimate purposes for the rest of humanity.[21]

This is reflected in the fact that the notion of Israel's election being in some way "for" the nations is only a highly indirect concern in some of Israel's central "election" texts.[22] In passages where this theme is usually discerned — particularly Deutero-Isaiah's account of the Servant as a light and covenant to the nations[23] — there is no consensus as to the extent to which Israel's direct engagement with the Gentiles can in fact be assumed.[24] If mission as a self-consciously willed activity therefore "plays a minor role if at all" in the Old Testament,[25] and so cannot be considered as a primary category for Israel's understanding of its election, how then are we to speak of the dynamic in which blessing for others is, as Genesis 12:2-3 makes clear, one of the foundational aspects of Israel's election?

One of the most insightful explorations of this theme is that of Christopher Seitz, whose account of the relationship between election, mission, and blessing draws together and richly develops key features of contemporary thinking on Israel's election.[26] It will become clear that while "representation" does not surface as an explicit term in the discussion, it is a concept that embraces the major elements of a growing consensus in understanding Israel's election.

Seitz acknowledges that the concept of mission must be radically rethought if it is to remain a viable term to describe the relationship between Israel as the elect people of God and the nations, and to remain part of the

---

21. These strands are helpfully summarized in Brueggemann, *Old Testament*, pp. 496ff.

22. A point made forcefully by MacDonald in *Deuteronomy;* see further p. 98 below.

23. So in particular, for example, Isaiah 42:1-9; 49:5-6.

24. For a brief survey of the options in the context of a discussion of election, see Kaminsky, "Concept of Election," pp. 139-41, and also his further discussion in *Yet I Loved Jacob,* chap. 9. Brueggemann (*Old Testament*, pp. 433-34) points out the persuasiveness of the suggestion that Isaiah 42:6 refers to the summoning of diaspora Jews rather than the Gentiles, before concluding that on the basis of Genesis 12:2-3 and Exodus 19:6, it is still legitimate to consider that Israel has a role towards the nations, and that this may be in view here.

25. Seitz's blunt summary, *Figured Out*, p. 146.

26. Seitz, *Figured Out*, chap. 11, *passim*. Bauckham *(Bible, passim)* takes up a similar nexus of issues.

common vocabulary of election between the Old and New Testaments. Taking a step back from the particular sociological expression of mission as proselytizing expansion, he offers a theological account of the source and purpose of mission as God's "sending forth" in response to a human situation gone awry. Understood as "God's address of blessing to the deficit and forfeit" brought about by humanity's rebellion, Seitz points out that "mission" may be described as *the* theme of the Old Testament and the supreme purpose of Israel's election.[27]

Seitz follows von Rad to describe the relationship between Genesis 1-11 and the commencement of the patriarchal narratives as God's response to human attempts to thwart his purpose of blessing. The election of Israel is "the means by which sinful creation receives the blessing originally intended for it, for all nations and people."[28] Summing up the relationship between election, mission, and blessing, Seitz remarks: "Blessing will come through election, and mission — God's word of blessing to the nations — will be the means by which God uses Israel to accomplish this."[29]

To the question of whether this election to bring blessing to the nations ought to entail a "missionary approach" as it is usually understood, and in the light of which Israel is found wanting, Seitz responds by asking us to deepen our concept of mission. In an insight to which we will frequently return, Seitz in effect asks us to consider that mission is essentially an *ontological* category before it is to be thought of in terms of particular "missionary" activities. The election that brings Israel into being and the

---

27. Seitz, *Figured Out*, pp. 146-48.

28. Seitz, *Figured Out*, p. 148. See also Bauckham, *Bible*, pp. 28-29, where he remarks that the narrowing of focus to Abraham is not God's "giving up" on the nations, but for the fulfillment of God's purpose of blessing. For Bauckham's discussion of blessing as God's purpose for creation, of the electing blessing to Abraham as God's intention that blessing will prevail over curse, and the fulfillment of this in Christ, see pp. 34-36. While his preference is to avoid using the category of election, Bauckham nevertheless acknowledges that he is seeking throughout to expound a scriptural view of election as God's singling out of particular individuals and groups to be "bearers of God's blessing for all" (p. 84).

29. Seitz, *Figured Out*, p. 149. Brueggemann (*Old Testament*, pp. 430ff.) follows Wolff to reach the same conclusion concerning the purpose of Israel's election. Israel has as "part of its vocation and destiny a role in the well being of the world" (p. 431), existing as God's response to humanity's disobedience, and as the expression of his insistent will "that the world should be brought to blessing" (p. 432). From a Jewish theological perspective, see, e.g., Wyschogrod, *Body of Faith*, pp. 102-4, for whom "The election of Israel and the biblical focus on the history of Israel are ... the means chosen by [God] for the redemption of humanity" (p. 104).

purpose of that election as "mission" — to be the channel of God's blessing — are mutually intrinsic and together constitute Israel's "ontological status in creation."[30] Insofar as Israel's election may be understood in some sense as "for" the nations, this takes place not through Israel's "self-consciously willed activity" but is inherent in its very being-and-act, in the unfolding of Israel's own relationship with YHWH as a nation encountering other nations.[31] *That* this elect community exists and lives out its covenanted life before God *is* God's missionary act of blessing.[32]

Seitz categorizes Israel's election to mission as having both "centripetal" and "centrifugal" elements. Rather than the usual geographical understanding of these terms, with Jerusalem as the focus, Seitz uses them to denote the two aspects of the ontology of election and mission. The former involves Israel (and *mutatis mutandi*, he notes, the church) living out its own internal life in unique relationship to God, and in and with this, therefore manifesting something of the nature of God. The latter involves Israel's interaction with other nations (and the church's explicit evangelistic witness).[33] Thus, in Grenz's description of the church's imaging of God, with its focus on the ecclesial community manifesting God's Trinitarian

---

30. Seitz, *Figured Out*, p. 152.

31. Seitz, *Figured Out*, p. 151. See also Bauckham, *Bible*, e.g., pp. 36ff.

32. ". . . mission has to do with the simple existence of Israel and the charge that gives its existence sense and purpose, a charge entailing election and promise" (Seitz, *Figured Out*, p. 151). See Bauckham, *Bible*, e.g., pp. 30-31, for a brief exploration of the notion that it is as Israel lives out its covenant-life with God that blessing will also flow to the nations. Pannenberg makes the same point when remarking that the principal "mission" of Israel's election, and so the principal way in which Israel serves God's purpose (which he here considers to be the manifestation of God's justice) is simply to be itself and to seek to live in accordance with Torah. Wolfhart Pannenberg, *Human Nature, Election and History* (Philadelphia: Westminster Press, 1977), p. 49.

33. It is with their respective accounts of centripetal and centrifugal "witness" or "mission" that both the similarities and differences between Seitz and Bauckham are most readily apparent. Bauckham retains the more usual understanding of mission as self-consciously willed "evangelistic" activity. He remarks that strictly speaking, none of the ways in which the Old Testament demonstrates the pattern of God's singling out of the particular for the sake of furthering his universal purpose of blessing can be called "mission" (*Bible*, pp. 46-47). He therefore uses the overarching concept of "witness" to embrace the "permanent value" of a non-geographical understanding of centripetal and centrifugal movement (p. 77; see pp. 72-80). So, in relation to the church, Bauckham speaks of a community sent out in centrifugal witness (which is "mission," properly speaking) and which by its life together is to manifest the presence of God in its midst in centripetal witness (which is not; see also pp. 79 and 103).

being-as-love in the dynamics of its own communion, we also see a central element of Seitz's definition of election, for Israel and the church. Grenz's definition of the image of God as the ecclesial self is also Seitz's understanding of election as "centripetal" mission.

Election to Representation

Significantly, Seitz's account of Israel's election also intersects with the major conclusion reached by contemporary Jewish and Christian engagement with key texts: that to fulfill the purpose of its election towards the Gentiles, Israel has to do nothing more than simply to be itself in relation to Yahweh. In Brueggemann's neat summary, Israel is a "theological phenomenon that has concrete socio-political embodiment."[34] Israel cannot be known apart from Yahweh, and neither can Yahweh be known apart from his dealings with and for Israel.[35] In MacDonald's analysis of election in Deuteronomy, a central "election" text for Israel, this is the *only* sense in which the existence of Israel may be thought to be "for" the nations. Any relationship that the nations might have with Yahweh is a byproduct of Israel's own existence before Yahweh as his elect people.[36]

On the basis of this wide-ranging convergence of opinion, Israel's election might therefore be summed up as an "election to representation." Simply by living out its existence as the chosen people of God, Israel is the

34. Brueggemann, *Old Testament*, p. 413.

35. As Wyschogrod remarks, "There is no relation possible for gentiles with [God] except in the context of their relations with the Jewish people. Conversely, every relation of the gentiles with the people of Israel is a relation with the God of Israel, whether so understood or not" (*Body of Faith*, p. 103).

36. In this central text for Israel's understanding of its election there is no suggestion whatsoever that Israel considers actively imparting the knowledge of Yahweh to others to be part of its role, still less that the fundamental distinction between Israel and the nations might be altered sufficiently to allow them to share in any way in the privileged relationship between Yahweh and Israel. MacDonald, *Deuteronomy*, esp. pp. 157-78, 174-75, 180-81. See Kaminsky ("Concept of Election," p. 141) for similar conclusions in commenting upon the parallels between Deutero-Isaiah and the Joseph narrative. So also, more broadly, Novak, who insists that the Jewish people are called first and foremost to "witness our election to ourselves" through faithful living (*Election of Israel*, p. 162; see pp. 157-62), and that it is through Jews living as the covenant people of God that God's love is experienced and revealed within the community, and that God's justice extends towards all (pp. 105-7). Israel's is to be primarily an "intensive" rather than an "extensive" love (p. 106) or, in Seitz's terms, it has a centripetal more than a centrifugal missionary existence.

locus of God's self-manifestation to the world and mediates his presence in the world, to use terms that remind us once again of Old Testament scholarship's account of the nature of the image. Moreover, in this ontology of representation — that simply by *being* Israel in the utter particularity of its covenant relationship with God, Israel represents God in and to the world — Israel also fulfills the electing purpose of God to be the channel of blessing (and judgment) to others. As the nations respond to Israel, so they are responding to the God of Israel. The nations receive blessing or judgment insofar as they respond rightly or wrongly to God's people. Israel neither has to intend this, nor even to be fully conscious of it. It is part of the *esse* of its election.

Hence, just as Israel's election is most fully expressed through but does not depend upon obedience, so the purposes that God intends to achieve through his election of Israel are not dependent upon Israel's obedience or thwarted by Israel's disobedience.[37] Seitz points out that God's purposes of mission through his elect people are achieved "in ways that neither Israel nor the nations fully comprehend," culminating in the supreme paradox that although Israel does not know it, exile itself becomes a "missionary activity."[38] In his brief discussion of Isaiah 40ff., Seitz suggests that the vision of the nations coming to acknowledge the law of God indicates that "[t]he something awry that it is God's missionary purpose to address, God addressed through the judgment of his own people" and their subsequent vindication. Hence, "In Israel's curse, to use the language both of Genesis 12 and Deuteronomy, there is God's missionary act of blessing. By becoming the sinful *goy* in judgment, being sent forth into the hands of the nations . . . there stands the paradoxical fulfillment of the promises to Abraham."[39]

If the enacting of God's purposes for wider blessing is intrinsic to Israel's election to *represent God to others,* however, what of the other side of representation as we have suggested with regard to the image: *representing others to God?* Does this notion have any place at all in the contours of Israel's election? As we have already noted, Brueggemann reminds us that Israel's role in representing God's loving justice and hosting God's holiness is almost exclusively an intra-Israel phenomenon. It may be observed by the nations; they might, perhaps, be drawn to share eschatologically in that which Israel represents to them. Nevertheless, Israel's election to represen-

37. Seitz, *Figured Out,* p. 152; see also, e.g., Levenson, "Universal Horizon," pp. 155-56.
38. Seitz, *Figured Out,* p. 152.
39. Seitz, *Figured Out,* p. 155; see also Bauckham, *Bible,* p. 40.

tation is rarely explicitly directed outwards specifically "for" or on behalf of the nations.

Yet Brueggemann several times refers to possibilities latent in Israel's own self-descriptions that point towards the idea that there is included in Israel's election at least the suggestion of representing others to God. Referring to the designation of Israel as a "kingdom of priests" in Exodus 19:5-6, Brueggemann remarks that while this does indeed primarily signify that Israel exists to point to Yahweh, there is also the tantalizing possibility that "perhaps this nation is offered as a priest for other nations, as mediator and intercessor for the well-being of other nations of the world. . . . And finally . . . to make communion between Yahweh and the world possible."[40]

Again, while acknowledging that the priestly mediation of God's presence is specific to Israel's cultus, Brueggemann is cautiously led to draw further conclusions on the broader basis of what he discerns to be the Old Testament view of human personhood. Israel has no concept of human being that is not utterly Yahwistic. That is, to be human is to be a person-in-relation to Yahweh who has created all people and all things.[41] Thus, there is an "overlap" between who Israel is and what Israel does, in conscious and uniquely covenanted relationship to God, and the situation of the whole of humanity.[42] On this basis, Brueggemann offers the suggestion that Israel's worship has a wider purpose: "the absence, abrasion and distance . . . between God and human persons are provisionally overcome in [Israel's] worship, and are finally overcome in the full restoration of creation."[43] As those who live in the knowledge of the sovereignty of Yahweh, and therefore the embodiment of the unrecognized condition of all, we might say that for Brueggemann, although once again

---

40. Brueggemann, *Old Testament*, p. 431 (see also p. 430). Nathan MacDonald has also pointed out in conversation the possible significance of Abraham's "intercession" for Sodom in this regard (Gen. 18:16-33, in relation to Gen. 12:1-3).

41. E.g., *Old Testament*, p. 450, where Brueggemann remarks that the Old Testament has no conception of an autonomous, general humanness. From creation onwards, humanity is considered only as it stands in relation to Yahweh. Humanity is wholly dependent upon Yahweh and owes him love and obedience, and on the basis of Genesis 9, all humanity in fact exists in a broad covenant relationship with Yahweh, whether it realizes this or not (pp. 453-54).

42. For a summary of the relationship between Jewish personhood and human personhood, with the latter as a derivative reflection of the former, see especially Brueggemann, *Old Testament*, p. 492.

43. Brueggemann, *Old Testament*, p. 481.

the word itself is not used, Israel provisionally *represents* the whole of humanity to God.[44]

There is no suggestion that election "for" others is the *only* purpose of God in setting Israel apart as his chosen people. Nor is the outworking of the election of Israel as it is presented in the Old Testament necessarily the final word on the subject; from a New Testament and Christian theological perspective, there is more that needs to be said. Nevertheless, on the basis of the dynamic of election discerned in the Old Testament, we can say that in the ontological linking of election and representation, and the binding of election and representation with the drawing of the "other" into God's of purposes of blessing, we are given a fundamental truth about the nature of election. With this in mind, we turn to N. T. Wright's account of the christological reorientation of election in Paul.

Election and Representation: A Pauline Perspective

In his *The Climax of the Covenant,* Wright traces the Pauline reconceiving of the Jewish categories of monotheism and election as they have been transformed under the impact of the death and resurrection of Christ, in the realization that Jesus the Messiah embodies both Israel's covenant faithfulness to God and God's covenant faithfulness to Israel.[45] On the basis of detailed exegesis of key loci, and finally, an overview of Romans 9–11,[46] Wright allows us to build a picture of the nature and role of Israel's

---

44. So, for example, Brueggemann remarks that because all persons are intrinsically situated in relationship to the holiness of Yahweh, "in a very general way the character and destiny of human persons replicates the character and destiny of Israel" (*Old Testament,* p. 451). In all of this, we once again find ourselves very close to the concept of the image and the idea that in concentrated form, the election of Israel articulates and encompasses the essence of the image as humanity-in-relation to God.

45. For a more recent synthesis of these themes, see N. T. Wright, *Paul: Fresh Perspectives* (London: SPCK, 2005), *passim,* in which, as he remarks ("Preface," pp. 9-10), he draws upon both *Climax* and also his "The Letter to the Romans: Introduction, Commentary and Reflections," in *New Interpreter's Bible in Twelve Volumes,* vol. 10 (Nashville: Abingdon Press, 2002), pp. 393-770. See also *Jesus and the Victory of God,* vol. 2 of *Christian Origins and the Question of God* (London: SPCK, 1996), Part III, "The Aims and Beliefs of Jesus," *passim,* where Wright develops the theme of Jesus as the representative Messiah of Israel, and as the embodiment of YHWH's saving presence and action.

46. It is worth noting that Wright stresses the near-unanimous position that Romans 9–11 cannot be interpreted as being "about" predestination or election as such and in the ab-

election and Christ's fulfillment of that election as Israel's representative Messiah, creating a compelling account of election from a New Testament perspective, which also intersects with and extends aspects of the Old Testament consensus we have presented.[47] At its heart is the category of representation, and above all the idea that the ontology of election fundamentally entails the representing of others to God.

Turning firstly to his account of Israel's election, we discover much that is familiar. On the basis of the intertestamental and rabbinic literature, as well as the language of blessing in Genesis, Wright notes that the election of Israel is considered to be God's response to the sin of humanity: as God's true humanity, "God's purposes for the human race in general have devolved on to and will be fulfilled in, Israel in particular."[48] With this we are reminded of the conceptual continuities already noted between the image and election, and the concept of "true humanity." The call of Abraham is "God's answer to the problem of evil: somehow, through his people, God will deal with the problem that has infected his good creation in

---

stract (*Climax*, pp. 235f.; "The Letter to the Romans," pp. 602, 620). Wright is at one with those who consider that the primary theme here is that of the righteousness of God through the question of how God in Christ has been faithful to his covenant with his chosen people Israel, in the face of Israel's rejection of Christ and the inclusion of the Gentiles in the people of God. For Wright's understanding of Romans 9–11, see *Climax*, chap. 13, "The Climax of the Covenant," *passim;* and also "Letter to the Romans," pp. 620-91. See also, e.g., Dunn, *Theology*, pp. 500ff.

47. While aspects of his exegesis in *Climax*, and of his wider work, remain controversial, many of the nerve centers of controversy — such as the issue of Israel's ongoing "exile" — do not bear directly upon the themes I wish to develop from Wright's work. One area of dispute that is significant for my use of Wright, however, is the extent to which Jesus can be identified not simply "with" Israel but, as Wright puts it in *Victory of God* (p. 538), as "Israel-in-person, Israel's representative, the one in whom Israel's destiny was reaching its climax." For a critique of this as too close to the older "corporate personality" approach associated with H. Wheeler Robinson, see, e.g., Ben Witherington III, *The Jesus Quest: The Third Search for the Jew of Nazareth* (Downers Grove, IL: InterVarsity Press, 1995), pp. 223, 230. Wright responds directly to Witherington's critique in *Victory of God*, p. 532; details of his covenantal understanding of the "incorporative" aspect of the term "Messiah," which distinguishes him from the earlier position, can be found in *Climax*, e.g., pp. 46-49 and chap. 7, *passim*. For a positive appraisal of Wright's position, see Paul R. Eddy, "The (W)Right Jesus: Eschatological Prophet, Israel's Messiah, Yahweh Embodied," in *Jesus and the Restoration of Israel: A Critical Assessment of N. T. Wright's Jesus and the Victory of God*, ed. Carey C. Newman (Carlisle: Paternoster, 1999), pp. 40-60, p. 54. Eddy also points to recent complementary developments in this area, including the work of Kaminsky, in a further indication of the convergence to be noted between Wright and the preceding account of aspects of Old Testament scholarship.

48. Wright, *Climax*, pp. 20-21.

general and his image-bearing creatures in particular."[49] Insofar as Israel walks rightly in its covenant relationship to God, "the nations will see . . . what it means to be truly human, and hence who the true God is."[50] In other words, it is the calling of God's elect people, in their being and action, to represent God in and to the world.

The predominant vision of intertestamental Judaism is that Israel's elect status as God's "true humanity" will issue in Israel's eschatological rule as God's vice-regent over the subdued nations. For Paul, however, Christ's death and resurrection have definitively revealed the nature and purpose of Israel's election. This is expressed particularly through his reinterpretation of the function of Torah, and with it the relationship of Israel to the rest of humanity.

As God's good gift, Torah demarcates and defines Israel's identity as the elect people of God. Nevertheless, elect Israel participates in the sinful condition of humanity as a whole, sharing in "the evil as well as the image-bearing vocation of the rest of humanity."[51] Thus, the very fact of being uniquely set apart for covenant relationship with God means that at one and the same time Israel under Torah is also elect to become the place in which human sin is exposed and concentrated, so that it can be "concentrated yet further, drawn on to Israel's representative Messiah — in order that it might be dealt with there once and for all."[52] It is Israel's "paradoxical vocation" to be the people of the covenant, even as this condemns all, including Israel, who are "in Adam," and through this to be the means of restoring relationship.[53] In effect Israel's is an election to bear rejection for the sake of wider blessing.[54]

---

49. Wright, *Fresh Perspectives*, p. 109; see, e.g., pp. 23-24 for the role of the call of Abraham in Genesis as a response to the sin of Adam and pp. 34-36 for binding this to the theme of the *imago dei:* the covenant with Abraham and his family is the means through which God will address the problems created by "the failure of human beings to be the truly image-bearing creatures God intended" (p. 35). See also "Letter to the Romans," pp. 399, 647.

50. Wright, *Fresh Perspectives*, p. 109.

51. Wright, *Fresh Perspectives*, p. 36.

52. Wright, *Climax*, p. 196. This is an oft-repeated theme throughout. For another characteristic example, see p. 39, in which Torah is described as having "the divinely intended function of drawing sin on to Israel, magnifying it precisely within the people of God . . . in order that it might . . . be drawn on to Israel's representative and so dealt with on the cross." See also, e.g., "Letter to the Romans," pp. 578-79, 625, 635, 643.

53. Wright, *Climax*, p. 198.

54. In Wright's terms, Israel is elect to be "cast away" that the world might be saved (e.g., *Climax*, pp. 243-49; "Letter to the Romans," pp. 625, 635, 643). Against the manifest

With this account of the Pauline reappraisal of Israel's election, a multitude of strands within Old Testament election scholarship are drawn together and extended. Once again, the election of Israel is understood as the means by which God responds to humanity's sinful rebellion and fulfills his purposes of blessing.[55] We are reminded particularly, perhaps, of Seitz's account of the "paradoxical and unexpected fulfillment" of the promise of blessing to the nations in and through Israel's exile and subsequent vindication.

We might also point to Levenson's account of the theology of chosenness as it is revealed in the patriarchal narratives and played out in the wider history of Israel: the pattern of the near-death and miraculous restoration of the beloved son.[56] As with the representative individual election of the patriarchs, so with the dynamic of the election of Israel as God's chosen son, Levenson speaks of election as utterly bound up with the concept of sacrifice, literal and metaphorical, and the bearing of suffering for the sake of, and as the channel for, God's promised blessing.[57] As Levenson remarks, from a Jewish perspective, the christological reorientation of election in the New Testament is a recognizable offspring of Israel's own understanding of election.

We have noted also the agreement that Israel simply has to live out its own unique relationship with God to fulfill the purposes of its election, and have summed up this consensus in terms of Israel's election *to represent God to others*. The implication of Wright's thesis is that for Paul, the fullness of Israel's election also includes the reality and supreme importance of Israel's election *to represent others to God*. Seitz's account of Is-

---

dangers of such terminology must be set Wright's Israel-christology, to be discussed below. This is *Christ's* calling also, as the representative Messiah of Israel, and the wider blessing that flows from this dynamic of election is one into which Israel, too, is taken up in the person of the Messiah; the blessing for the wider world that comes *from* Israel's paradoxical vocation is in turn *for the sake of* Israel.

55. Summarized, e.g., in *Climax*, p. 239, where Wright again describes God's choice to rescue the world by calling a people into covenant and through them dealing with sin, concentrating it in one place and condemning it there, such that it falls with full force not upon Israel itself, but Israel's representative Messiah. See also, e.g., "Letter to the Romans," p. 635, in which Wright re-describes this pattern in God's electing "for the extension of God's saving purpose to the whole world."

56. The tracing of this pattern is the focus of Levenson, *Beloved Son*.

57. See also, e.g., Kaminsky ("Concept of Election," p. 141) on the "theologically meaningful" suffering of the elect for the purposes of wider blessing in his comparison between Deutero-Isaiah and the story of Joseph.

rael's election describes how by the simple fact of its existence Israel accomplishes God's missionary purposes: by representing God to others, Israel is the channel of God's blessing for the nations. Here we see that from a Pauline perspective, it is central to the ontology of Israel's election that, likewise simply by living its covenanted life as the elect people of God, Israel has exercised a priestly representation, holding humanity as a whole in itself before God, and thereby fulfilling another aspect of its election to be, in Seitz's terms, "God's address to humanity's forfeit."[58] That which Brueggemann held out as an oblique possibility from within the contours of the Old Testament is now considered to be at the heart of the dynamic of Israel's election, of Christ's, and ultimately, as we shall see, of the church's as well.

Indeed, Wright makes clear that in Pauline terms, it is precisely because the entire human situation is representatively held and summed up in Israel that in Christ, in whom Israel itself is held and summed up, the fulfillment of the covenant promise of blessing to Israel and to the nations is made possible.[59] In his own faithfulness, Christ is the bearer of unfaithful Israel's sins in covenant judgment. It is because in its own election, Israel represents the whole of humanity, that Christ is also the bearer of the sins of the world. Thus, Israel's representative Messiah is the channel of the wider blessing that was God's promise and intention through the election of Israel, and the fullest expression of that election to be a light to the nations.

It therefore cannot be emphasized too strongly that Jesus' death is not the denial of Israel's role in the purposes of God but the fulfillment of that role and those purposes.[60] Moreover, in his resurrection Jesus also represents in his own person the eschatological role of Israel, vindicated after persecution and death, as the Messiah enacts in himself the expected victory of the nation as a whole.[61] In language that reminds us once again of

58. Seitz, *Figured Out*, p. 147.

59. This is a primary concern throughout. As an apt summary, he remarks that Jesus' death is "for sin" because "he represents Israel and Israel represents humanity as a whole" (Wright, *Climax*, p. 213). See also, e.g., Bauckham, *Bible*, pp. 48-49, 80, for his account of how the particularity of Jesus "repeated the particularity" of Israel and its seminal figures (p. 48), and precisely because of this, Jesus also holds within himself, and brings to its fulfillment, the universal trajectory which is integral to and intended by Israel's particularity.

60. Wright, *Climax*, e.g., p. 40; see also pp. 59ff. for Christ on the cross taking on "the role of Israel in the purposes of God": i.e., the means of responding to humanity's sinful rebellion.

61. Wright, *Climax*, p. 43.

the close conceptual links between the image and election, with regard to both Israel and Christ, Wright considers that for Paul, the role traditionally assigned to Israel has devolved onto Jesus Christ, so that it is Jesus himself and not Israel as such, who is God's true humanity.[62]

On the basis of this christological pattern, Wright speaks of Paul's "re-interpretation" of what it means to be the elect people of God, not in terms of a privileged status, but as a vocation to "dying and rising with the Messiah."[63] In fact, as Levenson's work in particular makes clear, this is not so much a reinterpretation of the shape of Israel's election for Paul, as his perception that in Christ is found the culmination and fulfillment of the pattern of God's electing that Israel itself has discerned.[64]

What must be emphasized here, however, is that at the heart of election there is not simply a pattern of (near) death and restoration for the sake of wider blessing, but an entire representational ontology in which this pattern is embedded and from which it derives its theological meaning. This representational ontology is vividly described by Wright with regard to Christ: "Because the Messiah represents Israel, he is able to take on himself Israel's curse and exhaust it,"[65] and as Israel's redeeming representative, "He *is* Israel, going down to death under the curse of the law and going through that curse to the new covenant life beyond."[66] This in turn makes sense only in the context of Israel's own representational election ontology: intrinsic to Israel's election is to bear in itself the rejection of the "other" in order to be the channel of blessing to the "other."

62. Wright, *Climax,* p. 88ff.

63. See Wright, e.g., *Fresh Perspectives,* pp. 127-28, and "Letter to the Romans," pp. 682-83, for further discussion of the "Messiah-shaped" pattern of Israel's history.

64. See Levenson, *Beloved Son,* chaps. 15 ("The Displacement of Isaac and the Birth of the Church") and 16 ("The Re-visioning of God in the Image of Abraham"), *passim,* for Levenson's interpretation of Paul's position, and that of the wider New Testament, in relation to the theme of election and the beloved son. See also Kaminsky, *Yet I Loved Jacob,* chap. 11.

65. Wright, *Climax,* p. 151.

66. Wright, *Climax,* p. 152; see also, e.g., p. 155: "the death of Jesus . . . draws Israel's destiny on himself . . . [as] the fulfilment . . . of the whole paradoxical history of Israel" so that the blessing promised through the election of Israel may also reach its fulfillment. See, e.g., his *Fresh Perspectives,* p. 120: "The Messiah has done that for which Israel was chosen in the first place. . . . He has done in Israel's place what Israel was called to do but could not, namely to act on behalf of the whole world," as the covenant faithfulness of God in person.

The Elect Community in Christ

Christ is therefore both the one in whose life, death, and resurrection are represented the whole of Israel's purpose and history as the covenant people, and the covenant faithfulness of God in person, in whom all the promises and blessings are contained. If this theme of election to representation — of God to others and others to God — reaches its climax in the person of Israel's representative Messiah, this also signifies for Paul that in Christ alone is now the way to enter into and remain within the elect people of God.[67] Jesus "represents and draws together in himself the physical family of Abraham, in order to be the focal point of a new community, the renewed people of God."[68] He alone is the one "in whom the true people of God are summed up and find their identity."[69] God continues, in Christ and in the people of Christ, to be faithful to his electing intention from the very beginning: "God's answer to the sin of humanity . . . is the people of Abraham"; through God's covenant faithfulness in Israel's representative Messiah, "Abraham's true people are now those redeemed in Christ."[70]

The consequence of acknowledging Christ as Israel's representative Messiah is therefore that the boundaries of the elect people of God must be redrawn. It is those who, through the Spirit by faith, "belong to"/are "in"/have "put on" Christ who alone belong to the family that shares in the promises to Abraham.[71] Wright neatly summarizes at once the new particularism and the new openness of election in Paul: "on the one hand . . . (only) those who *believe* in Christ belong to the community, and on the other . . . *all* those who believe in Christ, irrespective of racial background, belong."[72] To be the elect people of God is no longer demarcated by Torah and circumcision, but by being "in Christ" by the Spirit through faith. As we made clear in relation to the New Testament difficulties raised by

---

67. So, e.g., Wright, *Climax*, p. 36. See also *Fresh Perspectives*, e.g., pp. 113f., 119-21; "Letter to the Romans," e.g., p. 673.

68. Wright, *Climax*, p. 44.

69. Wright, *Climax*, p. 46.

70. Wright, *Climax*, p. 36.

71. So, e.g., Wright, *Fresh Perspectives*, p. 114. Hence, it is only those who believe in Christ who are within the covenant (p. 119). Wright summarizes that "Paul really does believe that those who do not believe the gospel are, to put it no stronger, given no promises of sharing in the life of the age to come" ("Letter to the Romans," p. 631; see also p. 673).

72. *Climax*, p. 3, Wright's italics.

Barth's christological reorientation of election, it is therefore the Spirit's work as well as Christ's that delineates those who are "in Christ."[73]

Wright's primary concern in *Climax of the Covenant* is the radical consequences of this for unbelieving ethnic Israel. He underlines that from Paul's perspective, for Israel to remain under Torah and apart from Christ is to remain in the place where sin was concentrated, and therefore not to participate in the bearing away of sin by Christ the *telos* of Torah.[74] Once again, however, we must recognize that here we have not the negation but the fulfillment of Israel's election, and thus the holding out of the promise of the pattern of election to unbelieving ethnic Israel even as it appears to be withdrawn.

Thus, just as Seitz points out that, although initially unbeknownst to Israel, through the apparent rejection of exile comes God's missionary act through Israel to the nations *and* the promise that the faithful God will restore Israel, so in his account of the sweep of Romans 9–11, and especially the import of Romans 11, Wright reminds us that for Paul, too, the pattern of Israel's election, and of God's faithfulness, is as it has always been. Israel's rejection of Christ is the paradoxical outworking of the promise that through the election of Israel will come blessing for the nations. Moreover, as Israel's stumbling opens the way for the Gentiles to enter into the covenant blessings, so *their* entry is for the sake of holding out the promise again to unbelieving ethnic Israel.

With this note of continuing hope for Israel, we need to turn to a distinction between Wright and J. D. G. Dunn, who otherwise share a similar understanding of the dynamic of Romans 9–11. The difference between them lies in their answer to the question "Who is Israel?" — in other words, "To whom does the term 'elect' apply?" — and is encapsulated in their interpretations of the "all Israel will be saved" of Romans 11:26. How each responds will draw out important themes to be taken up when we turn to the ways in which theology might speak of election on the basis of scriptural patterns.

---

73. See Chapter 3, pp. 66-69 above. For Wright's insistence upon this, see *Climax*, chap. 10, *passim* (with regard to Romans 8); and pp. 255f., 267; *Fresh Perspectives*, pp. 123-25. Wright's consideration of the shape of the church's election will be pursued in the following chapter.

74. As such, and as one of the major sub-themes of the whole, Wright is adamant in rejecting any notion that, either in Romans 11 or elsewhere, Paul lends any support to a "two covenant" theory in which Gentiles are to find salvation in Christ but ethnic Jews may remain "in covenant" under Torah apart from Christ; e.g., *Climax*, p. 173, chap. 13, *passim*, pp. 252ff. See also "Letter to the Romans," e.g., pp. 621, 627ff., 672-74, *Fresh Perspectives*, pp. 125-28.

Wright maintains that "all Israel" here signifies all who believe in Christ, since the elect community has now been redefined around Christ, God's covenant faithfulness in person.[75] Dunn considers that, for Paul, God's covenant faithfulness requires that unbelieving ethnic Israel must still be considered to be "elect," with the existence of the "remnant" from ethnic Israel who believe in Christ as the link that makes this continuing designation possible.[76] Crucially, however, Dunn and Wright both insist that election is ultimately to be defined in terms of faith in Christ, and that the work of the Spirit forms the boundary marker of the people of God. As such, Dunn considers that Paul has in view the eschatological conversion of all or most unbelieving Jews at the parousia.[77] Wright is adamant that there can be no eschatological event of salvation, but only the coming to faith that takes place in the present time.[78]

To anticipate some of the conclusions of this chapter, and aspects of those to follow, it seems to me that in terms of how theology is to use the language of election, *only* the new covenant community of those united to Christ by the Spirit through faith may now be called "elect," since *only* those who are "in Christ" now stand in the particular set of relations to God and the rest of humanity that allows them to be the locus and channel of the covenant promises and blessings. Nevertheless, the intricate relationship between ethnic Israel and the Gentiles in the unfolding of God's purposes in election, as this is described in Romans 11, suggests a greater openness to eschatological possibilities than Wright is prepared to allow.

Returning to the overall dynamic of Romans 11, once again we are reminded of the wider pattern of election that has already been noted: that election is always intrinsically *for* the other, whether this is fully recognized by the elect people of God or not, and always participates in the fulfilling of God's wider purpose of blessing. This is the way in which Israel's stumbling accords with the pattern and promise of election in the Old Testament, and it is at the heart of the role that Paul considers the incoming of the Gentiles will play in the purposes of God, by continuing to hold out God's promises and possibilities to Israel. Moreover, it is important to note that, although the Roman Christians are now aware of it, thanks to Paul's

---

75. See Wright, *Climax*, pp. 249ff.; "Letter to the Romans," e.g., pp. 672-74, 676-82.

76. For Dunn's account of Rom. 9–11 see his *The Theology of Paul the Apostle* (Edinburgh: T. & T. Clark, 1998), §19, *passim*, in addition to his detailed exegesis in *Romans 9–16*, Word Biblical Commentary 38B (Dallas: Word, 1991).

77. E.g., Dunn, *Romans 9–16*, pp. 680ff., 692ff.

78. E.g., Wright, "Letter to the Romans," pp. 688-91.

explanation here, Gentile believers themselves do not in fact *need* to know that their election is part of the fulfillment of God's purposes for Israel for this nevertheless to be intrinsic to the reality of their election. On Paul's terms, the Gentiles in effect represent God to Israel simply by existing as the elect people of God in Christ, in the same way that in the Old Testament Israel, by living out its existence as the elect people of God, was playing its part in God's purposes of blessing for the nations, whether with self-conscious intent or not.

With this in mind, we return to Old Testament scholarship, and to another area both of significant consensus and of pressing concern.

Beyond "Particularism" and "Universalism"

As the pattern discerned by Seitz reminds us, Old Testament scholarship seeks a far greater recognition that intrinsic to Israel's election is its role in God's purposes of wider blessing. At the same time as asking for more credit to be given to the "universal horizon" of Israel's election, Old Testament scholarship also demands that those who look primarily to the New Testament to define their understanding of election acknowledge that the New Testament account of election makes claims that are as "particularistic" and "exclusivist" as its Old Testament counterpart. This reflects a desire from the Old Testament scholars we have mentioned for an implicit and explicit assumption in much Christian reflection to be acknowledged and rectified: that Judaism essentially represents an "exclusivist" and "particularist" approach to election, while Christianity is lauded for its supposedly "universalistic" outlook.[79]

The element of truth within this — that election in the New Testa-

79. The crude caricature of Israel's understanding of election as "particularistic" and "exclusivistic" (and therefore "bad") and the Christian approach to election as "universalistic" (and therefore "good") has been an unfortunate and pervasive default tendency, and one that owes more in tenor and content to Enlightenment preoccupations than to the scriptural data (so, e.g., Seitz, *Figured Out,* p. 146; Levenson, "Universal Horizon," where the concern is pervasive, but see esp. pp. 157ff.; Kaminsky, "Concept of Election," pp. 136-37, 140, and his *Yet I Loved Jacob,* "Introduction to the Topic," and chap. 11, "New Testament and Rabbinic Views of Election" and "Concluding Reflections" in particular, although it is a significant theme throughout; and MacDonald, *Deuteronomy,* pp. 213-15). Dispelling this notion, and also the idea that the particular and the universal must necessarily be seen as mutually exclusive or contradictory, is also a key concern in Bauckham, *Bible,* made explicit, e.g., pp. 47, 77.

ment is not tied to race or ethnicity — is more than outweighed by a failure to acknowledge that the New Testament is as particularistic as the Old Testament in its understanding of the identity of the people of God. As Wright's work makes clear, Paul is working with the same basic division of humanity as Judaism, between those who belong within the covenant family of Abraham and those who do not.[80] What is at issue is not *whether* election entails membership of the family of Abraham, but *how* the terms of that membership are to be understood.[81] As we have already suggested in relation to Barth, however Christian theology attempts to articulate the dynamic of election, neither the term itself nor its New Testament equivalent of "in Christ" can straightforwardly bear any kind of universal application. Wright correctly insists that election language can refer *only* to a very particular community: those who find themselves "in Christ" by the Spirit through faith.

While election in both the Old and New Testaments includes within it a "universal horizon," a well-defined and utterly irreducible particularism is therefore central to both.[82] Moreover, as Kaminsky wisely notes, the issue is not to be papered over by the suggestion that this reflects a straightforward affirmation of the goodness of particularity in general, as we might ironically put it.[83] It is an affirmation of the very deliberate singling out of one community for a unique relationship to God and for a role that can be shared by no other.[84]

80. A major theme of Levenson, e.g., *Beloved Son,* p. 217, where he goes on to remark that "The division between the circumcised and the uncircumcised, between Israel and the nations . . . has become the division between the baptised and the unbaptised, between the Church and the world, between those who have accepted the gospel and those who have not." He insists elsewhere that if both Judaism and Christianity are to remain true to their founding documents, they must "continue to affirm the essential dichotomy between insiders and outsiders" ("Universal Horizon," p. 166). See also Kaminsky, *Yet I Loved Jacob,* e.g., pp. 170-72.

81. Kaminsky neatly sums up the relationship between the Old Testament account of Israel's election and its New Testament counterpart as issuing in "two equally particularist faiths who have a genuine disagreement about who the elect are and what election implies" ("Concept of Election," p. 142).

82. See, e.g., Kaminsky, "Concept of Election," further developed in *Yet I Loved Jacob;* Levenson, "Universal Horizon," *passim;* MacDonald, *Deuteronomy,* esp. pp. 158, 167, 213-15.

83. Kaminsky, "Concept of Election," p. 137.

84. As Kaminsky also points out ("Concept of Election," e.g., pp. 136, 141), however, the Old Testament categories of elect and non-elect do not necessarily imply the "saved" and the "lost," as the inference is generally drawn from the New Testament. Instead, the nations are, and will always remain, non-elect — they cannot *be* Israel — but in their own particularity as non-elect may still be the recipient of God's blessing. This is a major theme taken up in

The complex interrelationship between "universalistic" tendencies within two particularistic conceptions of election leads to yet further agreement within Old Testament election scholarship: the call for biblical scholars and theologians alike to recognize that these very categories which have long dominated the discussion of election are profoundly inadequate and exceedingly unhelpful.

Constructively speaking, however, the discussion appears to have reached something of an impasse. While "universalism" and "particularism" are stifling and unhelpfully freighted categories, the question remains unanswered as to how we are to speak of the biblical contours of election without allowing the language of election to continue to be dominated by them. What is required is an alternative conceptual framework that is able both to hold together these polarities and to transcend them.

Representation holds out rich potential as just such a category. Unlike "universalism" and "particularism," which are alien hermeneutical impositions on the scriptural texts, the concept of representation is itself rooted in scripture, offering a governing biblical context to shape and relativize the continuing use of these disputed terms. More particularly, the category of representation encompasses both key elements of the scriptural election dynamic across the Old and New Testaments: it honors the utter exclusivity of election as signifying one clearly defined and distinctive community set apart to be and to do what no others can be and do, and also suggests a dynamic within which election can be seen as intrinsically for the sake of the other.

Conclusion: Three Scriptural Guiding Principles

On the basis of the scriptural contours of election that have emerged in this chapter, we are also in a position to set out a broad framework within which to situate our attempt to rearticulate the doctrine. Three guiding principles both summarize the agreement on the shape of election that has

---

Yet I Loved Jacob, where Kaminsky develops a threefold typology of election in the Old Testament: the elect (Israel), the non-elect (the majority of the Gentiles, not hostile to Israel), and the anti-elect (the enemies of Israel), and suggests that Judaism is in fact more hospitable with regard to the fate of the non-elect than is Christianity, with its insistence that salvation is through Christ alone (see esp. pp. 107-36, 175-77). See also, e.g., Wyschogrod, "Israel, the Church and Election," in *Abraham's Promise: Judaism and Jewish-Christian Relations,* ed. R. Kendall Soulen (Grand Rapids: Eerdmans, 2004), pp. 179-87, pp. 185-87.

been outlined here, and provide a series of interwoven themes that will mold our account of the church's election to representation.

The first is the constancy of God's purpose in election: *God sets apart an elect people as the means by which his purpose of blessing will be fulfilled in the face of human sinfulness.*

So the insistence of Seitz and Brueggemann, for example, that election in the Old Testament is the means by which humanity and the whole created order will receive God's intended blessing is matched by Wright's account of the Pauline interpretation of God's faithfulness to his electing intention from the outset. In God's election of the people of Abraham — from ethnic Israel, culminating in Israel's representative Messiah, to its outworking in the eschatological redefinition of the people of Abraham in Christ — we find God's response to human sin and the means by which God will bring about the healing of the world.

Second, *representation* is a significant category through which to understand the nature and purpose of election.

From an Old Testament perspective, we have seen that Israel's election to representation includes the notion that simply by living out its covenanted relationship with God, Israel represents God to others in a way that radically includes God's purpose of blessing for others. We have also noted that this representational election ontology hints allusively at the idea that again, simply by being human, set apart to live and worship in recognition of its relationship with the holy God, Israel also represents humanity to God.

The Pauline reinterpretation of election discussed by Wright pushes this dynamic of election to the full expression of the notion that Israel represents in itself the whole human situation before God, such that we might say that a major purpose of Israel's election is to hold non-elect and apparently rejected humanity within itself, and so within the sphere of the promised blessings of God. For New Testament scholarship and Christian theology, this is at once definitively made known by and brought to its climax in the person of Christ, the embodiment of Israel, God's true humanity; *and* as we have already suggested, the image of God who represents God to us supremely by representing us to God.

Once representation has been acknowledged as a significant category by which to understand the dynamic of election in Israel and in Christ, we must go on to say that it also remains a significant category through which the church is to explore its own election in Christ. There is continuity in the shape as well as the purpose of God's election.

Finally, my reappraisal of the doctrine of election will proceed on the basis that *the believing community and the believing community alone can be described as elect in Christ.*

Old Testament scholarship insists upon the utter particularity of election with regard to Israel, as well as (and as the basis for) its "universal horizon," asking also that New Testament scholarship and Christian theology recognize the same basic pattern in their own accounts of election. In turn, we have noted that Wright is adamant that the language of election can refer only to those who are in Christ by the Spirit through faith. To be in Christ by the Spirit is the new "boundary marker" of the covenant people of God — and not ethnicity, Torah, or for that matter a universal christological anthropology.

The first two guiding principles — that there is continuity in the purpose and shape of God's election — should prove relatively uncontroversial. The last may well be viewed with considerable suspicion, suggesting not so much a basis for the renewal of the doctrine as a straightforward return to a previous orthodoxy, an unraveling of the themes developed by Barth in his christological reorientation of the doctrine. In due course, we will reexamine and challenge both Owen's Reformed orthodoxy and Barth's reformulation of the doctrine in the light of what has been suggested here. For the moment, however, as the shape of the church's election to representation begins to unfold in the following chapter, it cannot be emphasized too strongly that each of these principles is inseparable from the others, and in particular that the last cannot be taken in isolation from the other two. It is as we are constantly mindful that the elect community exists to further God's purpose of wider blessing, and the representational dynamic of this, that we will be in a position to examine further the implications of an insistence upon confining the concept of election exclusively to the believing community.

CHAPTER 5

Election, the Spirit, and the Ecclesial Imago Dei

In a considerable departure from the framework within which the doctrine is usually formulated and discussed, contemporary biblical scholarship has therefore opened out rich possibilities for a fresh approach to election, and its relationship to the notion of the *imago dei,* through the category of representation. It will be the task of this chapter to move towards an account of what such a doctrine of election might look like for the church by drawing the preceding biblical discussion into conversation with contemporary theology's interest in describing our imaging of God in terms of "perichoretic" personhood. It is Wright's description of the dynamic of election in Israel and Christ, and his suggestions concerning the pneumatological outworking of this in the church, that point towards the fruitfulness of a dialogue between the two.

The Pneumatological Dynamic
of the Church's Election: Some Hints

We have seen that in *The Climax of the Covenant* Wright's focus is almost entirely upon Christ as the hermeneutical key to Paul's understanding of Israel. Nevertheless, at the close of his exposition of Romans 9–11 Wright offers a brief excursus to draw out some of the implications of his analysis for the church's self-understanding as the elect people of God in Christ.[1]

Wright remarks that it has always been God's covenant purpose "to

---

1. N. T. Wright, *The Climax of the Covenant: Christ and the Law in Pauline Theology* (Edinburgh: T. & T. Clark, 1991), p. viii, chap. 13, "Hermeneutics and Theology," pp. 252-57.

choose a people in and through whom the world would be healed. That purpose, reaching its climax in the Messiah, is now to be worked out through his people."[2] In undeveloped but highly suggestive hints, he then sketches an outline of the shape of the church's election in continuity with the pattern that he has already discerned with regard to Israel and Christ. For the church to be true to its vocation "it will find that its role is Christ-shaped: to bear the pain and shame of the world in its own body, that the world may be healed. . . . The church is called to do and be for the world what the Messiah was and did for Israel. . . . The church must find out the pain of the world and must share it and bear it."[3]

Wright has already described the role of Israel's representative Messiah as holding Israel in himself, taking upon himself its disobedience and embodying that which it was called to be, in order that the promises to Israel, and through Israel for the world, might be proleptically fulfilled in and through himself. Wright's assertion is that the church, as the people of Christ, is called to stand in such a relation to the world, as the means by which the redemption that has been accomplished in Christ is worked out in and for the world.

He goes on to indicate that the dynamic of the church's election in this regard is explicitly pneumatological, and that it also entails fulfilling a parallel role towards the world to that of Israel. As the one by whom we are brought to be "in Christ" and so to belong to the new covenant people of God, the Spirit "accomplishes within the church what, *mutatis mutandi*, the Torah accomplished within Israel. Just as the sin and death of the world were concentrated by means of Torah on Israel . . . so now the pain and grief of the world is to be concentrated by means of the Spirit on the . . . family of the Messiah, so that it may be healed."[4]

Much care will need to be taken in developing this trajectory of thought to ensure that a clear distinction is maintained between the saving work that has been accomplished once-for-all in Christ and the secondary and derivative role that the church is given to play in the unfolding of that completed work. Nevertheless, Wright's brief sketch of the shape of the church's election indicates that the concept of representation remains central: to hold the other's alienation from God in the self so as to represent the other to God is for Wright the characteristic pattern of God's electing

2. Wright, *Climax*, p. 256.
3. Wright, *Climax*, p. 256.
4. Wright, *Climax*, p. 256.

activity in Israel, in Christ, and in the church. It is in this fundamental election dynamic, and in his presentation of the Spirit as the one who constitutes the church's representational being, that Wright invites dialogue with the notion of the ecclesial *imago dei* as pneumatologically constituted "perichoretic" personhood. Before exploring further the implications of Wright's biblical scholarship for a renewal of the doctrine of election, we therefore turn to some of the problems and possibilities created by this understanding of the image of God, finding in it an approach that will enrich Wright's insights, and to which Wright in turn will help to provide a vital corrective.

The Spirit, "Perichoretic" Personhood, and the Ecclesial *Imago Dei*

As the previous chapter has indicated, for Grenz, the image of God as the ecclesial self entails the coming-to-representation in the human sphere of the eternally loving being-in-relation of the triune God. The ecclesial form of human relational personhood is, for Grenz, the closest creaturely approximation to the inner-divine perichoresis. Alongside Grenz's sketch of ecclesial "perichoretic" personhood we will refer to the complementary and more extended reflections of Miroslav Volf, whose exploration of related concepts in *After Our Likeness* intersects with and supplements Grenz's rather briefer presentation.[5] Both point us towards the possibilities offered by this way of understanding the ecclesial imaging of God, but also to the difficulties that the general notion of human relational personhood raises for the particular shape and role of "perichoretic" personhood among those who are in Christ by the Spirit in the community of the church.

An obvious but extremely important clarification must be made at the outset. The spatio-temporal limitations of creatureliness mean that we can

---

5. Although Grenz only nods briefly in Volf's direction (*The Social God and the Relational Self: A Trinitarian Theology of the Imago Dei* [Louisville: Westminster/John Knox Press, 2001], p. 334, n. 150), Volf had already explored similar questions and reached similar conclusions in *After Our Likeness: The Church as the Image of the Trinity* (Grand Rapids: Eerdmans, 1998). For a complementary treatment of the concept of "perichoretic" personhood as it is developed by Grenz and Volf, which sets this in the context of a carefully qualified understanding of perichoresis as a transcendental category, see Colin E. Gunton, *The One, the Three and the Many: God, Creation and the Culture of Modernity* (Cambridge: Cambridge University Press, 1993), part 2, "Rethinking Createdness," *passim*.

speak only analogically of the concept of perichoresis outside the being of God. Perichoresis is the term that seeks to describe the "mutual reciprocity, interpenetration, and interanimation" by which the triune God is one, a dynamic within which the particularity of Father, Son, and Holy Spirit is not lost but established by mutual indwelling.[6] Obviously and crucially, we do not share one *ousia* with God or with one another; there can be for us no such mutual indwelling.

Our creaturely and analogical equivalence to the inner-divine perichoresis can be expressed only in the reality that our personhood is constituted and shaped as one of particularity-in-relation. First and foremost, this is in the relationship established by the Creator God with us as his image-bearing creatures.[7] Second, we have also been created such that our personhood is mutually constituted through our relations with others. In our limited creaturely correspondence to the triune God, we too are who we are only in relation.[8]

At this point it is probably as well to acknowledge the significant doubts expressed by those who are wary of what Bruce McCormack terms the "creeping perichoresis" in contemporary theology, understood as the "uncritical expansion" of the term to refer to anything beyond inner-Trinitarian relations.[9] McCormack's preference is for the term to be confined to describing only that which is *dissimilar* in the analogy between the triune relations and human relations, or our relationship to God in Christ, precisely because the latter two can never involve unity of substance. Nevertheless, the continuing, qualified use of the concept outside the sphere of describing the inner-Trinitarian relations will be important in the development of election to representation, and is rooted in the concept of the relational *imago dei*.

6. The citation is from Gunton, *The One, the Three and the Many*, p. 163.

7. In this regard, we must also note that not only can there be no human sharing in the divine *ousia*, neither is there the mutual constitution of personhood that characterizes the inner-divine perichoresis. We do not co-constitute the being of God. Rather, our personhood is constituted by the God who in his love and freedom chooses human beings as the created other able to exist in relationship with him.

8. Volf is considerably more careful than Grenz in qualifying any use of concepts borrowed from Trinitarian discourse for ecclesiology and setting out the limits within which we can speak of human "perichoretic" personhood (*After Our Likeness*, pp. 198-200, 210-11).

9. Bruce McCormack, "What's at Stake in Current Debates over Justification? The Crisis of Protestantism in the West," in *Justification: What's at Stake in the Current Debates*, ed. Mark Husbands and Daniel J. Treier (Downers Grove, IL: InterVarsity Press, 2004), pp. 81-117, esp. 111.

If we speak of divine interrelatedness as *perichoresis,* then we may find in this some justification for speaking of aspects of the dynamic through which our particular personhood is relationally constituted as "perichoretic." The term *perichoresis* holds two poles together with regard to the inner being of God: that the *unity* of God's *ousia* is what it is as the *relationally constituted distinctiveness* of Father, Son, and Holy Spirit. While the analogous use of "perichoretic" language with regard to human beings excludes a unity of *ousia,* it offers a way of speaking of human/divine and human/human relations that emphasizes that our personal particularity is both constituted and preserved in the closest *possible* relationship (i.e., short of unity of substance, which is precisely a violation of divine and created distinctiveness). It is in this way that the concept of "perichoretic" personhood will be used in the development of election to representation, and, as shall be noted shortly, this is closely bound to the way in which the Spirit's role is understood, as the one through whom personal particularity is established and sustained in and through relation.

With these qualifications in place, we may take up with Grenz and Volf· the notion that the mutual constitution of Father, Son, and Spirit in their particularity through a relational ontology of persons-in-communion is the foundation upon which to maintain that relational personhood is ontologically basic to human being, and constitutive of our personal particularity.

Understood in this way, "perichoretic" personhood is the ineffaceable *imago dei* in which the whole of humanity shares.[10] With this as a given, Volf and Grenz focus upon the church as the anticipation of the eschatological consummation of the image, on the basis of the fullness of perichoretic personhood into which it is called and which it is to express. As the church is drawn to participate in the dynamic of the triune life, it is the sign and foretaste of the eschatological communion between God and human beings.[11] As it is transformed into a community whose loving mu-

---

10. As Volf reminds us, while our relational being as the image of God in us may be misdirected, it cannot be lost, since it depends not upon the particular quality of our relations, either with God or others, but upon the ontologically basic fact of God's establishing a relationship with us, and setting us within a network of relationality (*After Our Likeness,* p. 206). We are therefore close to Barth's position, outlined in Chapter 2 above.

11. Volf, *After Our Likeness,* e.g., p. 174; see also pp. 128-29. We will give consideration to John Webster's critique of ecclesiologies founded upon Trinitarian relations below. Here, though, we must note his reservations about the concept of "participation." For him, the church does not "participate" in God, but is elected to fellowship with God ("The Church and the Perfection of God," in *The Community of the Word: Toward an Evangelical*

tuality points towards the nature of true human personhood-in-relation, it is the prolepsis of the eschatological communion between human beings before God.

In this regard, Grenz offers a summary that reminds us, in its linking of the image and the shape of salvation history, of the close ties between the language of election and the image when both are seen not as isolated loci, but in relation to the dynamic within which God fulfills his purpose of blessing. So it is that the Spirit shapes the ecclesial community in order that its members may reflect in "their communal life the kind of love that characterizes the triune God. In this manner, the Spirit brings the ecclesial community to fulfill the divinely given mandate to be the prolepsis of the new humanity as the *imago dei,* which is the goal of the biblical salvation-historical drama."[12]

Ecclesiology, ed. Mark Husbands and Daniel J. Treier [Downers Grove, IL: InterVarsity Press, 2005], pp. 80, 91). The crucial issue for Webster is whether "participation" language implies the loss of the Creator/creature distinction. That this is not necessarily the case is suggested by Webster's own definition of the church's "essence" as "participation in the divine communion" ("The Visible Attests the Invisible," in Husbands and Treier, eds., *The Community of the Word,* pp. 96-113, p. 97). It would therefore seem that, for Webster, while we do not participate "in God" in such a way that proper ontological distinctions are lost, we may graciously participate in the triune life of communion without this being the case. The work of Julie Canlis is extremely helpful here ("Calvin, Osiander and Participation in God," *IJST* 6 [April 2004]: 169-84).

12. Grenz, *Social God,* p. 334. John Webster objects strongly to "communion ecclesiologies" founded upon ecclesial reflection of the inner relations of the triune life, as threatening the aseity of God and the asymmetrical relationship between Christ and the church (see esp. "Perfection," pp. 80-87). He suggests that *election* rather than communion be seen as the "master concept" for speaking of the church (see, e.g., "Perfection," p. 89; "Visible," p. 105), since election makes clear that it is the free decision of God, rather than any necessity in God, to dignify creatures by calling them to his service ("Perfection," p. 80). I will be suggesting that while election is indeed the "master concept" for ecclesiology, with all that this implies about the ontological distinction and ordering of relations between God and the church, it remains possible — and indeed central — to use the relational categories about which Webster expresses reservations. My contention is that it is precisely the relations in which the church is given to stand — its participation in the communion of the triune life and the unique relationship with the rest of humanity that flows from this — that identify and shape the church's chosenness, and that these relations are crucial to the nature and purposes of its election. Moreover, I shall argue that this is so in a way that does not undermine the ontological separation and asymmetrical relationship of unity-in-*distinction* between Christ and the church, nor does it compromise the freedom and aseity of God in relation to the church. These latter issues will be the particular concern of the following chapter.

Grenz also reminds us that the central category for the church's imaging of God — and also, as we have noted, the central category for its election — is union with Christ. As the one who unites us to Christ, it is therefore the Spirit who is the source and shaper of ecclesial personhood. The Spirit "constitutes the church ontologically to be the prolepsis of the *imago dei*" and "constitutes the 'self' of those who are in Christ and therefore are participants in the ecclesial community."[13] In a passage to which we have already referred, "the Spirit-fostered mutuality of unifying love — the perichoretic life — within the ecclesial community marks a visual, human coming-to-representation of the mutual indwelling of the persons of the Trinity."[14]

Volf likewise elaborates on the dynamic of "perichoretic" personhood in the church by exploring the pivotal nature of the Spirit's role. Ecclesial selves are perichoretic in the qualified sense that we have noted, not on the basis of a mutual interiority to each other that is foreign to our being as creatures, but because the Holy Spirit is interior to each: "It is not the mutual perichoresis of human beings, but rather the indwelling of the Spirit common to everyone that makes the church into a communion corresponding to the Trinity."[15]

The Spirit is the one person in many persons as personal counterpart (so preserving his own and others' particularity) and personal presence (thereby establishing union).[16] Because the same Holy Spirit is interior to all believers, and because they are therefore "in Christ," on the one hand all are drawn to participate in the triune life of communion, and on the other, there is a pneumatologically created, christologically grounded "perichoretic" relationship between those in ecclesial communion. As Volf points out, here we have not simply a formal, but an ontological and soteriological correspondence between Trinitarian and ecclesial relationships, grounded in communion with the triune God in Christ by the Spirit.[17]

A Particular Ecclesial Personhood?

What, then, is the particular nature of the ecclesial personhood that the Spirit forms in those whom he unites to Christ? For Grenz, the indwelling

13. Grenz, *Social God*, p. 336.
14. Grenz, *Social God*, p. 336; see Chapter 4, p. 91 above.
15. Volf, *After Our Likeness*, p. 212.
16. Volf, *After Our Likeness*, p. 189.
17. Volf, *After Our Likeness*, p. 195.

Spirit accomplishes the goal of transforming the ecclesial community after the pattern of the divine life as, "by means of incorporating them 'into Christ,' [he] places participants in one another."[18] Here we have, in effect, a restating of Paul's description of the body of Christ — that those who are in Christ by the Spirit are members of Christ and therefore of one another. As a result, he remarks that "In this perichoretic in-one-another, 'traces' of the others are taken into oneself, and each participant finds (or 'refinds') one's own self in the others. . . ."[19]

Again, we find a more detailed exploration in Volf, who redescribes the divine perichoresis and human perichoretic relations in terms of what he calls "catholic personhood." Within the Trinity this signifies that each person is not only distinct and particular, "but carries within itself also the other divine persons, and only in this indwelling of the other person with it is it the person it really is."[20] In the human sphere, the equivalent is the pneumatologically created and sustained catholic personhood within the church, described in detail as follows:

> In personal encounters, that which the other person is flows consciously or unconsciously into that which I am. The reverse is also true. In this mutual giving and receiving, we give to others . . . a piece of our-selves. . . . Each person gives of himself [or] herself to others and each person in a unique way takes up others into himself or herself. *This is the process of the mutual internalization of personal characteristics occurring in the church through the Holy Spirit indwelling Christians. The Spirit opens them up to one another and allows them to become catholic persons in their uniqueness. It is here that they, in a creaturely way, correspond to the catholicity of the divine persons.*[21]

At this point, however, we must ask both Grenz and Volf in what way, if at all, the shape of "perichoretic" personhood in Christ by the Spirit differs from that of human beings who do not belong to the believing community. Both describe what they present as the particular dynamic of selfhood shaped by the Spirit in the church, yet both are also simply restating a process of mutually constituting personhood which they regard as universal.

---

18. Grenz, *Social God*, p. 335.
19. Grenz, *Social God*, p. 335.
20. Volf, *After Our Likeness*, p. 209.
21. Volf, *After Our Likeness*, pp. 211-12, my italics.

So, Volf is quite clear that every believer is a catholic person by virtue of the indwelling of Christ through the Spirit.[22] He is also clear that all human beings are "catholic" persons: "Every person is a catholic person insofar as that person reflects in himself or herself in a unique way the entire, complex reality in which the person lives."[23] Yet he equally wishes to maintain a strong distinction — not least an absolute *soteriological* distinction — between ecclesial catholic personhood and non-ecclesial catholic personhood, between those who are in Christ by the Spirit through faith and those who are not.[24] What, if anything, is distinctive about the dynamic of personhood for those who are constituted as persons in Christ by the Spirit?

One obvious answer, shared by Grenz and Volf, is that those who are in Christ by the Spirit are brought to participate now in the dynamic of the divine communion of love, partially and proleptically embodying this within the communion of the church, and awaiting its consummation at the eschaton. With regard to the dynamic by which perichoretic personhood is shaped between human beings, however, it might be argued that there is no need to posit a difference between those within and those outside the believing community, and that indeed to do so might undermine the notion that in relational being we see the universal and ineffaceable *imago dei.*

Volf is clearer than Grenz in recognizing and responding to the difficulty. As he remarks, "The way one becomes a person (anthropology) and the way that one becomes a Christian (soteriology) both differ and correspond to one another" in that one is already a subject when one becomes a Christian, but the dynamic within which one becomes a Christian is relational, as it is for human personhood in general. The difference is precisely that a Christian is not constituted by relationality in general, but by ecclesial relations in particular.[25] While all human beings are mutually constituted by their relations — and while human beings may in fact choose to live in isolation from and hatred of other human beings and not lose their status

---

22. Volf, *After Our Likeness,* e.g., p. 280.

23. Volf, *After Our Likeness,* p. 212.

24. Volf is repeatedly insistent that ecclesial being, marked by a professed and lived-out faith that is itself the gift of the Spirit, is soteriologically indispensable. It is those who ultimately share in *this* perichoretic personhood who will participate in the fullness of communion with God and one another at the eschaton. See *After Our Likeness,* chap. 4, "Faith, Person and Church," *passim.*

25. Volf, *After Our Likeness,* p. 185.

as human beings — a Christian precisely cannot *be* a Christian except in relation to other Christians.[26] This is both an ontological fact — as the Spirit
unites a person to Christ, so that person is united to all others who by the
Spirit are likewise "in Christ" — and an ecclesiological one. Christians are
Christians in the community of the church.

While this responds to the question of how one *becomes* an ecclesial
person, it does not respond to the question as to whether the Spirit constitutes a distinctive *kind* of relational personhood in the church. The extensive attention that both Grenz and Volf devote to describing the work of the
Spirit in constituting the particular personhood of those within the church,
even as it appears to describe nothing other than the dynamic of mutually
constituting relational being that is shared by all, seems to point towards a
need to be able to say that there *is* something specific to the ecclesial community in this regard, even if the form of the distinctive relationality that
the Spirit forges in those who are in Christ remains unclear.

Viewing the central issues at stake through another theological lens
suggests how to frame a possible answer. It also exposes a christological
problem for both Grenz and Volf, and makes clear the importance of
Volf's reminder that we are to see his *Exclusion and Embrace* as a companion volume to *After Our Likeness*.[27]

Christ, "Perichoretic" Personhood, and the Ecclesial *Imago Dei*

For both Grenz and Volf, it is our being "in Christ" by the Spirit that forms
the ground of the particular "perichoretic" personhood which constitutes
the ecclesial imaging of God. In neither of the two works discussed is this
line of thinking pursued to discuss the notion that we are thereby brought
through the Spirit to participate in the *true humanity of Christ*. If *this* is
kept to the forefront, then questions concerning what constitutes "ecclesial
perichoretic personhood" are give a somewhat different — and a somewhat clearer — focus.

---

26. Volf, *After Our Likeness*, p. 206.

27. Volf (*After Our Likeness*, p. 7) asks us to recognize the limits he has imposed upon
himself in *After Our Likeness*, which are precisely that he here confines his presentation to
the formal features of the relationality created within the church and not to its material
character, and to the inner nature of the church, rather than its outward focus. For this reason, he sees *Exclusion and Embrace: A Theological Exploration of Identity, Otherness, and Reconciliation* (Nashville: Abingdon Press, 1996) as a necessary companion volume.

With regard to Barth, and again in the previous chapter, we noted the significance of the concept of "true humanity" for election and the image, and the culmination of both in the person of Christ. Drawing that discussion into the context of the present chapter, we might say that as the one true image of God, the incarnate Son is the embodiment of the divine relations *ad intra,* living out in the human sphere his relation as the eternal Son to the Father and the Spirit; he is also the perfect embodiment of human relatedness to God and to others.

As we are transformed into his image by the Spirit, this clearly includes being conformed more and more into the likeness of his human relational personhood. One aspect of our sharing in this true humanity of Christ merits particular attention in this context: Christ's imaging of God is intrinsically outward-focused and other-directed. So, we might say, is any corresponding account of the image of God in us as relational, and this is true insofar as it goes. With regard to the church's imaging of God in Christ, however, we need to pay particular attention to the fact that Christ does not simply image the relational dynamic of the Trinitarian being of God *ad intra.* This is indeed one aspect of Christ's perichoretic personhood: as we have just observed, in his humanity the incarnate Son lives out of, and reveals to us, the dynamic of inner-Trinitarian relations. Self-evidently, however, by the very reality of incarnating this among us, Jesus Christ expresses to us the relational dynamic of the triune God *ad extra.* His imaging of God among us is the manifestation that God does not exist in pure self-relation, but is also God-for-the-other, God-for-us.

In declaring that in Christ we see the true image of God, we are affirming that to image the relational God is not and cannot be solely an end in itself.[28] Christ demonstrates that the imaging of God in the created order

---

28. Barth gives powerful expression to the christological reality that the church is radically and intrinsically for the world in *CD* IV/3/2, §72, 2, "The Community for the World." Although not placed directly in the context of a discussion of the image, the themes of God's self-election in Christ and Christ's true humanity, and the implications of both for the church, are never far from the surface. So, e.g., "That it exists for the world because for God, follows . . . directly from the fact that it is the community of Jesus Christ and has the basis of its being and nature in Him. . . . For in Him God is not for Himself but for the world. In Him God has given Himself to and for the world to reconcile it to Himself. . . . This decides the orientation, meaning and purpose of His community. As the people created by Jesus Christ and obedient to Him, it is not subsequently or incidentally but originally, essentially and *per definitionem* summoned and impelled to exist for God and therefore for the world" thereby living out its own existence in itself and for the world in correspondence with the fact that "Jesus Christ expresses His own true divinity precisely in His true humanity" (p. 763).

is focused outward to the one who is radically "other." As in the dynamic of God's own being the triune God exists as and for communion, so in the sphere of human brokenness and sin, Christ's imaging of God is the expression of a reconciling, redemptive purpose to restore alienated humanity to communion with God.[29]

What we find, however, when we look at the way in which Grenz describes ecclesial personhood as the *imago dei*, is that he is exclusively concerned to explore the concept of "perichoretic" personhood as the dynamic of relations *within* the church. When he posits that the heart of the ecclesial *imago dei* is representing in human form the love of the triune God, he describes this wholly in terms of the love *between* members of the believing community.[30]

It is inevitable, given Volf's particular concerns in *After Our Likeness*, that his emphasis here should likewise fall very much upon an intra-ecclesial dynamic.[31] Thus, even when referring to the relationship between

---

29. So, for example, Pannenberg, who places his discussion of election in the context of the *imago dei*, remarks that the shape of our imaging of God must reflect the purpose of Christ's, which "consists in reconciling to God what had been separated from God." Wolfhart Pannenberg, *Human Nature, Election and History* (Philadelphia: Westminster Press, 1977), p. 25.

30. So, typically, "the indwelling Spirit *shapes the fellowship of Christ's followers* after the pattern of the love that pre-exists in the triune life" (*Social God*, p. 336, my italics). Ironically, therefore, while Grenz sees in his account of the relational image the overthrowing of the "inward focused, individually oriented self" (p. 331), the ecclesial *imago dei*, while it is indeed centered upon Christ, nevertheless appears to be as collectively self-enclosed in that relationality as the isolated individual he deplores. He goes on to remark that the communal ontology and narrative formation of the ecclesial image means that the self is no longer the product of an inward turn, but is instead *the fellowship of those who share the Jesus story* (p. 332, my italics). While this is obviously both true and important, he provides no redress for the ecclesial "inward turn" in his own account. This is all the more to be regretted in that preceding his description of the ecclesial image is the assertion that Jesus reveals the love of God as Trinity, and therefore images of God, supremely through his self-giving love for the world (pp. 314ff.).

31. With his hostility to the notion of an earthly "universal" church as a single "subject," a key emphasis for Volf is that the constitution of ecclesial personhood does not take place as the Spirit incorporates the individual into this supposed "whole," but through the Spirit-shaped dynamic of each person's relations to other Christians (*After Our Likeness*, p. 280). His priority, therefore, is to build an ecclesiology focused upon the local church, and his exploration of ecclesial correspondence to Trinitarian perichoretic relations sets about to emphasize that this takes place supremely within *intra*-ecclesial relations between Christians, only secondarily and with qualifications *inter*-ecclesially, and not at all in relation to the misconceived notion of the earthly "universal" church.

those within and outside the church, he too speaks above all of how the personhood of *those within the church,* if it is to be truly catholic, must also involve the internalizing of their whole environment, not simply their relations with fellow-Christians.[32]

While this intra-ecclesial understanding of "perichoretic" personhood is quite clearly foundational to the being of the church and to its imaging of God — mutual love is, after all, the touchstone by which all are to recognize Christ's disciples — it is nevertheless only part of the dynamic of the church's being and imaging. If the ecclesial self is truly to image the triune God made known to us in Christ, then intrinsic to this must be an account of the church's imaging of the *ad extra* dynamic of the triune life in reaching beyond itself.

With this, all the issues we have raised concerning the shape of ecclesial personhood come to a head. On the one hand, an intense focus on "perichoretic" personhood within *intra-ecclesial life* reflects a lopsided emphasis upon the church imaging the dynamic of the triune life *ad intra* at the expense of imaging God's relational being *ad extra.* This leads to a model in which the Spirit's role is to enable members of the believing community to hold *each other* within themselves and mutually constitute *each other's* personhood in Christ.

On the other, as has been noted, the manifestation of "perichoretic" personhood in the church is bounded by the same limitations in which all humanity shares. Thus, if the perichoretic relationality in the church is presented simply in terms of the basic reality that all human beings are mutually constituted by one another, this aspect of personhood is essentially the same inside and outside the church. To focus wholly on intra-ecclesial relations is therefore inadequate in terms of describing how the ecclesial self is to image God and equally inadequate in helping us articulate the distinctive form of personhood constituted by the Spirit among those who are in Christ.

It is in his *Exclusion and Embrace* that Volf draws out something of the significance of this *ad extra* dynamic for ecclesial "perichoretic" personhood, speaking of the triune God's reception of hostile humanity into divine communion as the model for how we in turn should relate to the one who is other.[33]

---

32. Volf, *After Our Likeness,* p. 212.

33. So, e.g., Volf, *Exclusion and Embrace,* p. 100. While "the divine self-donation for the enemies and their reception into the eternal communion of God" (p. 23), and the way in

He first refers specifically to "catholic" personhood as the foundation and dynamic of the intra-ecclesial life in terms with which we are familiar. It is the Spirit who in uniting us to Christ sets about transforming us so that each becomes a "catholic personality" within a "catholic community," in which openness and responsiveness to, and enrichment by, otherness and difference make us a microcosm of the eschatological new creation.[34]

Later, however, this is explicitly linked to the dynamic of embrace in the context of a brief discussion of perichoresis, worship, and the will to embrace the enemy-other.[35] Speaking of Christ's passion as the "self-giving love which overcomes human enmity and the creation of space in himself to receive estranged humanity," Volf first establishes this as the expression, in the sphere of human alienation from God, of the "giving of the self and receiving of the other" that characterize the internal life of the Trinity.[36] The perichoretic relations of the Godhead, as the mutual interiority of love that establishes "nonself-enclosed identities" within the Trinity, are opened outward for humanity, the beloved "other" who has become "enemy." Space is made for us within the eternal triune embrace.[37] In turn, those in the church are called to "make space in ourselves for [the enemy-other] and invite them in — so that together we may rejoice in the eternal embrace of the triune God."[38]

Although the Spirit's role in this regard is not directly mentioned, we must assume that for Volf it is the Spirit who forges *this* aspect of ecclesial

---

which this translates into the sphere of human interaction, and its relation to questions of truth and justice, are the themes of the whole, his direct application of triune relations and ecclesial personhood to these issues is concentrated in "Space for the Other: Cross, Trinity, Eucharist" (pp. 125-31).

34. Volf, *Exclusion and Embrace*, p. 53.

35. Volf, *Exclusion and Embrace*, pp. 126-31.

36. Volf, *Exclusion and Embrace*, p. 127.

37. Volf, *Exclusion and Embrace*, pp. 128-29.

38. Volf, *Exclusion and Embrace*, p. 131. The model for this — and the context for the citation — is the Eucharist. So also, e.g., p. 129, "We would most profoundly misunderstand the Eucharist . . . if we thought of it only as a sacrament of God's embrace of which we are simply the fortunate beneficiaries . . . we can be made its recipients only if we do not resist being made into its agents. . . . Having been embraced by God, we must make space for others in ourselves and invite them in — even our enemies." This is true insofar as it goes, but there are wider christological issues at stake than the one that concerns us here, which is simply the christological requirement for an *other*-directed, as well as inwardly focused, ecclesial imaging of God. For a brief but pointed christological critique of *Exclusion and Embrace* see John Webster, *Word and Church: Essays in Church Dogmatics* (Edinburgh: T. & T. Clark, 2001), pp. 217-19.

"perichoretic" personhood, just as it is also the Spirit who shapes the "perichoretic" personhood of those within the church. Here we have suggested to us the concept of holding the alienated "other" in the self before God, described in terms of ecclesial "perichoretic" personhood, which we have already suggested lies at the heart of a fresh scriptural approach to election and the image of God.

To return to the way in which the previous chapter illustrated the convergence of the notions of the image of God and election in the person of Christ: his imaging of God, and therefore that of the elect community in Christ, is for the sake of God's wider purpose of blessing. As a central element of that dynamic, and as a summary of the narrative structure in which it is in redeeming humanity that Christ most fully images God, we suggested that part of what it means to say that Christ is the image of God is that he *represents who God is to us* precisely by *representing us to God*. It is with this specifically representational aspect of the dynamic of the image and election in mind that we now return to Wright.

Scriptural Guiding Principles for Election and Ecclesial Personhood: 1) The Purpose of Election

Wright's outline of the church's election offers the same vital corrective to the concept of ecclesial personhood as that demanded of us if we take our bearings from the notion of being brought to share in the true humanity of Christ. For Wright, as we have seen, it is intrinsic to the nature of election to hold the other in the self, but this is expressed not primarily in terms of a dynamic *within* the elect community, but of a dynamic *between* the elect and the rest of humanity. With this we take up the first of our scriptural guiding principles: that the church's election must be considered in the light of and in continuity with God's purpose in election as it is revealed in Israel and in Christ.

On this basis, the church is to be the instrument through which God continues to work out his wider intent of blessing beyond the elect community. We have seen that Wright's account of the Pauline understanding of election shares with Old Testament scholarship the consensus that from the outset, God's election of a people for himself is his counter to human rebellion, in order that his promise of blessing shall not be thwarted.[39] In

---

39. So, God's covenant with Israel is designed "to address the problem of human sin and

the overarching intention of God, we may therefore say that the elect community is brought into being both to be a sign and foretaste of the fullness of redeemed communion with God and to be the instrument of furthering that restored communion between humanity and God which will carry with it the renewal of a creation cast into disorder by the broken relations rooted in human sin.[40]

It follows that, from the outset, the elect community itself is not the sole focus of God's purposes in election. That the elect exist radically and intrinsically for the sake of the other, and to bring blessing to those who apparently lie outside the promises of God, is part of election's fundamental purpose.[41] Election can never simply be reduced to a vision of, or way of accounting for, personal salvation, but has in view the entire sweep of God's purposes for the whole created order.[42] This leads to a concept of ecclesial personhood that is not simply an example of the general notion

---

the failure of creation as a whole to be what its Creator had intended it to be," such that the covenant becomes the means of "bringing God's justice to the whole world" (Wright, "Letter to the Romans," in *New Interpreter's Bible in Twelve Volumes,* vol. 10 [Nashville: Abingdon Press, 2002], p. 399). For the same reason, Pannenberg remarks that the church serves "the same function that was intended for the chosen people of Israel. The election of Israel was aimed at the blessing of all . . . and this vocation continues" (*Human Nature,* p. 30).

40. Newbigin offers the threefold summary of the church's identity as sign, instrument, and foretaste of the kingdom of God in *The Open Secret: An Introduction to the Theology of Mission,* rev. ed. (London: SPCK, 1995), e.g., pp. 110, 113, 150. For the themes here, see also, e.g., Wright, *Paul: Fresh Perspectives* (London: SPCK, 2005), pp. 34-39.

41. A key theme also for Bauckham, e.g., "God's purpose always begins with . . . singling out but never ends there. It was never God's intention to bless Abraham purely for his and his descendants' sake. It was never God's intention to reveal himself to Israel only for Israel's sake . . . God's purpose in each of these singular choices was universal: that the blessing of Abraham might overflow to all the families of the earth" (*The Bible and Mission: Christian Witness in a Postmodern World* [Carlisle: Paternoster, 2003], p. 46; see also p. 49). This is also a significant concern for Newbigin, the influence of whose *Open Secret* is gratefully acknowledged by Bauckham (p. 83). So Newbigin summarizes that the elect are the "bearers" but not the "exclusive beneficiaries" of God's promises (e.g., *Open Secret,* pp. 17, 32), as "trustees" of God's wider purposes of blessing on behalf of others (p. 17).

42. The present focus is upon developing the notion of election to representation in relation to human beings. Although it cannot be explored here, never too far from the surface of a discussion of election and representation, as the account of Owen has suggested (see Chapter 1, n. 57 above, and also the suggestion concerning the naming of the animals, Chapter 4, n. 14 above), is the tradition of the "priestly" role of human beings in relation to the created order as a whole, and the intimate binding that we see from Genesis to Revelation, of the relationship between human beings and God and the present and future state of all creation.

of mutually constituting relational personhood, but is the expression of the particular *representational* dynamic that is at the core of election as God's chosen means of furthering his purposes of blessing.

Scriptural Guiding Principles for Election and Ecclesial Personhood: 2) The Shape of Election

One of the primary aspects of election as we have discerned it in Israel and in Christ is to hold the apparently rejected and alienated in the self, that they may be drawn into the sphere of God's promise. It is here, as we noted in the previous chapter, that Wright's interpretation of Paul and Brueggemann's suggestions concerning the priestly role of Israel towards the rest of the world come together. Through the explicit covenanted relationship with God enshrined in Torah, Israel is the place in which both the gracious reality that God chooses relationship with human beings and the sinful reality of human rebellion and alienation from God are concentrated and focused. Israel embodies in itself the whole human situation before God, in order to be the instrument of God's wider blessing. In turn, it is of the essence of Christ's election to representation that his own covenant faithfulness entails bearing Israel's disobedience and rebellion. It is by being Israel's representative Messiah that Christ bears in himself the sins of the world.

In keeping with the second scriptural principle — continuity in the shape as well as the purpose of election — it is therefore into this priestly, representational dynamic that the church enters by the Spirit in order to play its particular role in the unfolding of God's purposes of blessing. In Wright's words, as we noted at the start of this chapter, the Spirit forges a community to do and be for the world what the Messiah was and did for Israel, and so also to stand in a relationship to the world that corresponds with the election dynamic seen in Israel. The Spirit "accomplishes within the church what, *mutatis mutandi,* the Torah accomplished within Israel. Just as the sin and death of the world were concentrated by means of Torah on Israel . . . so now the pain and grief of the world is to be concentrated by means of the Spirit on the . . . family of the Messiah, so that it may be healed."[43]

Once again, the same cautionary note must be sounded concerning

43. Wright, *Climax,* p. 256.

the need to uphold a clear distinction between Christ's work and that of the church. This is an issue that will be taken up in the following chapter. For the moment, however, in focusing specifically on the notion that the world's pain, grief, and shame are to be concentrated in Christ's people, Wright's express concern is to counter any triumphalist or imperialistic tendencies within the church's conception of itself as God's elect people in Christ, and his warning is well taken.[44] In doing so, he helps to illustrate several significant aspects of the church's understanding of the nature and purpose of its election.

In the first instance, Wright reflects the point made in the previous chapter that in the new covenant community there is a more self-conscious fulfillment of the outward-focused aspects of the dynamic of election. Wright is clear that the church is not only the place where the pain, grief, and shame of the world are concentrated. It is also called by virtue of its election in Christ to *seek out* the pain and grief of the world, in order to play an active role in the unfolding of the loving justice, redemption, and reconciliation of the gospel.[45] We might say that action on behalf of others is therefore intrinsic to the election — and the imaging — of the church.[46] While the church cannot build the kingdom, the church, as the community that lives out of the redemption won in Christ, is nevertheless to bring a foretaste of the kingdom to the world, and is inseparable from the coming of the kingdom.

Binding this closely to the notion of our imaging of God in discussing Romans 8:29, Wright remarks that "those in Christ are conformed to the image of the Son . . . standing between the pain of the world and the love

---

44. Wright, *Climax*, p. 256.

45. So, for Wright, the church is to evince a "passionate concern" that the loving justice of God as it has been revealed in the gospel be made known in the world (*Climax*, p. 256). See also, e.g., Bauckham, *Bible*, pp. 101-3, for the inseparability of the church's mission from its counter-cultural, cross-shaped life in the world, and p. 53 for sensitivity to the injustices and inequalities of the world as integral to the church's existence as God's people.

46. In this regard, as Webster reminds us, the church's activities are not the self-generated acts of a self-constituted group of people "with a lively sense of the need for alternatives to oppression and marginalisation." The church plays its part in the unfolding of the ministry of reconciliation because this task is given to it as intrinsic to its constitution as the elect community that acknowledges and lives by God's accomplished work of reconciliation in Christ (*Word and Church*, pp. 221-22, 224-25). It does all of this, therefore, not as if adding to God's work, but because it has been given to play its part in the unfolding of that which God has already accomplished. This aspect of the dynamic of election to representation will be explored in more detail in the following chapter.

of God," such that in their growing conformity to Christ, they become "the vessels and vehicles of God's redeeming love."[47] Reminding us once again of the centrality of the concept of "true humanity" for election and the image, and of the dynamic nature of our imaging, he later speaks in relation to the same verse of our growing conformity to the image of the Son as our progress towards becoming true human beings, such that as his image-bearers, we are given to play our part in bringing to creation "the healing, freedom and life for which it longs."[48]

Wright's focus in speaking of the church's role to seek out and bear the pain, shame, and grief of the world is upon the continuity of the church's role in a covenantal relationship designed from the outset to play a significant part in God's intention to bring "salvation and justice to the ends of the earth."[49] Although Wright himself does not explore its possibilities, his suggestion that the church participates in the same dynamic as characterizes the election of Israel and Israel's representative Messiah — of bearing in the self the alienation and rebellion of the apparently rejected — also opens the way for the doctrine of election to take with absolute seriousness the brokenness and continuing sinfulness of the church.

On the basis of our discussion so far, it might be all too easy to consider the church as a somewhat idealized entity. The focus of Grenz, and of Volf in *After Our Likeness,* has been on describing the ecclesial imaging of God supremely in terms of what the church *should* be and what it eschatologically *will* be. This naturally tends to imply a rather more realized eschatology than that suggested by the realities of life within the body of Christ and the church's engagement with wider society.

An account of the church's election based primarily upon its coming perfection will inevitably struggle to find room for, and therefore to take proper account of, the mixed reality of its present condition. An account of the church's election that emphasizes the church's representational role offers a way of seeing what we know to be the sinfulness, brokenness, and inadequacy of the community of Christ *not only* as the shameful falling away from the fullness of its calling which it self-evidently is, but *also* as an element *within* its election. This is not to minimize the seriousness of the church's sin, which, like that of Israel, is magnified by the fact that it takes place within an explicit covenant relationship with God. Nevertheless, the

47. Wright, "Letter to the Romans," p. 591.
48. Wright, "Letter to the Romans," p. 602.
49. Wright, *Paul: Fresh Perspectives,* p. 24.

reality that the elect community shares in the sinfulness of humanity as a whole continues to play a part in the redeeming dynamic of election.

With this, we once again see at work in the church the same pattern of election as has been noted in Israel. Part of the significance of the ontology of election is that it is in the full reality of the elect community's being and doing, as it lives out of its covenant relationship towards God in the world not only in its obedience but also in and through its disobedience, that God continues to work out his purpose of wider blessing. It is through the representational dynamic of election that the elect community in its own sinfulness also representatively holds the sinfulness of alienated humanity as a whole in itself before God.

Nevertheless, there is more to be said concerning the nature of the church's election than the albeit central notion of bearing and seeking out the pain and shame of the world, if we are to apply to the church the full contours of election discerned by Wright with regard to Israel and Christ. As the particular place in which the redeeming work of God in Christ is concentrated and through which it is mediated, the church shares both in Christ's suffering and also in the fruits of his victory. It exists to hold out the promise of humanity's intended destiny as well as to hold the whole of humanity before God in its sinfulness and rebellion.

To be the locus of God's decisive redeeming work and the first fruits of his promised blessing therefore means that the church is also called to be the community that rejoices in the triumph of God over sin and death. We might therefore say that the church is called to seek out and hold in itself before God not only the pain and grief of the world, but also the world's joy and celebration. Joy and celebration are the eschatological destiny of redeemed humanity in the fullness of the presence of the triune God. It is therefore in the community of Christ in particular that the true joy of humanity is known, and the pulse of that true joy is to be found.

The elect new covenant community is called to discern, delight in, and act to further that which is good and true in the world, as signs and hints of the intention of God for humanity, but also to recognize that its celebrations of goodness are equally in need of reorientation and redemption. As it is to bear in itself the rejection of the alienated other, so also the elect community of Christ is called to take into itself and hold before God the joys of the world, redirected in Christ by the Spirit to their proper end in the praise and glory of God. Through the representative personhood that characterizes the elect community, the whole human situation is therefore held up to be healed and purified, and we are given intimations of creation's promised destiny when all things are to be brought by the Spirit to their consummation in Christ.

In all of this, we are reminded of the significance of the two sets of "perichoretic" relations through which, by union with Christ, ecclesial personhood is shaped. We are drawn in Christ by the Spirit to share in the communion of the triune God, which is to be reflected within the communion of the church; and we are shaped in Christ by the Spirit for "perichoretic" relationships with others. Once the full significance of this other-focused aspect of the ecclesial sharing in Christ's true humanity is recognized, the twofold dynamic of election to representation is seen to be at the fulcrum of both sets of relations in the purposes of God. God's promised blessings are poured out upon and mediated through the new covenant people in Christ, who are called to represent God to others. In turn, because it is intrinsic to the elect community to represent the other to God, it is by the "perichoretic" personhood which entails holding still-alienated humanity in itself that the apparently rejected are drawn into the sphere of God's promised blessing.

Scriptural Guiding Principles for Election and Ecclesial Personhood: 3) The One Elect Community

The following chapter will explore further the nature of this dynamic and engage with some of the questions that it raises. For the moment, however, we need to note how an account of the church's election in the light of the first two guiding principles from the previous chapter is inseparable from the third. That is to say, election to representation, with election understood as God's chosen means to fulfill his purpose of blessing, entails a clearly defined elect community set apart to be and do for the world what no other community can be and do, as the place in which that promise of blessing is proleptically realized and through which it is mediated. God's purpose of blessing cannot be separated from God's elect.

Wright draws this to our attention by his very direct description of the church's mediating role in the unfolding of God's saving purpose. It is through the body of Christ by the Spirit that the redemption and reconciliation achieved in Christ are worked out within the world.[50] This matches his insistence throughout that it is only those adopted into the eschatologi-

---

50. Wright, *Climax*, p. 256.

cally defined family of Abraham in Christ by the Spirit through faith who are the heirs, recipients, and mediators of the promises of God.

This is *not* of necessity to suggest that there is no presence of Christ and the Spirit outside the church, but it *is* to insist that just as God does not act to fulfill his purposes for the world apart from Christ, so he does not work those purposes out in the world except through the elect people of Christ. Nor, again, is this to suggest that because this one community is the locus of the blessings and promises of God, all others are excluded. It must be repeated that all three of these guiding principles must be held together: the dynamic within which the setting apart of the elect community is situated is the furthering of God's redeeming intent for the world. It is through its representational role that the church is given to be instrumental to — and indeed an instrument of — the world's healing.

Two points in particular need to be made in relation to this strong interpretation of the believing community's mediating role. The first is to note again the continuity between this way of understanding the church's election and the shape of God's election as it is discerned by Old Testament scholars in the previous chapter: that in the face of human sin and alienation from God, God's intentions for humanity and the created order as a whole are focused upon and mediated by the elect community, as the locus and channel of God's self-revelation and God's blessing. The pattern of election is the pattern of God's dealings with the world: the one elect community is set apart for the sake of God's redeeming and restoring purpose for humanity and for creation as a whole.

The second, central point that will help us to think through what it might mean to say that God's promised blessing is not worked out apart from the church is the question of election's ontology.

As the previous chapter indicated, a key element of consensus within Old Testament scholarship and between Old Testament scholarship and Wright's account of election is that simply by living out its existence as the elect people, Israel fulfills the purpose of God to be the channel of blessing to others. Seitz expresses this consensus in his account of centripetal and centrifugal mission in Israel and, like Wright, he offers a "brief word" concerning the implications of the pattern of election he has discerned for people of God in Christ.[51]

As was the case with regard to Israel, Seitz points to the ontology of

---

51. Christopher Seitz, *Figured Out: Typology and Providence in Christian Scripture* (Louisville: Westminster/John Knox Press, 2001), pp. 156-57.

election: it is simply by *being* the elect community in Christ that the church engages in centripetal mission. Like Israel, the church "must live out its own destiny within its own life, as the body of Christ, not allowing itself to be metamorphosed to the world. This is its elect missionary act, or, non-act!"[52] We have already noted the similarity between the way in which Seitz defines this aspect of election and Grenz's description of the ecclesial *imago dei*.[53]

Like Wright, however, Seitz also reminds us of the self-consciously outward focus of the church's election. The contrast between Israel and the church is located in the dynamic of centrifugal mission. As the previous chapter made clear, centrifugal mission is indeed at the heart of God's purpose of election, and is likewise intrinsic to the being-and-doing of Israel. Nevertheless, this is largely the by-product of the relationship between God and Israel rather than a self-consciously willed activity of the people of God. It is following the New Testament's understanding of Christ's climactic role in the unfolding of God's covenant purposes that a much more self-conscious centrifugal mission becomes intrinsic to the distinctive being of the elect community.

Although not explicit in Seitz's brief account, the difference between Israel and the church in this regard might be seen in terms of the shift that the New Testament perceives to have taken place in the eschatological time. There is no suggestion of the supposed "failure" of Israel to fulfill the purpose of its election by not engaging in active "mission"; rather, the New Testament reconsideration of election stems from the understanding that the death and resurrection of Jesus and the outpouring of the Spirit mark the inauguration in the present age of the promised new covenant. Following this, the elect community's "centrifugal" mission, presented within the Old Testament as the eschatologically oriented promise that the nations will recognize the God of Israel, now takes on a more explicit form and a more prominent role. With the proleptic inbreaking of the eschatological new age in Christ, it is of the *esse* of the church, in a way that it was not for Israel, that to be the covenant people of God entails the impetus to missionary proclamation and activity.

Thus, it is specifically the promised eschatological Spirit of the new covenant who creates and empowers the distinctive dynamic of the church's election to centripetal and centrifugal mission. As the one who brings the elect community into being by uniting believers to Christ and

52. Seitz, *Figured Out,* p. 157.
53. Chapter 4, pp. 97-98 above.

who forms the community as the body of Christ, the Spirit is the source of the church's centripetal mission; as the one who impels that community outward, the Spirit is likewise the source of its centrifugal mission. In Seitz's summary, the "alternative, transforming work of God the Holy Ghost in the church has a purpose that propels the church . . . into the world to witness."[54]

Again we see that it is the very ontology of election, now understood as constituted and shaped particularly by the Spirit, that holds centripetal and centrifugal mission in unity-in-distinction as intrinsic to the being of the people of God and to the fulfilling of his purposes of blessing. Here, too, we have in effect a description of the pneumatological dynamic by which ecclesial "perichoretic" personhood is formed into the *imago dei*: caught up into the dynamic of communion with the triune God in Christ, the church is brought to express, in its inner relations, something of the loving relationality that characterizes the life of Father, Son, and Spirit; sent outward into the world, it is called to image the *ad extra* dynamic of God's relational being.

In all of this, we find Seitz encapsulating the notion that intrinsic to the ontology of election is the concept of representing God to others. When we also consider the notion of representing others to God we can discern the same pattern at work. So the church is indeed summoned to a more self-conscious fulfilling of the task to represent others to God, illustrated most obviously perhaps in intercessory prayer for those outside the elect community.[55]

Particularly in the light of the claim that it is only in and through the church that God channels his promises of blessing, we also need to emphasize that the full implications of election's representational ontology apply equally to this aspect of the church's being. As we have noted, just as

---

54. Seitz, *Figured Out*, p. 157.

55. We will turn again to intercessory prayer in the following chapter. Much might be said concerning the relationship between the dynamic of election to representation as I am developing it here and the nature of the church's worship, as the locus in which the whole of its life is supremely concentrated. The primary task of the present work is to lay some foundations for seeing representation as a key category for rethinking the doctrine of election, and to sketch the outline of what such a doctrine of election might look like. There is only space to hint at how a self-understanding in terms of election to representation might be reflected in the church's life, in its worship, and its engagement with the world. These are themes to which we will return briefly in the Epilogue, as directions in which this way of looking at election might be further developed.

through its covenant relationship with God and the sinfulness that it shares with the whole of humanity, it is intrinsic to Israel's being as the elect community to hold the situation of the non-elect in itself before God, so also simply by existing as those reconciled to the Father through the Son by the Spirit, and yet still sharing in the brokenness and rebellion of the world, the church represents others to God. By its very existence as the elect community, as well as through its self-conscious activity towards others, and in both facets of the twofold dynamic of representation, the church is the instrument through which the healing that has been proleptically accomplished in Christ continues to unfold, partially and provisionally, in the "in between" time.

Conclusion

We have remarked upon how closely Grenz's description of the image as ecclesial personhood approaches the language of election: the outworking of the image of God, like the unfolding of the purpose of election, is described as the goal of the entire biblical salvation-historical drama. How might the dynamic of ecclesial personhood itself contribute to the outworking of this goal? In a remark that is undeveloped but full of promise, Grenz suggests that the Spirit's shaping of ecclesial personhood results not simply in the church being the foretaste and present sign of the fullness of the eschatological *imago dei,* but also *in the shaping of the personhood of the whole of humanity.* For Grenz, by forming the eschatological new humanity in the church after the pattern of Christ the one true image, the Spirit is also "in the process of constituting the 'self' of all humankind in fulfillment of Genesis 1:26-7, and by extension the being of all creation."[56]

How is it that in and through the process of constituting the "perichoretic" personhood of those in the church, the Spirit is also drawing all people and all things towards their consummation in Christ? This is a question that Grenz's own account of the shape of ecclesial personhood struggles to answer; nevertheless, it is in the insight *that* the ecclesial *imago dei* as "perichoretic" personhood lies at the heart of the unfolding of God's purposes for the whole created order that the network of ideas linking the image and election, perichoretic personhood and election to representation comes together.

56. Grenz, *Social God,* p. 336.

As we have seen, a difficulty arises in seeking to assert that the Spirit forms a particular kind of relational personhood among those who are in Christ, and at the same time being able to distinguish this sufficiently from the relational constitution of human personhood in general. On the one hand, if relational personhood constitutes the ineradicable and universal image of God in us, how *can* we posit that this is in some way particular to the church without denying the image of God to humanity as a whole? On the other, if there is no particular kind of relationality that both relates ecclesial persons to and distinguishes them from those who are not in Christ by the Spirit in the believing community, then it becomes all but impossible to suggest how the formation of "perichoretic" personhood in the church can play the particular role in the unfolding of God's saving purposes that Grenz suggests the ecclesial imaging of God entails.

In the dynamic of election to representation we have the resources both to continue to affirm that mutually constitutive relationality is fundamental to human being and constitutes the image of God in all humanity, and at the same time to posit a particular shape to this "perichoretic" personhood, and therefore the imaging of God that flows from it, among those who are in Christ by the Spirit in the church. At its heart is a notion of "perichoretic" personhood that is not simply to be understood as mutual relations within the church, nor is it simply a more truly oriented and loving example of the same dynamic of mutually constituted personhood shared by all human beings. It is all of these things, but is also a very specific relationship *between* the church and the rest of humanity, which entails most particularly the holding of the alienated, non-elect, apparently rejected before God and so within the sphere of God's promised blessings, worked out in and through the new covenant community in Christ.

In the language of election, it is therefore this Spirit-shaped representational dynamic that sets this particular community apart to be and do what no other community can be and do. In the language of the relational *imago dei*, ecclesial perichoretic personhood takes its bearings from, and is the outworking of, our being conformed by the Spirit to the true humanity of the one true image of God. In his person, Christ incarnates for us both the inner-Trinitarian perichoretic life of love and the *ad extra* dynamic of God's relationality which intends the bringing of the alienated other into communion with himself.

As a result, not only does the dynamic of election to representation illustrate how there can indeed be the kind of distinctive ecclesial personhood that Grenz and Volf are seeking, but also makes clear that this very particular expression of relational personhood plays a pivotal role in the unfolding of God's purposes for the rest of humanity and the whole created order. In the twofold representational ontology of election in which the church, simply in its being-and-doing, as well as in its self-consciously other-focused actions, represents God to others and others to God, and especially in the holding of the other in the self before God that is intrinsic to the very being of the elect community, we find the overall dynamic within which Grenz's hints can be developed: that in and through the Spirit's shaping of ecclesial personhood, the Spirit is also at work to shape the personhood of all humanity in Christ.

Quite how this might take place, and in particular how it might take place in such a way as not to compromise both the once-for-all nature of Christ's work on the one hand, and the particularity of those who in themselves are not "in Christ by the Spirit" on the other, is one of the themes to be taken up in the following chapter as we discuss some of the challenges that the concept of election to representation must face. It is in this context that we will also offer a "parable" to help us reflect on the ontology of representational personhood and the particular dynamic of the church's election, before suggesting how the dynamic of election to representation might shape our thinking about the parousia.

PART III

Election to Representation in Dialogue

CHAPTER 6

Some Problems, a Parable, and the Parousia

By drawing upon the concept of "perichoretic" personhood, the development of the idea of election to representation has intersected with, challenged, and extended aspects of a key theme in contemporary theology — the relational *imago dei* and its particular expression in the community of the church. In turn, however, Volf's exploration of ecclesiality points us towards some of the most significant problems that confront the dynamic of election being proposed here.

Volf reminds us of the strict limitations to be placed on the church's understanding of its role in the outworking of God's purposes of salvation, and in doing so, draws together some serious challenges that might well be put to the understanding of election I am developing. The issues raised also bring us to a brief consideration of some of Farrow's concerns in *Ascension and Ecclesia*. In effect, does this way of understanding election attribute too much to the elect community, compromising both the uniqueness of Christ's incarnate and ascended work and the necessity and integrity of personal response?

Responding to the nexus of issues raised by both Volf and Farrow will help to clarify the relationship between christology and ecclesiology in election to representation, and then between the elect community of the church and the rest of humanity. In turn, this will lead to a synthesizing and extending of the suggestions found in previous chapters concerning the Spirit as the one who shapes and sustains the dynamic that characterizes this approach to election.

Having outlined the christological shape and pneumatological dynamic of election to representation in the unfolding of God's purposes in time, it then becomes possible to sketch out the significance of this understanding of Christ's role and the Spirit's for the way in which we might conceive of the eschatological consummation of election at the parousia.

Ecclesial Hubris? Christ and the Church

In *After Our Likeness,* Volf offers a brief analysis of the nature and role of the church in the context of his discussion of the church's "motherhood" as the "motherhood of all believers."[1] In the process, he raises issues that are highly pertinent to the dynamic of election being developed here. He is adamant that while the church exists to *attest* to the salvific activity of God in Christ by the Spirit, it must never think of itself as in any way a secondary subject of that activity. His repeated and insistent contention is that while the church mediates the cognitive content of faith and the process of learning how that faith is to be understood and lived, nothing can be permitted to suggest that the church might participate actively, even if in a secondary and derivative sense, in God's saving work.[2]

The reason lies in Volf's emphasis upon the absolute soteriological indispensability of the personal confession of faith. The church is not and cannot be a "secondary subject" in the saving work of God "[b]ecause one does not receive faith *(fiducia)* from the church . . . but rather *through* the church."[3] The goal of the church's mediating work is precisely that which the church itself cannot give: the faith which is *fiducia* or personal trust, and which is exclusively the gift of the Spirit.[4] This is the saving work of God, in which the church can have no part. In the strongest possible terms, "the church is not the subject of salvific activity with Christ, rather Christ alone is the subject of such activity."[5]

---

1. Miroslav Volf, *After Our Likeness: The Church as the Image of the Trinity* (Grand Rapids: Eerdmans, 1998), pp. 162-68, in dialogue with Ratzinger and *Lumen gentium.* Volf is raising objections to the notion of the "universal church" as a historico-temporal "subject" by rejecting a model in which the institutional church is seen as a "universal" mother "over against" individual Christians, and in which the functions of its motherhood are concentrated in the institutional priesthood. His alternative is a concept of the "motherhood of all believers," in which each Christian fulfills the role of mediating the content of the faith to others.

2. Volf, *After Our Likeness,* pp. 163-68.

3. Volf, *After Our Likeness,* p. 166, Volf's italics.

4. Volf, *After Our Likeness,* p. 163.

5. Volf, *After Our Likeness,* p. 164. This forms part of Volf's rejection of the notion of Christ and the church as the *totus Christus.* Webster too expresses strong objections to the

Farrow expresses similar ecclesiological caveats from a different starting point: the paradigmatic significance of approaches to the ascension for ecclesiology.[6] Nestorian tendencies in theologies of the ascension, coupled with the concept of Christ and the church together as the *totus Christus,* lead to an "inflationary factor" for ecclesiology in which the church as an institution comes to fill the vacuum created by an inadequate account of the ascended humanity of Christ.[7]

Among the many dangers created when the church appears to become "joined to the divine Christ in such a way as to supplant his humanity with its own,"[8] Farrow points to a particularly important example in the present context, drawing our attention to the consequences of downplaying Christ's continuing high-priestly ministry in his humanity. In its place, the church as an institution comes to assume an intercessory role and exalted status distinct from its members, attracting to itself "the mediatorial function belonging to Jesus."[9] We will return to the subject of the church and the ascended ministry of Christ later in the chapter. For the moment, we turn to the concern over a tendency to create a dichotomy between the church as institution and the church as its members, before focusing on the central christological issues at stake.

---

notion of the *totus Christus* as part of his rejection of any ecclesial compromising of the uniqueness of the incarnation ("The Church and the Perfection of God," in *The Community of the Word: Toward an Evangelical Ecclesiology,* ed. Mark Husbands and Daniel J. Treier [Downers Grove, IL: InterVarsity Press, 2005], pp. 75-95, 94-95), and of any suggestion that the church and Christ can be seen as co-constitutive (see esp. pp. 85-86). As will be seen, the concept of election to representation likewise rejects the notion of Christ and the church as the *totus Christus.*

6. Douglas Farrow, *Ascension and Ecclesia: On the Significance of the Doctrine of the Ascension for Ecclesiology and Christian Cosmology* (Edinburgh: T. & T. Clark, 1999).

7. Farrow, *Ascension and Ecclesia,* p. 123. For a discussion of the implicit and explicit transfer of Christ's humanity to the church, such that it becomes the "prolongation of the incarnation" and attracts to itself "more and more of the essential functions of Jesus" (p. 122), see pp. 121-23. For Farrow's exploration of the ecclesiological issues raised through a critique of the development of Marian doctrine, see, e.g., pp. 130-31, 152-64. As we have seen, the "inflation of ecclesiology" ("Perfection," p. 77) is also a key concern for Webster in his critique of the tendency of ecclesiologies founded upon inner-Trinitarian relations to distort the asymmetrical relationship between Christ and the church (see above, Chapter 5, n. 11).

8. Farrow, *Ascension and Ecclesia,* p. 164.

9. Farrow, *Ascension and Ecclesia,* pp. 130-31; see also, e.g., p. 123.

Election to Representation: The Humility of the Church

It is readily apparent that the ontology of election as we have presented it accords well with Volf's concept of the "motherhood of all believers," noted above. To represent God to others and others to God is intrinsic to the very being of all the elect, as individuals and as a community. This way of understanding the nature of election leaves no room for the notion, which troubles both Volf and Farrow, that the church may be considered as an institutional "subject" in contradistinction to its members, and in which, for example, some aspects of its election devolve particularly upon the former rather than the latter. All that can be said of the institution with regard to the nature and dynamic of election to representation can and must be said of its individual members, and cannot be said of the elect community except as it can be said of all its members.

Farrow also rightly remarks that with the glorification of the institutional church as "subject" in contradistinction to its members comes limited scope for self-criticism in the light of the cross, and the danger of denying the "spotted actuality" of the church at an institutional level.[10] As the previous chapter has suggested, election to representation allows us to take full account of the broken, sinful reality of the church as a whole as well as in the individuals of which it is comprised.[11] As was the case with Israel, the church's disobedience as well as its obedience is taken up as part of the dynamic by which God fulfills his purpose of blessing for the wider world. The continuing sinfulness of the covenant community is both its reproach and also, through its sharing in the sinfulness of humanity as a whole, an aspect of its representational role.

If the approach to election being suggested here therefore does not permit an over-inflated notion of the church as an institution, nevertheless, is not that which Volf so vehemently denies — the active participation of the elect in the saving work of God — exactly that which election to representation claims for itself? Is there any way to conceive of such a role for the people of God that does not immediately compromise the *solus Christus* of salvation?

---

10. Farrow, *Ascension and Ecclesia,* pp. 128 and 160, n. 286, respectively.
11. Chapter 5, pp. 133-34 above.

Election to Representation:
The "Secondary Subjecthood" of the Church

The first of our scriptural guiding principles is of considerable assistance here. It will be recalled that this understands election to be the means through which God's purpose of blessing shall be fulfilled in spite of human sinfulness. On the basis of the biblical scholarship that we have discussed, this entails a far greater involvement of the elect in the unfolding of God's saving activity than theological caution might wish to allow. If we were to summarize the conclusions to which we are led with regard to both Israel and the church, then we could hardly do better than to say that the elect are set apart to act precisely as secondary and dependent acting subjects in the outworking of God's saving purposes.

From what may be known of the nature and dynamic of election in Israel, in Christ, and in the church, God's intentions for humanity as a whole are not simply made manifest by but also *enacted through* his elect. Both Old and New Testament scholarship suggest that Israel and the church exist not only to mediate knowledge of the nature of God and of his dealings with humanity, but also to be at the heart of the dynamic by which God *works out* his purposes in and for the world.

This takes place, we have argued, not simply in and through the unfolding of the history of the relationship between God and his chosen people and their interaction with others, but also because in the light of Christ we are able to see that part of the meaning and purpose of election is to bear the rejection of the alienated other in the self before God. In this regard we drew from biblical scholarship the concept of an ontology of election, in which it is through the very existence of the elect community — and in particular its representational role — that humanity as a whole is caught up in the continuing dynamic of God's promise in the face of the continuing reality of human rebellion.

We must therefore be careful not to take it upon ourselves to place stricter limits on our participation in the purposes of God than the contours of the scriptural witness hold open to us. This leads, however, to specifically christological questions. If the very reason for the calling into being of the elect community is to be the means through which God accomplishes his purposes of blessing, and if election is therefore nothing less than God's choice to allow the elect to be "secondary subjects" in his saving activity, how does the election of Israel and the church relate to — and in particular, differ from — that of Christ? How are we to speak of this "secondary subjecthood" without undermining the absolute priority of Christ's election and the *solus Christus* of salvation? The danger here must surely be that election effectively becomes an overarching category of which Christ is simply one — albeit the supreme — example, and Israel and the church another.

Election to Representation: Christ's Election and Ours

The concept of election being developed here asserts that the election of Israel and the church is embraced within that of Christ the self-election of God, to borrow a Barthian idiom, although one that is also appropriate for the earlier Reformed tradition. As we have seen, for all the differences in the way that the content of the electing decree of God is understood, both Barth and Owen insist that God's self-election in Christ is the all-encompassing act of election that establishes the character and content of all God's dealings with the world, and thus, the nature of our election as well.

On this basis, the notion that our election and Christ's can be considered as differing only in degree but not in kind is wholly unsustainable. God's self-election in the person of Jesus Christ is the demonstration, enacting, and proleptic accomplishment of the entirety of God's eternal determination towards human beings and the whole of creation. The election of Israel and the church is of a different order entirely. Fundamentally secondary and wholly derivative, the election of Israel and the church has no independent status, validity, or content.

It is therefore only on the basis of what we know in the person of the incarnate Son that we are able to affirm what election entails and signifies in Israel and the church — and indeed that election itself *is* the means that God chooses to fulfill his saving purposes. The notion that election is the way in which God works out his intentions for the world, and that election may be understood as the setting apart of the covenanted one for the sake of the alienated many, may be discerned as one of several strands in Israel's self-understanding, but it is affirmed for us as the true purpose and character of election only in the life, death, and resurrection of Jesus, Israel's representative Messiah and the incarnate Son. That the dynamic within which God's purpose in election is accomplished involves the twofold ontology of representation — representing God to others and others to God — is again discernible in aspects of Israel's role towards the nations, but it is only in the light of Jesus that this can be claimed as a defining element in the shape of election.

The attempt in the previous two chapters to follow the contours of the scriptural witness allows theology to posit an intricate but consistent relationship between Christ's representational role and that of Israel and the church. In particular, it is not the case that Christ and the church together form the *totus Christus,* but rather that we are enabled to speak of Christ and the church as two acting subjects, with Christ alone as the one saving agent.[12] The asymmetrical relationship between the two acting subjects must never be lost, but neither must the gracious gift of an active, although secondary and dependent, role for the church in the unfolding of God's purposes in and through election.

By way of summary, the previous two chapters have indicated that in Christ, who definitively represents God to us and us to God, we see the covenant faithfulness of God in person, and also the perfect covenant partner whose loving obedience includes representatively bearing in himself the rejection of an alienated and rebellious humanity. It is the nature of God's eternal self-election in Christ that gives the election of Israel and the church its particular shape and representational dynamic. God's self-election, and rooted in this, his setting apart of the elect communities, is the expression of God's eternal determination to bring blessing, and the means through which that purpose of blessing is furthered.

Intrinsic to Israel's existence as the elect covenant people of God is both that Israel represents God to the nations, and also that Israel holds in itself the whole of humanity in its situation as those created for and in rebellion against the covenant relationship established by God. Within this dynamic of election for the sake of wider blessing, Jesus' humanity is representative humanity because it is elect, covenanted Jewish humanity. As Bauckham has reminded us, it is as Jesus repeats the particularity of Israel that he repeats also the "universal trajectory" of Israel's election.[13] The shape of God's elect-

---

12. I owe the expression "two acting subjects and one saving agent" to George Hunsinger, who offered it in conversation as a summary of the relationship between the actions of individuals and the action of God in the unfolding of God's purposes. In this context, it likewise encapsulates the relationship between Christ and the church in the unfolding of the accomplished saving work of Christ. For Hunsinger's application of this concept with regard to the Eucharist, see George Hunsinger, *The Eucharist and Ecumenism: Let Us Keep the Feast* (Cambridge: Cambridge University Press, 2008), pp. 162-65.

13. Richard Bauckham, *The Bible and Mission: Christian Witness in a Postmodern World* (Carlisle: Paternoster, 2003), p. 48; see above, Chapter 4, n. 59.

ing is such that in representing in himself the covenant people Israel, Jesus Christ represents Gentile as well as Jewish humanity before God.

So too when we turn to the eschatological shift in the ages following the Christ-event, we find the church by the Spirit fulfilling an equivalent role to that of Israel within the outworking of God's electing purpose, as the community set apart to represent God to others and others to God, and in whom the entire human situation, now understood in relation to the life, death, and resurrection of Christ, is concentrated.

Hence, just as before the incarnation Israel provisionally and partially reveals and enacts the purpose and dynamic of election as it is definitively made known to us in Israel's representative Messiah, so between ascension and parousia, the church is the people through whom his representative election provisionally and partially unfolds in and for the world. As through Israel the promises of God were to reach beyond the covenant people to the nations, so it is because there is a community of the new covenant — a people united to Christ by the Spirit, and so participating already in the salvation which has been wrought by God in him — that those who are as yet outside that community are also held provisionally within the sphere of God's promised blessings.

To speak of election in this way is not to suggest that Christ's representation is incomplete, or that in the elect communities there is another work taking place alongside Christ's, to complement or supplement it. The church's election does not add anything to what is accomplished in Christ any more than Israel's election "preempts" it. Jesus Christ is the eternal election of God in person. He is thus the origin of our election, the source of its shape and purpose, and also the perfect expression of what election signifies in the sphere of the created order. Above all, proleptically in the resurrection, and as we shall explore a little further later in this chapter, in its fullness at the parousia, Jesus Christ is himself the ultimate goal and consummation of election. In their subordinate election, the covenant communities are graciously given to participate in the representational dynamic of the saving activity of God, as those set apart to express and enact — albeit brokenly — in the ongoing life of the world all that is intended in and has been proleptically accomplished by the election of Christ.[14]

---

14. This understanding of the church's role in the unfolding of election therefore has much in common with Webster's appraisal of the nature and role of the church's ministry in relation to Christ's. Reflecting on T. F. Torrance's account of the relationship between Christ's ministry and the ordained ministry of the church, Webster concurs that while the

Election to Representation: The Ascended Christ and the Church

An aspect of the church's election mentioned briefly in the previous chapter provides a paradigm for how we may both speak of the active participation of the elect in the saving work of God, and maintain that this role is indeed wholly secondary, in no way undermining the absolute priority and primacy of Christ. Moreover, it engages directly with an issue so far left somewhat ambiguous, and with the crux of Farrow's concerns with regard to the relationship between the church and the ascended Christ. Is election to representation guilty of allowing an ecclesiological takeover of the high-priestly role of Christ in his ascended humanity?

While we have maintained that the representational role of the church adds nothing to Christ's election, it might still be thought that the church's election to representation implies a suspension in the unfolding of Christ's own election between resurrection and parousia. It seems as if Christ's community in the world exists to further the outworking of what *has been* done in Christ until all things *shall be* brought to their consummation by and in him at the eschaton. Since this is far from the case, how are we to describe the relationship between the church's election to representation and Christ's continuing ascended high-priestly ministry?

In the previous chapter, it was suggested that intercessory prayer is one locus within the context of the church's worship that reflects the more self-conscious fulfillment of the character of election to representation in the new covenant community, in comparison with that of Israel. Here, the dynamic of intercession is also offered as a paradigm for the way in which the elect participate as secondary subjects in God's saving activity, and in particular for the relationship between the church's election to representation and the continuing high-priestly ministry of Christ.[15]

"indirectness" and asymmetry of the relationship between Christ and the church must be retained, this is "not a denial of the real participation of the church" in Christ's ministry (John Webster, *Word and Church: Essays in Church Dogmatics* [Edinburgh: T. & T. Clark, 2001], p. 201). It is not that the church and Christ are co-constituting, or that there is cooperation between divine and human agency. The church's activity is "neither self-generated nor self-sustaining; both its origin and its telos lie wholly beyond itself" (p. 201). Nevertheless, the *solus Christus* includes the fact that Christ in his sovereign freedom appoints the church to its "real (though limited)" activity in the unfolding of his work (p. 200).

15. In so doing I am particularly following the direction set by J. B. Torrance in *Worship, Community and the Triune God of Grace* (Carlisle: Paternoster, 1996), in which, within his overall development of the theme of our worship as the gift of participating by the Spirit in

Unequivocally, Jesus is the one true Intercessor before the throne of the Father, in the continuing outworking of his all-encompassing election for the sake of God's purpose of blessing. Farrow is correct in his insistence that it is a confusion of christological and ecclesiological categories to suggest the church can in any way assume to itself Christ's role in this regard.

Nevertheless, as we are commanded to pray for others, so our intercessions, in all their flawed and broken inadequacy, are taken up by the Spirit into Christ's, rightly ordered and purified, without for a moment suggesting *either* that our intercessions are needed to "complete" Christ's prayers, *or* that they are redundant. Intercessory prayer offers a framework within which it becomes thinkable that the elect may represent others to God, not in place of or in addition to Christ, but in dependence upon and with Christ.[16]

Thus, we see here *in nuce* the claim of election to representation in relation to Volf's objection to any notion of the church's "secondary subjecthood." We also see in this paradigmatic pattern the response that election to representation might make to the concerns raised by Farrow. The elect community is not called to assume the mantle of Christ's ascended humanity. Instead, intercessory prayer makes explicit that at God's command, and by God's gracious enabling, those who are in Christ by the Spirit are both invited and granted to participate in the enacting of God's saving activity in and for the world. The ongoing priestly work of Christ is the continuing expression of God's self-election for us, and the gift of sharing in its unfolding within human history is the nature and ground of our own election in relation to his.

---

the Son's communion with the Father in his ascended humanity, he draws attention to the dynamic of intercession as the expression of the way in which our worship is taken into the dynamic of his continuing high-priestly ministry (e.g., pp. 8, 73). Torrance himself summarizes the entire ministry of Christ as representing God to us and representing us to God (e.g., pp. 46,77), interpreting the church's pneumatological sharing in this twofold dynamic in terms of enabling us to encounter God in worship, and enabling our response and joining it to Christ's (p. 77). Election to representation as I have been developing it might well be understood as taking Torrance's aim — to help the church understand its participation by the Spirit in the ongoing priestly work of Christ and his twofold representational ministry — and seeing in it not simply the shape of the church's worship, but the very dynamic of its election as a whole.

16. So, e.g., Torrance, *Worship*, p. 73, "By grace we are given to participate in his intercession for all humanity. So in our corporate worship we are called to be a royal priesthood, bearing in our hearts the sorrows and cares and tragedies of our world as our heavenly High Priest does."

Ecclesial Hubris? The Church and the World

If this is how election to representation might begin to respond to the theological question marks suggested by Volf and Farrow — that the church cannot possibly participate actively in God's saving work without trespassing upon christology — it must also confront what we might call Volf's "anthropological" objections.

Crucial to the dynamic by which the elect community participates in the unfolding of God's saving purpose is the notion of a perichoretic relationship between the elect and the rest of humanity, in which the elect bear in themselves the rejection of the alienated other, provisionally holding the other before God and so within the sphere of God's promised blessing. This makes no claim to mediate or bestow the "all-decisive faith . . . that the church cannot give to a person,"[17] but does it not apparently replace, displace, or at the very least minimize the centrality of the cognitive and volitional dimensions of faith?[18]

In this regard, it will be recalled that the heart of the earlier critique of Barth was to draw out the scriptural and Trinitarian difficulties of asserting any understanding of what it is to be "in Christ" apart from the work of the Spirit, who alone unites us to Christ. One of the central elements of this attempt to rethink election is to maintain that only those who are in Christ by the Spirit in the community of the church may now be considered to be "elect" in Christ. How then does election to representation understand the notion of "in Christ"? Can those outside the elect community be considered to be "in Christ" in a way that does not entail bypassing the decisiveness of the Spirit's role, ecclesiologically in this case, rather than christologically as we have suggested with regard to Barth? And yet, if only the elect are "in Christ," what meaning does the church's election to representation ultimately have for those outside the elect community?

Some of these issues will be dealt with when we call upon a "parable" to help us think through the dynamic of election to representation, and in the discussion of the Spirit's role and the parousia to follow. Here we need to note the importance of the way in which the third of our guiding principles is understood. This affirms the exclusivity of the elect community as those in a unique relationship to God, set apart to be and do what no other

---

17. Volf, *After Our Likeness*, p. 163.

18. See Volf, *After Our Likeness*, e.g., p. 171: "Faith, with its cognitive and volitional dimensions, is soteriologically indispensable."

can be or do. The church cannot believe for others in such a way that they become part of a community whose very being is defined precisely as those who are in Christ by the Spirit through faith. Moreover, election to representation emphatically asserts that since Jesus Christ is the covenant of God in person, there can be no participation in the covenant promises apart from him. The new covenant community of those united to Christ exists as the locus of the promises of God in Christ in the world.

Here we are reminded again of Wright's remarks concerning the church as the community through which alone that which has been accomplished in Christ is worked out in the world. With this we confront explicitly the weighty negative and positive realities of election, understood as God's ongoing purpose of blessing in the face of humanity's sin. Negatively, it means that without the existence of the elect, there could be no reconciliation and no blessing; the only possibility of either in the situation created by human rebellion is the decision of God to set apart a people for himself. Positively, that which God intends for the world *is* brought about in and through the existence of the elect; it is precisely because there is an elect community, as both the pledge of his promise and the means through which it is at work, that reconciliation and blessing continue to be operative in the world.

With this in mind, a shift in perspective needs to be made very clear. Volf's emphasis is upon the soteriological decisiveness of the confession of faith, and therefore upon the church primarily as the community of the saved. To be in Christ by the Spirit through faith is to be among those who alone will ultimately share in the fruits of Christ's work.

The emphasis here is somewhat different. Although strongly affirming that those united to Christ by the Spirit now will enjoy that communion eternally, the focus is not only upon the soteriological status of those within the community but also upon election as intrinsically including being-for-the-other, and as always participating in the fulfilling of God's wider purpose of blessing.[19] God has chosen to enact his intention to bless not only *for* the elect community, but also *beyond* the elect community; it is not only *in* the elect but also *through* the elect that the fullness of God's saving will is accomplished.

---

19. Gunton's pithy remark is apt: "the elect are not primarily those chosen for a unique destiny out of the whole; rather they are chosen out of the whole as the community with whom the destiny of the whole is in some way bound up." Colin Gunton, "Election and Ecclesiology in the Post-Constantinian Church," *SJT* 53 (2000): 212-27.

The term "elect" therefore cannot simply be explicated as "all those whom God has determined to save." Instead, it delineates the community set apart within human history in explicit covenanted relationship with God, on the understanding that the election of the covenant community specifically and directly concerns not only the eschatological destiny of its members, but the intention of God to enact his purpose of blessing for all people and all things.

The discussion of the parousia to follow will sketch the nature of the eschatological hope that may be held out beyond the boundaries of those who belong to the elect community in human history. For the moment, however, Volf leaves us with one further question. As well as his concern for the integrity of the church's identity as the community of believers, he also reminds us of the need to respect the self-understanding of those outside the church. Volf sharply remarks upon the oppressiveness, as well as the scriptural difficulties, of any suggestion that those outside the confessing community are members of the "latent church" or "anonymous Christians."[20]

It might well seem that the dynamic of representing others to God as we have described it entails just such a tacit absorption of those outside the community of Christ. Election to representation's claim, however, is that the Spirit-shaped "perichoretic" relationship between the elect and the rest of humanity creates a dynamic in which the elect hold the apparently rejected before God *without compromising their particularity,* as those still caught up in alienation, rebellion, indifference, or ignorance. It does so in a way that does not suggest that humanity as a whole is "elect in Christ," yet in such a way that humanity as a whole is held in the sphere of God's promised blessing. How is such a dynamic to be conceived?

A Parable: Some Preliminary Remarks

One way is by turning to a "parable," in which aspects of the general relational dynamic that characterizes human existence allow us to reflect upon the nature and possibility of this kind of relationship between the elect and the rest of humanity. Two elements of the previous chapter allow us to clarify the reasons for, and limits of, the use of such a parable in this context.

On the one hand, it was suggested that while it is particularly made known in and expressed by the body of Christ, mutually constituting rela-

---

20. Volf, *After Our Likeness*, p. 151, n. 96.

tional personhood may be thought of as the universal and ineradicable *imago dei*. On the other, much was also made of the uniqueness of the "perichoretic personhood" forged by the Spirit between the elect community and humanity as a whole. It was argued that there is a distinctive relational ontology and representational dynamic that is peculiar to the elect, and which is at the very heart of election's role in the outworking of God's purposes of blessing. This stems from the particular relationship to God and to the world that characterizes the covenant community; it is this set of relationships for which it has been brought into being, and in which no others can stand. Thus, nothing can replicate the unique dynamic of these relationships in the saving work of God.

Nevertheless, with great care and in full recognition of the partial nature of the correspondences to which they point, there are some situations that assist us in conceptualizing this dynamic between the elect and the rest of humanity. One such is offered here. For this parable to help us think of how the elect may hold the apparently rejected in themselves before God without compromising their particularity, we are required to enter into a situation that in itself is in many respects quite literally unthinkable. It is the situation of dementia, and with it, we allow one of the most extreme challenges to any conventional understanding of relational personhood to teach us more about how the "perichoretic" personhood of the elect and the role of the Spirit in the dynamic of election to representation might be expressed.

Before beginning to explore how this might be the case, however, an obvious but extremely important point must be made. To suggest that in this disease we might find help in expressing a theological concept is not an attempt to rationalize the tragedy of dementia, nor to imply that the suffering it causes to victims and those who care for them might be mitigated by the idea that something "meaningful" may be drawn from this most inexplicable of diseases.[21] Instead, it is to join with others in suggest-

---

21. Inexplicable in so many ways — its causes are unclear; official confirmation of the diagnosis is possible only after death; there is no "cure" and little can be done to stem its progress; by its very nature, after a certain time, its sufferers cannot take us any further into the mystery of what is happening to them; and it results in what is often deeply painful, "inexplicable" behavior towards family, friends, and carers. See Malcolm Goldsmith, *In a Strange Land . . . People with Dementia and the Local Church: A Guide and Encouragement for Ministry* (Southwell, UK: 4M Publications, 2004), pp. 25-30 for a brief, accessible account of current medical research into conditions covered by the term "dementia" and chaps. 3 and 4 for the ways in which its symptoms unfold.

ing that in aspects of this condition we are also confronted with an extreme expression of truths about our own existence and the nature of personhood.[22] It is also to suggest that there are very particular insights here into the "perichoretic personhood" that we are positing as central to the dynamic of election to representation.

Relational Personhood and Dementia

As the degenerative process of dementia reaches its nadir, almost all that is usually associated with the uniqueness of individual identity and the concept of "personhood" is seemingly annihilated.[23] Conventional modes of communication, recognition, and response towards others are lost; so, gradually, is the sense that the person with dementia has any awareness of unique self-hood.

Medical, psychological, and pastoral debate continues as to whether it is correct to say that the elements which make up the "personhood" of a dementia victim are gradually "lost" or whether they remain trapped but inaccessible, as triggers are less and less successful in helping sufferers to access their own identity.[24] For our purposes, we need only acknowledge

22. A theme that recurs throughout David Keck's *Forgetting Whose We Are: Alzheimer's Disease and the Love of God* (Nashville: Abingdon Press, 1996), first articulated on p. 17; see also, e.g., Goldsmith, *In a Strange Land*, pp. 201-8. There is no space here to begin to touch upon the enormous range of questions and concerns that dementia forces theology to confront. In addition to those already mentioned, recent resources that reflect on the questions raised by dementia for systematic as well as pastoral theology include Albert Jewell, ed., *Spirituality and Ageing* (London: Jessica Kingsley, 1999); Suzanne McDonald, *Dementia and a Theology of Holy Saturday*, MHA Aspects of Ageing Papers, no. 1 (Derby, UK: Methodist Housing Association, 2003); Donald McKim, ed., *God Never Forgets: Faith, Hope and Alzheimer's Disease* (Louisville: Westminster/John Knox Press, 1997); James Saunders, *Dementia: Pastoral Theology and Pastoral Care* (Cambridge: Grove Books, 2002).

23. It is here that theological recognition of the centrality of our physical bodies for who we are as persons is particularly important (e.g., Stephen Sapp, "Memory: The Community Looks Backward," in McKim, ed., *God Never Forgets*, pp. 38-54, pp. 44-51) and care for the physical appearance and dignity of dementia patients becomes a vital expression of their personal integrity and worth (see, e.g., Mary C. Austin, "Joy in the Moment: Immediacy and Ultimacy in Dementia," in Jewell, ed., *Spirituality and Ageing*, pp. 115-24). It is also here in particular that we feel the full force of the reality that our lives — and our true personhood — are hid with Christ in God (Col. 3:3).

24. For a useful summary of developments in this area, see Goldsmith, *In a Strange Land*, pp. 17-21.

the painful truth that when we, as friends, family, and carers, are in the presence of those with end-stage dementia, that which makes them uniquely themselves is to all intents and purposes lost to their own perception. Without the structures and content of memory, they can no longer hold together in and for themselves a perceptible sense of their personal identity, and they retain no recognition of the relationship of others to them. They literally do not know "who" they are.

What is the relational dynamic at work here, as reciprocity becomes increasingly tenuous and fleeting, and finally disappears altogether? The extreme situation of dementia shows us the most profound and poignant possibilities inherent in the concept that human identity in general is constituted through relationship. In severe dementia, the dynamic of that relational personhood is essentially *representational*. The only way that the unique identity and personhood of someone with severe dementia can be preserved is as it is held in being for them, and continually re-bestowed upon them, by others.

It is here that the reality that human being is relationally constituted has a significance that is rarely noted. Not only, as is usually remarked, does it mean that "I" cannot be "me" without being in relation to "you" as other; it also has profound implications if the time comes when I myself cannot be "me" anymore. To assert that our being is intrinsically relational means that even on a human level I am not the only source or guarantor of my own personhood. It cannot be emphasized too strongly that the foundational relationship within which all others take place, and which is the ultimate source and guarantee of our personhood, is the relationship of God to us. The point here concerns the significance, for our being and personhood, of the human relationality that God has likewise made constitutive of our being. Because my identity and personhood are bound up with that of others at this ontological level, others are able to hold my very personhood and identity in being for me when I cannot.[25]

This sustaining of the personhood of another in the self takes place self-consciously, in the attempt to help dementia patients recall aspects of

---

25. This is *not* to say that the dementia sufferer is not a person, but it is an extreme reminder of the situation that *none* of us can be a person without others. Moreover, while the narrative that makes up my awareness of my personhood may still be trapped within a disintegrating brain, if it is, by any means that it is possible to determine, inaccessible to me and incommunicable to anyone else, then while it may theoretically still "exist" in me, it seems legitimate to claim that for all practical purposes "my" personhood is in fact being held in being not so much *by* me, but *for* me by others.

their identity, and unself-consciously in the simple unfolding of the continuing relationship. Moreover, it does not entail the absorption or dissolution of the other's personhood; rather, it is the very possibility of preserving that person's true identity in its uniqueness. By what they know of someone with dementia, and in their ongoing relationship to that person, relatives, friends, and carers hold together the integrity of who the person with dementia has become — which is no longer the full, true self that s/he has been — and preserve something of that full, true self that would otherwise be irrecoverably lost.

Two more related points must be made. First, to stress the obvious, this remains true even if those with dementia can no longer know anything either of what constitutes their own personhood, or the fact that others are upholding it for them. This representational, relational ontology is a reality even if there is no awareness and no reciprocity — or if, as is often the deeply distressing reality when dementia takes hold, the only response is one of hostility or violence.

Second, and again to stress the obvious, while we can provisionally and partially hold in ourselves the personhood of those with dementia, we cannot restore to them the fullness of personhood that has been lost to their awareness. To that extent, we might say that for all its being an ontological reality, this holding of the personhood of the other in the self may make no perceptible difference to the person with dementia, who remains unaware of it. We cannot make them "whole" persons by virtue of the fact that we stand in this relation to them. Nevertheless, by continuing to sustain in being for them that which they are no longer capable of knowing and therefore of preserving in themselves, we also sustain and continue to dignify their fundamental individuality and irreducible worth, demonstrating that we honor and care for both who they have been and who they have now become.

Making Some Connections

With this, we begin to see how the experience of many may help us conceive of the possibility of a relationship in which personhood is able to be held in being in and through another, in the painful reality of all its genuine otherness and radical difference. An extreme situation in the context of human relational being in general offers us a framework for thinking further about the representational dynamic we have been developing with regard to election through the concept of the "perichoretic" personhood of the ecclesial *imago dei.*

Of course any attempt to make direct parallels between the dynamic of election to representation and the situation of dementia begins to break down almost immediately, in particular because dementia involves the loss of an identity of which the person was once cognizant, and because only in the sphere of close relations is the kind of representational dynamic to which we have alluded possible. Nevertheless, the relational dynamic of dementia allows us at the very least to ask the question: If it is possible to hold the personhood of a dementia victim in my own in such a way that it has ontological force, and if all this suggests the structural reality of what it is to be human beings in relation, what might this mean theologically, in the "so much more" of God's grace?

We begin with some immediate resonances with several key themes from our exploration of the scriptural witness. The way in which biblical scholarship has presented the nature of election in Israel, in Christ, and in the church likewise suggests a representational dynamic with ontological dimensions. As we have maintained, representation in both its forms — of God to others, and of others to God — is quite literally of the *esse* of election. It is intrinsic to the very being of the elect. This is so precisely in order that the elect covenant people may bear in themselves the rejection of the other, that those who exist in alienation from God might nevertheless be held where they otherwise could not be — within the sphere of the promised covenant blessings of God.

The parable of dementia also points us back to another central element of biblical scholarship: that this representational dynamic remains a reality whether it is known and acknowledged as such or not, either by humanity as a whole or by the elect themselves. Hence, as was indicated in Chapter 4, Israel represents God to others and holds the whole of humanity in itself before God without necessarily being fully aware that it is doing either, or of quite how it is that as a result, blessing will come to the Gentiles. Likewise, neither do the Gentiles necessarily have any conception that in and through Israel they too are the intended recipients of God's promises, or that they might be provisionally blessed in any way through the existence of Israel.

Seitz reminded us of this by pointing to the example of the exile, in which neither Israel nor the nations are fully aware of the way in which the unfolding of God's covenant relationship with rebellious Israel is also the working out of his intention to bring blessing to Israel and the world.[26] In turn, we noted that Paul points to a similar pattern for the church: even if they remain unaware of it, the very existence of Gentile Christians is central to the dynamic by which God intends blessing for unbelieving ethnic Israel.[27]

To put this in terms that recall our description of the situation of dementia, the elect community therefore does not have to intend this representational being and doing, or even to be fully conscious of it. Nor does it need to be able to discern what "difference" this being and doing is making, or the nature of its present and ultimate contribution to the unfolding of God's purposes. In turn, neither can the rest of humanity be aware of how their existence before God is bound up with the being and doing of the elect. It is simply as the elect community and the rest of humanity engage with each other in their integrity and particularity that the intentions of God in and through election continue to unfold.

This brings us to another vital theological consideration for which dementia offers a parallel. At the most radical level, our true personhood is inaccessible to *all* of us. We have already noted that the *imago dei* is relational through and through, consisting primarily in our having been set apart as the creature able to live in conscious, covenanted relationship with God, and secondarily in our mutually constituting relationships with others. Since our true being is grounded in the relationship established with us by God, to the extent that people continue to live in rebellion and alienation from, indifference to, or denial of that relationship, not only are all their relations to other human beings and the created order as a whole fundamentally distorted, neither can they know the true nature of their own identity and personhood. Of themselves they cannot rightly know who they were created to be, and so cannot truly know who they are. Neither can they know that in Christ is kept who they shall be.

Only in the new covenant community can there be recognition of what constitutes true human personhood. Here we are able to acknowledge that in the incarnate Son we see embodied the perfection of human relatedness to God for which we were created, and that through him is revealed all that denies and distorts our true personhood even as he takes it into himself and redeems it. It is in union with Christ by the Spirit that we begin to become most fully our true selves, growing into the free,

---

26. Christopher Seitz, *Figured Out: Typology and Providence in Christian Scripture* (Louisville: Westminster/John Knox Press, 2001), pp. 153ff.; see Chapter 4, p. 99 above.

27. See Chapter 4, pp. 109-10 above.

faithful obedience and love towards God that characterizes his true humanity; and it is in this glorified humanity that God intends us ultimately to share.

To those outside the new covenant community this truth about their own personhood, created for right relationship with the Father in Christ by the Spirit and eternally embraced within the intention of God to bless in his self-election in Christ, is as unknowable as the sense of identity that a dementia victim has lost. It is the reality of this true personhood in Christ that the elect hold in keeping for the rest of humanity, to whom it is otherwise wholly inaccessible.

Nevertheless, we must also be clear that *all* knowledge of who we are remains distorted, partial, and provisional, because we do not know yet who we shall be. Personhood is rightly considered to be an eschatological concept.[28] None of us will know ourselves or others as we and they truly are until we know each other in the fullness of God's relationship to us in Christ and ours to God in Christ. Our lives and our true personhood are hid with Christ in God. We will know who we really are only at the parousia, when we will know ourselves as we are known by God, and when in beholding face to face we will also be fully transformed into who we were created to be.

The Spirit and the Dynamic of Election to Representation

It is to the parousia that we shall shortly turn, but for the moment, we might summarize by saying that the parable of dementia has raised three fundamental concepts that pertain to election to representation: that the reality of our true personhood may be quite radically beyond our knowing; that it may be partially and provisionally held representatively for us by another in ways that have ontological significance; and that this does not compromise our personal particularity, but rather allows another person to become the space in which both who we presently are and the truth about who we are that is beyond us may be held.

This latter point allows us to consider a little more closely the question of how election to representation understands what it means to be "in

---

28. A frequent theme in Gunton. See, e.g., his *The Triune Creator: A Historical and Systematic Study* (Grand Rapids: Eerdmans, 1998), p. 209 and chap. 9, "Creation and New Creation: in the Image and Likeness of God," *passim.*

Christ," and with this, to spell out something of the richness of the Spirit's role. Newbigin aptly summarizes the eschatological Spirit's work in election and mission as the "prevenience" of the kingdom, and as "hope in action," not just for ourselves, but for the fulfilling of God's purposes of blessing for the whole created order, which is the intention of election from the outset.[29] To examine the nature and significance of the Spirit's work in the particular election dynamic being developed here, we return to the previous chapter's account of the *imago dei,* election, and "perichoretic" personhood, this time with its pneumatological implications particularly in view.

To be elect in Christ is above all to be constituted by the Spirit in a very particular set of relations. As the one who alone unites us to Christ, the Spirit draws us up into the dynamic of the triune life of love. At the same time, the Spirit likewise creates the particular relations across time and space by which all who are "in Christ" are also "in one another," as the one body of Christ and the communion of saints. Just as all human personhood is "perichoretic" in the sense that it is mutually constituting, so it is this set of relations that particularly constitutes the being of Christians.

The Spirit is also the one who continues to shape us through the relations into which he gives us entry. Transformed more and more by the Spirit into the image of Christ the image of God — and so into the realization of our true humanity — the church is to express more and more fully its election to image the divine life of love simply by *being* this pneumatologically constituted community, as well as by the Spirit's shaping of its self-conscious witness. We are elect to image God by representing God in and to the world, and the work of the Spirit is to enable this to happen.[30]

In suggesting that the ontology of election in Israel, in Christ, and in the church includes representing the other to God by holding the apparently rejected before God, we have insisted upon extending the concept of "perichoretic" personhood to posit a unique relationship between the elect and the rest of humanity, and upon placing this relationship at the center of the dynamic through which election furthers God's wider purpose of blessing.

The shape of this particular form of "perichoretic" personhood con-

29. Lesslie Newbigin, *The Open Secret: An Introduction to the Theology of Mission,* rev. ed. (London: SPCK, 1995), chap. 6 *passim.*

30. As we have noted, this is the conclusion of Volf and Grenz; and for all their differences, this might also stand as a summary of the positions of Owen and Barth, to whom we will return in the following chapter.

tinues to reflect the person and work of the Spirit who creates it. Above all we might say that the Spirit is the one whose especial role is to enable, preserve, and bring to its fullest flourishing distinctive personal identity in and through relation. Volf and Grenz have emphasized this aspect of the Spirit's activity with regard to our union with Christ, and to the ecclesial "in-one-another" created by the Spirit among those who are in Christ.[31] Gunton in particular draws out wider systematic reflections on this aspect of the Spirit's identity to include the suggestion that within the inner-Trinitarian perichoresis we understand the Spirit not only as the expression of the unity of the Father and Son, but as the one who is the focus of the distinctiveness of Father and Son.[32] One of the chief ways in which to characterize the Spirit's person and work might therefore be as the one who shapes and sustains particularity-in-relation within the Godhead, in our union with Christ, and within the body of Christ.[33]

Election to representation states that the Spirit creates just such a relationship between the elect and the rest of humanity in the saving purposes of God. It is between the elect community in (and indeed, *because of*) the particularity of its unique covenant relationship with God, and the rest of humanity in the particularity of *its* continuing rejection of God and separation from Christ, that the Spirit forges a representational dynamic for the blessing of the alienated other. This too can be seen as consonant with the characteristic nature of the Spirit's work as a whole: always to allow space for the inviolable distinctiveness of the other and always to be seeking the fullness of the personhood of the other, through the shaping of personhood-in-relation. In election, no more and no less than in any other sphere of his activity, this is part of who the Spirit is and what the Spirit does.

31. So, e.g., *After Our Likeness*, pp. 188-89, for Volf's discussion of the Spirit-created unity-in-distinction and differentiated communion in both regards; and Grenz, *The Social God and the Relational Self: A Trinitarian Theology of the Imago Dei* (Louisville: Westminster/John Knox Press, 2001), pp. 333-36, for a similar account of the nature of the Spirit's work.

32. Colin E. Gunton, *The One, the Three and the Many: God, Creation and the Culture of Modernity* (Cambridge: Cambridge University Press, 1993), p. 190. See chap. 7 ("The Lord Who Is the Spirit: Towards a Theology of the Particular," pp. 180-209) for his scripturally shaped account of the Spirit as the one who "is not a spirit of merging or assimilation . . . but of relation in otherness . . . which establishes the other in its true reality" (p. 182).

33. So also Gunton sees the notion that the Spirit is the one who enables this form of "perichoretic" relationship between us and God as the expression *ad extra* of the Spirit's identity within the Godhead (see *The One, the Three and the Many*, e.g., p. 185).

This has considerable implications for what is meant by that key phrase for election, "in Christ by the Spirit." As we have repeatedly insisted, it is now in Christ alone that the promised covenant blessings of God are concentrated, and to be "in covenant" is possible only as one is "in Christ" by the Spirit through faith. On this basis, it appears that in and of itself the rest of humanity can have no part in those promises. Yet at the heart of God's self-election in Christ — and therefore of the nature and purpose of election as a whole — is the notion that part of what it means to be elect is always and intrinsically to exist *for the sake of* those who are alienated from God, and therefore outside the sphere of covenant blessing.

Thus, in accordance with the shape of Christ's election as the one who, in covenant faithfulness and for the sake of the covenant promises, bears in himself humanity's rejection of God and God's rejection of human rebellion, so the elect communities of Israel and the church are the place in which not only the covenant promises of blessing but also the alienation and rebellion of humanity as a whole are concentrated, as part of the dynamic by which God refuses to allow human sin to thwart his intention to bless. Thus, the covenant community exists as a sign of hope for the apparently rejected, and not of the radical exclusion of those outside its boundaries. Therefore, God's purpose of blessing can never be interpreted as if it is to be confined to those who are "in Christ by the Spirit"; rather, those who are "in Christ by the Spirit" exist to be the channel of that blessing to those who as yet are not.

The work of the Spirit is the lynchpin of this understanding of election. It is the Spirit who creates the elect community in Christ; it is the Spirit who shapes the unique personhood through which the elect are united to and exist for the rest of humanity. The very heart of what it means for the elect to be "in Christ by the Spirit" is precisely that in the elect, by the same Spirit, those who themselves remain apart from Christ are nevertheless provisionally held in Christ.[34]

The very personhood that the Spirit constitutes, by which the elect

---

34. It is worth noting at this point that Gunton sums up his critique of Barth's understanding of election "in Christ" as his "questionable" decision to see "the whole human race as *immediately* in Christ rather than *mediately*" through the historical outworking of election in the communities of Israel and the church, and that this is brought about by the Spirit's "eschatological enabling" ("Election and Ecclesiology," p. 23). The present undertaking seeks to provide some detailed contours to illustrate what the dynamic of just such an alternative account of election might look like, in the pneumatologically enabled representational dynamic between the elect community and the rest of humanity.

community is set apart from all others, is one which allows the elect to hold the rest of apparently rejected humanity in themselves in Christ in such a way that the particularity of both the elect community and of those outside it is preserved. Those outside the believing community are not anonymous Christians; neither can they in any way be considered to be "elect" in Christ. To be elect, as we have made clear, is to be constituted in a particular set of relations as the explicit covenant community, and it is to be set apart to be and do in and for the world what no other can be and do. In themselves, those outside the elect community are not "in Christ" — this is possible, as we have repeatedly insisted, on the basis of the New Testament witness, only by the Spirit through faith. Nevertheless, through the work of the Spirit in the dynamic of election to representation, those outside the covenant community are held, in their continuing alienation, where otherwise of themselves they could not possibly be: within the sphere of God's covenant promises of blessing in Christ.

The Parousia: Tracing Some Patterns

Until now, we have been speaking almost exclusively of the way in which election to representation furthers the unfolding of God's purposes in the arena of human history. What, though, are we to make of its significance when the provisional gives way to the ultimate, and the purposes of God in election are consummated at the eschaton? What will election to representation finally mean for those who have been drawn by the elect into the sphere of their own communion with the Father in Christ by the Spirit?

We must proceed with great caution here. All that any attempt to speak of the eschaton can legitimately do is to sketch some tentative patterns for our thinking on the basis of what we have already been given to know of the character of the triune God. In this regard, the supreme enacting of God's covenant faithfulness within history provides us with an important reminder for our thinking about the eschaton. Just as none could have anticipated the perfect enacting of that redemptive faithfulness in incarnation, cross, and resurrection, neither can we know in advance how at the parousia the fulfillment of God's purposes shall be accomplished. The most that an account of the eschatological unfolding of election to representation can do, therefore, is to trace some patterns by reflecting on what its foundational concepts might signify in the final outworking of God's faithfulness to his promises.

In the first of our three scriptural guiding principles, we have affirmed that election is God's chosen means to bring about his wider purpose of blessing. The other two offer some hints as to how this takes place: that election consists in the setting apart of the uniquely covenanted *one* for the sake of the alienated *many,* and that a representational dynamic is fundamental to the accomplishing of election's task in the redemptive and reconciling purpose of God.

If this is so, then there can be no question whatsoever of *whether or not* the representational dynamic of election will ultimately make a difference to those outside the elect community as this is known in the unfolding of human history. Without hesitation, it must be affirmed that it will. As we have insisted, the elect themselves are not the only focus of God's electing. Rather, they are also the instrument of his wider saving purpose. It is God's eternal determination that through the elect, blessing will flow to the rest of humanity and, indeed, as Romans 8 reminds us, to the whole created order. While we cannot know *how* this will unfold, we can certainly be confident *that* the existence of the covenant community has a part to play in the eschatological purposes of God for those who remain outside it.

With this we are taken back to the claim that the representational dynamic of election has implications for the very being of those whom we represent. The situation of dementia has helped us to understand that it is possible to hold the personhood of others in being, when in themselves they are incapable of preserving or even knowing their own true identity. We noted that in many instances it is not at all apparent that this makes any perceptible "difference" to the people concerned. We nevertheless continue to do this because it is the expression of a relationship in which we seek to honor the integrity and worth of who they have been and what they have painfully become.

Election to representation suggests that the elect exist in part to hold in being the reality of true human personhood — created for and restored to right relationship to God in Christ — for those who in themselves cannot be aware of or share in it. To do so is to honor the integrity and worth of who they have been created to be, who in their separation from God they have become, and also who, by grace, and in the light of the promise held out in Christ, they may yet be.

We also have to say, however, that in this we are doing what we exist to do and are summoned to do, and we do it without knowing the final outcome of our being and doing — without knowing, in effect, what "difference" we are making and shall make. We do not know exactly what God will ultimately accomplish through us or how he will accomplish it.[35] All that we can know is that the elect community has been brought into being precisely in order to participate in the fulfillment of God's promise of wider blessing. With regard to the eschatological implications of our election for others, we can only repeat the promise of blessing for those outside the covenant community which is the very reason for election, and speak of the dynamic within which it currently unfolds.

The Parousia: The Spirit and Our Eschatological Personhood in Christ

As the one who creates and sustains that dynamic and who constitutes our personhood in Christ, we may also look particularly to the Spirit's work in the present to suggest some further contours for our thinking about election to representation and the eschatological future.

Although the notion cannot be developed fully here, the dynamic of election to representation suggests that the parousia must be considered as a *pneumatological* as well as a christological event. With this we take up the scriptural hints that posit a close association between the fullness of participation in the eschatological new covenant and the work of God's Spirit, and in particular the implications of Joel 2:28-29 ("Then afterward I will pour out my spirit on all flesh. . . . Even on the male and female slaves, in those days, I will pour out my spirit"), taken up in Peter's Pentecost speech in Acts 2. What we see in the extraordinary outpouring of the Spirit upon the apostles at Pentecost represents the partial, proleptic fulfillment of this promise. The final outpouring of the Spirit upon all flesh is still to come. This outpouring we may surely consider to be part of the Trinitarian fullness of the parousia-event.

When this full and final outpouring takes place, we may assume that the outcome will be consistent with what we have come to know of the Spirit's person and work in the present. Our hope for the eschatological outworking of election to representation is shaped by the expectation that

---

35. As Webster comments, the actions of the church are not "causative"; rather, the church is simply appointed and empowered to play its part in "that whose accomplishment lies entirely outside the church's sphere of competence or responsibility" (*Word and Church*, p. 201).

whatever the Spirit accomplishes then will be consistent with the nature of his work in the unfolding of election now.

First and foremost, even then — especially then — the same dynamic will be at work as we have emphasized throughout. There can be no union with Christ that does not include the work of the Spirit, and no reconciliation with God except as one is in Christ. This is the clear implication of the New Testament understanding of the shape of God's covenant faithfulness and of our participation in the promised covenant blessings. As the Spirit's work now in this respect is above all to enable confession of Christ, to constitute our personhood in Christ, and to transform us in Christ-likeness, so we must assume that at the parousia it will likewise be by the Spirit alone that any of us will confess Christ as Lord, be drawn into fullness of communion with the triune God and with one another in him, and come as a result to the fullest realization of our true personhood.[36]

Second, however, we also need to recall that it is no less the work of the Spirit in election that participation in this communion and the realization of this true personhood is provisionally anticipated for those who as yet remain alienated from God in Christ. The Spirit's work in election now is the outworking in the in-between time of the purpose of election to bring blessing to the apparently rejected. He does so as the one who forges rela-

---

36. See Gunton, "Election and Ecclesiology," p. 222, for the reminder that the perfection of personhood in Christ is eschatological, and for the relationship of this concept to election and the Spirit: "Only the Spirit can relate lost human beings to God the Father through Christ — election — yet the Spirit's otherness, modeled on the New Testament depiction of his relation to Jesus, generates an openness according to which the Spirit can determine a relation through . . . election which is yet uncompelled because it is the means of the realization of the sinner's true being in Christ." Once again, Gunton has pointed us to the crux of the matter: that the Spirit's work is necessary if we are to be united to Christ, and that in this work, the Spirit does not infringe our freedom or particularity, but enables the fullest flourishing of our true being. This is profoundly true, and Owen, to whose pneumatology he refers in this context, strongly upholds both. This, however, is also the problem. If, as Gunton rightly points out, it is *only through the Spirit* that we are united to Christ, then, from the Reformed perspective which he shares, only those upon whom the Spirit is bestowed to this effect can be in right relationship to the Father and so brought to the fullness of true human being in Christ. We therefore find ourselves once again, by implication, in the realm of individual double predestination. Gunton explicitly wishes to avoid this and, as we have noted several times, quite clearly understands the elect community in history to be those through whom God's wider saving purposes are accomplished. Nevertheless, he nowhere suggests a dynamic by which this can be reconciled with the nature and necessity of the Spirit's work as he rightly describes it. It is precisely such a dynamic that is being suggested here, rooted in what can be known of the person and work of the Spirit in the present.

tionships that both honor personal distinctiveness and seek to bring about the fullest flourishing of personhood in Christ.

As a result, as we have stressed, the work of the Spirit in election to representation does not override but preserves the particularity of those outside the covenant community. We also know that in the process of constituting and shaping our own personhood by bringing us into union with Christ, the Spirit does not undermine or violate our freedom or our particularity, but brings both to their highest realization. We do not know what the eschatological outcome of the Spirit's role in election to representation will be. What we may say with confidence, however, is that in the full outpouring of the Spirit on all flesh at the parousia, the Spirit will continue to be the one who both establishes and preserves particularity-in-relation, and who works to bring about the fullness of redeemed personhood in Christ which is God's highest purpose for humanity.

Therefore, as we anticipate the consummation of all human personhood in Christ, we do so in the awareness that our own personhood in Christ is as yet incomplete, and that even where that personhood is unrecognized, denied, or rejected, it may be provisionally held in being by others in the very integrity of their negation of it. We do so also in the hope and expectation that stem from what we know of the saving purpose of God in Christ and the nature of the Spirit's work, awaiting the eschatological outpouring of the Spirit upon all flesh and the revealing of the fullness of our identity and personhood in Christ.

The Parousia: The Consummation of Election in Christ

This leads us back to a significant issue raised earlier in this chapter — that just as he is the self-election of God in person, and the perfect expression and fulfillment of the nature, shape, and purpose of election within the created order, so Christ himself is the consummation and goal of election. We have already issued the reminder that the object of God's electing is not only the elect in themselves, but also the apparently rejected; now we also need to recall the secondary, derivative, and provisional nature of our election in relation to Christ's. With this we once again turn to the biblical scholarship of Chapter 4, to note another instance of how the shape of election in the church corresponds to the pattern made known in Israel.

The Old Testament suggests that the full realization of the significance of election — for Israel, and through Israel for the Gentiles — will be eschatological. The restoration of Israel and the incoming of the Gentiles (in those strands of the Old Testament that envisage a positive place for the nations) are seen as inextricably linked, but also as a matter for the end times. From a New Testament perspective, the Christ-event is the climax of the covenant, and the proleptic inbreaking of the eschatological fulfillment of God's purposes for Israel and the world. Thus, in the person of Christ is revealed the true nature and significance of Israel's election, for itself and for the whole of humanity. Thus, too, we have maintained that the New Testament re-envisaging of election stems from the realization that the promised new covenant has been inaugurated in time in Christ, and is entered in union with him by the Spirit.

While Christ and the Spirit now define the identity of the new covenant community, the dynamic of election into which the church enters once again remains the same. Only at the eschaton will the nature and significance of its election for the rest of humanity and the world be known, and only then will the way be fully open for the rest of humanity to recognize how it is that the church, by its representational being-and-act, has been intrinsic to God's purpose of wider blessing. Moreover, just as it is in the person of Christ the incarnate Son that the nature and purpose of Israel's election is definitively made known and proleptically fulfilled, so it will be precisely in the person of Christ at the parousia that the church's election for the world will be made known and its purpose reach its final consummation.

The relationship between Israel's election and the life, death, and resurrection of Christ suggests that at the parousia, too, Christ will take into himself, rightly order, heal, and redeem that which is disordered and broken within the elect community and that which is distorted in the elect community's dealing with the world, so that in him the goal of election in the overflowing of blessing for the world will be realized in all its fullness.

Until such time, that which can be known to the church is the basic pattern of election, made known in part by Israel, definitively revealed and accomplished in its fullness in Christ, and into the unfolding of which the church has been summoned to play its part between the ascension and the parousia: that whether the elect community fully recognizes it or not, in, through, and in spite of its flawed imaging and the distortion and poverty of its representation, election is the means that God has chosen to bring about the overcoming of human sin and its consequences, and so to fulfill God's purpose of blessing through the reconciliation of sinful humanity to himself and the restoration of the whole created order.

One final remark: at the parousia there will be no further need for the dynamic of election to representation. Representation is by its nature a feature of the created order and a necessity of our distance from God. If we were to speak of its correlate in the being of the triune God, it would be in terms of the perfect self-presence of Father, Son, and Spirit to each other in loving, self-giving communion. The expression *ad extra* of this perfect self-presence is the drawing of others into that presence through redemptive representation, in God's self-election in Christ, and then derivatively in the representational role of the elect communities in history.

Election's particular task of representation in the here and now has no place when we come to behold face to face, and to know as we are known. Nevertheless, the outward-reaching, other-embracing dynamic of presence and representation made known to us by the triune God now offers at least an indication that we might conceive of our eternal rejoicing in the sheer presence of the triune God as part of the same pattern that we have glimpsed and have been caught up in here. In ways towards which election to representation can only point, to uphold one another before God and to be upheld by others will be part of our fullness of joy.

CHAPTER 7

Owen and Barth: Beyond the Impasse

The preceding chapters have sought to sketch the contours of a fresh approach to the doctrine of election through an engagement with contemporary biblical scholarship and theological reflection on the ecclesial *imago dei*. This closing chapter returns to our point of departure by bringing the concept of "election to representation" into dialogue with Owen and Barth. Doing so will draw together some of the themes developed so far, and will raise again the key questions with which we began.

We turn firstly to the way in which the concept of representation itself functions within Owen's and Barth's approaches to election. While Owen's use of the category has already been noted, Barth also explores the concept of representation in his discussion both of human nature and of election. Following the previous chapter's account of some of the challenges that the representational dynamic of election being developed here must meet, the issues raised by Owen and Barth require us to clarify further the nature of an election ontology that entails representing others to God as well as God to others.

Finally, we will consider election in Owen and Barth in the light of the three scriptural guiding principles that shape election to representation. In the process, that which has been implicit throughout much of the preceding account will be made clear. An understanding of election in which it is intrinsic to the very being and doing of the one elect community to further God's wider purpose of blessing offers full scope for a rich election pneumatology such as that exemplified in the early Reformed tradition while likewise moving us beyond the apparent impasse that Owen and Barth exemplify.

Representation in Owen: A Summary

Chapter 1 gave considerable attention to the significance of the category of representation for Owen, and the rigor with which he pursues the relationship between election and the *imago dei* in this connection. In summary, human beings are for Owen the creatures uniquely able to represent the righteousness, holiness, and love of God in and to the world. Created for right relationship with God, once that relationship is distorted by sin, we are no longer able to exercise our representational function and have essentially lost the capacity to image God. It is as the Spirit transforms the elect more and more to the likeness of Christ, the one true image of God, that they are able to fulfill their calling by representing Christ in and to the world in their lives and by their proclamation.

The notion that the elect might also have a role in representing the apparently rejected to God, however, would be for Owen a complete *non sequitur*. This, too, can be stated very briefly. Even if a way might be found to speak of the concept without appearing to impinge upon the sole High Priesthood of Christ, the idea at the heart of election to representation — that the elect represent in themselves before God those who remain alienated from God — is wholly redundant. For Owen and Reformed orthodoxy, the concept of being represented before God is tied to the double decree. The incarnate Christ represents only the elect, just as the ascended Christ is mediator only for the elect. The sole purpose of Christ's representational work and mediation, including the gift of the Spirit, is to bring the eternally elect to salvation. Neither Christ nor therefore his people can be said to represent the non-elect to God. Those who are not elect to salvation have no mediator: that is the definition of their situation.

Representation in Barth

Like Owen, Barth also binds the concept of representation to election and the *imago dei*. Turning firstly to the latter, we find that this takes place in the context of a careful distinction between existing "with" and "for" others, which distinguishes our humanity from the unique humanity of Christ. Barth insists that Jesus Christ alone exists *for* others as the fundamental determination of his being.[1] As such, "he is the image of God, in a

---

1. So, e.g., "there can be no question of a total being for others as the determination of any other . . . but Jesus," *CD* III/2, p. 243.

way that others cannot even approach. . . . For of no other . . . can we say that from the very outset and in virtue of his existence he is for others . . . to be and act in their place . . . as their representative."[2]

This being-for-others as their sole representative is nothing less than what it means for Jesus Christ, the incarnate Son, to be the self-election of God, and is a fundamental truth about his being that can be shared with no other. All other human beings are therefore *with* but not *for* others in this basic sense.[3] For Barth, to say anything more than that we are "with" others is to say too much.[4]

There is nevertheless a carefully qualified "being for others" without which we are not truly human.[5] To render one another mutual assistance and to be at the disposal of another is the way in which our humanity corresponds with Jesus' unique ontological determination for others.[6] In this analogous correspondence Barth is careful to maintain the strict difference between Christ and us, and the touchstone for this difference is the concept of representation. In particular, there is a reciprocity about all human "being for" the other — we are mutually in need of, as well as able to give, assistance — that cannot arise in relation to Christ. "God alone, and the man Jesus as the Son of God, has no need of assistance, and is thus able to render far more than assistance to man, namely *to represent him*."[7] On the other hand, "I cannot represent [the other]. I cannot make his life-task my own. He cannot expect this from me. He must not confuse me with God."[8]

Representing others to God is therefore very strongly identified with the unique being-for-others of Christ as the supreme expression of his election and his existence as the incarnate image of God. *Representing God to*

2. *CD* III/2, p. 222.

3. *CD* III/2, §45, 2, "The Basic Form of Humanity," *passim*. E.g., "With this . . . expression we distinguish humanity generally from the humanity of Jesus . . . only the humanity of Jesus can be absolutely exhaustively and exclusively described as being for man" (p. 243).

4. "We could not say more than 'with.' To say 'for' would be . . . to say too much. It can and must be said of the man Jesus, but of Him alone" (*CD* III/2, p. 317). This is not to deny that for Barth, as we have noted, the church exists fundamentally "for" the world (see above, Chapter 5, n. 27). It is how Barth understands the nature and limits of the concept of "being for" that will be a matter for discussion.

5. "There is a being for one another, however limited, even in the relationship of man and man in general. And human being is not human if it does not include this being for one another" (*CD* III/2, p. 260).

6. *CD* III/2, pp. 260-62.

7. *CD* III/2, p. 262, my italics.

8. *CD* III/2, p. 263.

others, however, is at the core of Barth's account of our election. We have seen that in his mature doctrine of election, the role of the elect community of Israel and the church (and even of the outer circle of election, the "rejected") is precisely to represent the different aspects of the one election of Christ. The particular election of the church is a further, self-conscious exercising of this aspect of representation: the church exists to *witness,* declaring God's self-election in Christ and the reality that all are given to share in his election to bear our rejection.

It will be recalled that here, above all, we see Barth speaking of the Spirit's role in election: the Spirit is the one who enables proclamation and faith, the speaking and the hearing of the gospel. As this is worked out further in the doctrine of reconciliation, the themes of the Spirit, representation, and the church's election are taken up once again.[9] Here, Barth speaks respectively of the role of the Spirit with regard to the church's calling to be the provisional representation of the whole of humanity justified in Christ,[10] and of the church's election as sharing by the Spirit in Christ's self-declaration, as the representation of his prophecy in the world.[11] The church exists for the world as the community that, by the Spirit, knows and embodies the reality of God's self-election for us in Christ and is called to proclaim it.

Barth is forthright in insisting, however, that the church's ministry — the nature of its "being for" the world — can *only* consist in this understanding of representation as witness. The church

> is not commanded to represent . . . bring into play or even in a sense accomplish again in its being, speech and action either reconciliation, the covenant, the kingdom or the new world reality. . . . In doing so it would do despite to Jesus Christ himself as the one Doer of the work of God. . . .[12]

---

9. Most particularly in §62, "The Holy Spirit and the Gathering of the Christian Community," and §72, "The Holy Spirit and the Sending of the Christian Community."

10. This stands as part of the *Leitsatz* to §62, *CD* IV/1, p. 643.

11. *CD* IV/3/2, p. 794; see pp. 792-95, where Barth situates this representational aspect of the church in relation to its existence as the image and likeness of Christ, and where he pursues the idea, stated in the *Leitsatz* of §72, that in being the provisional representation of Christ's prophecy in the world, the church is also therefore the provisional representation of the calling of all humanity (and the whole creation) to the service of God in Christ.

12. *CD* IV/3/2, p. 836 (with particular reference to Roman Catholic and Eastern Orthodox ecclesiologies); see also pp. 834ff.

Barth's discussion of the Christian as witness in the context of his account of vocation sets out the issues at stake.[13] Here he poses the question, "What kind of an action is it in which [the Christian] assists the action of Jesus Christ and thus has an active part in the history of salvation?"[14] Before describing this action of the church, he points to the kind of action in which the church has no part whatsoever. Nothing can be added to the sole sufficiency of what Christ has done in representing all people in the act of reconciliation on the cross. Christ is the one High Priest in whom all are reconciled, justified, and sanctified whether they realize this or not, and Christ indwells not only Christians but also non-Christians as their sole Mediator, Head, and Representative.[15]

Since Barth insists that the representational, priestly aspect of Christ's work is wholly completed in the reconciliation of the world on Golgotha, the ascended Christ's ongoing work is not so much as Priest, but as Prophet.[16] Barth identifies the role of Christ the Mediator with the making known of that which has been accomplished in cross and resurrection, and it is into this continuing prophetic ministry of Christ, not his fully accomplished priestly ministry, that the church is called to play its part.[17] The work of Christ moves towards its consummation at the final form of the parousia through the church's witness to this all-embracing act, in its role as the herald of Christ by the Spirit.[18]

The connections between this position, his earlier account of Christ's unique "being for" others, and his mature doctrine of election are clear. In Christ we see the one elect human being, in whom alone the entirety of election is exclusively concentrated. In turn, the whole of humanity shares, whether consciously or not, in his one, "all-inclusive election [which is] universally meaningful and efficacious."[19] The fundamental distinction in election is therefore between Christ and the rest of humanity. Hence Barth

13. *CD* IV/3/2, §71, 4, "The Christian as Witness," *passim.*

14. *CD* IV/3/2, p. 603.

15. *CD* IV/3/2, pp. 604-5.

16. *CD* IV/3/2, pp. 604-8.

17. So, e.g., while Christ's priestly work of reconciling the world was fulfilled once for all on Golgotha, "this work . . . is not exhausted in the action of his passion. . . . His work goes forward *in presentation of what took place then*" (*CD* IV/3/2, p. 605). For the detailed identification of Christ's role as Mediator with his office as Prophet, see *CD* IV/3/1, §69, "The Glory of the Mediator," *passim.*

18. E.g., *CD* IV/3/2, pp. 606-7.

19. *CD* II/2, p. 117.

makes no distinction between the elect community and humanity as a whole in his account of Christ's being "for" and humanity as a whole's being "with" others, but rather distinguishes Christ's representational role from the rest of humanity's mutual rendering of assistance.

That which sets the elect community of the church apart from humanity as a whole is the Spirit's gift of recognizing the reality of the entire human situation in relation to God's self-election in Christ, and of living in accordance with and witnessing to it. As such, the church therefore stands in solidarity with the rest of humanity in sharing in the *outcome* of this unique election, bearing witness to the inclusion of all in the election of Christ; it does not participate in any way in the actual *dynamic* of election by which this reality is brought about.

Barth's account of what it means to be "with" or "for" the other is intended to avoid the collapse of anthropology into christology.[20] The danger of his position is that there is too near an identification of anthropology and election. We have already noted that among other issues, the inclusion of the whole of humanity in the one all-embracing election of Christ struggles to do justice to the full distinctiveness of the elect community in its relationship to God and to the rest of humanity.

These are matters to which we will return later in the chapter. For the moment, it is because election to representation holds strongly to the absolute particularity of election, confining the concept exclusively to the covenant community, that it cannot accept Barth's stark either/or between christology and a general anthropology.[21] Instead, this approach speaks of a particular ontology of election, established in God's self-election in Christ, in which the covenant communities are graciously given to participate. It is to a response to both Owen and Barth from the perspective of this approach to election that we now turn.

The Relationship Between Election and Representation

On the one hand, election to representation as I have been developing it here shares with Owen and Barth the notion that representing God to oth-

20. Barth begins his account of the basic form of humanity by elaborating precisely this point (*CD* III/2, p. 222).

21. So, for example, it is precisely in the contrast between christology and a "general anthropology" that Barth insists that human beings as a whole are "with," but only Christ is "for" others (*CD* III/2, p. 317).

ers, through active witness and in terms of simply living out its existence as the covenant community, is a fundamental aspect of election. To borrow Seitz's terms once again, here we see the centrifugal and centripetal mission of the elect.

On the other, the choice appears to be a stark one: *either* the church must understand its role only in terms of witness *or* it is guilty of an evil denial of the very foundation of the gospel by presuming it can add to or take the place of Christ's work.[22] In representing God to others, it fulfills the former; in the notion of representing others to God, it seemingly cannot help but fall into the latter.

As was noted in the previous chapter, it cannot be asserted too strongly that the church adds nothing to what has been done in Christ. To suggest anything of the sort is indeed wholly to undermine a basic premise of the gospel. We have nevertheless suggested that it is possible to conceive of a secondary and derivative, but nevertheless active, participation in both sides of the representational dynamic that characterizes God's self-election in Christ without trespassing on the priority and primacy of that election.

This allows us to clarify a central difference concerning the relationship between election and representation with regard to Owen and Barth on the one hand, and the concept of election being put forward here on the other. We have referred to the idea that for Barth, the elect community of the church, like humanity as a whole, shares in the *outcome* of Christ's work in representing others to God, but does not itself participate in that aspect of the representational *dynamic*. In fact, for all their differences, the position of both Owen and Barth might be summarized in terms of seeing election as the outcome of representation. For both, the elect in Christ may be defined as those whom Christ represents.[23] Anyone who is represented by Christ shares in his election; anyone whom Christ does not represent does not. For Owen this is the outworking of the eternal double decree; for Barth it reflects the inclusion of all, at least provisionally, within the one election of Christ to bear our rejection.

The hints we have taken up from biblical scholarship, however, suggest a somewhat different approach to the relationship between representation

---

22. *CD* IV/3/2, p. 605.

23. The difference, of course, being that for Barth there is in theory no one whom Christ does not represent. See Chapter 3 above for a discussion of the ambiguities in Barth's presentation of election in terms of "Jesus and . . . the people represented in Him" (*CD* II/2, p. 25).

and election. Rather than considering election solely as the *outcome* of representation in this way, the concept of representing others to God, as well as God to others, is also fundamental to the *dynamic* of election itself, in Israel, in Christ, and in the church.

That is to say, whereas Barth and Owen identify election and representation, the approach to election being developed here distinguishes the two by seeing representing others to God as part of what it means to be elect. Rather than equating the two terms (all/some are represented by Christ, therefore all/some are elect), election to representation therefore maintains the restrictiveness of the concept of election (this applies only to the covenant community), but in and through this it affirms the radical openness of the dynamic of representation.

As we noted in the previous chapter, for election to representation, the term "elect" cannot simply be replaced by the phrase "all those whom God has determined to save," but refers to those set apart within human history to be and do what no other can be and do. The scriptural witness leads us to suggest that part of what this entails is that election is the means God has chosen to further his purpose of blessing not only *for* the elect community, but also *beyond* the elect community as it exists in history.

Unlike both Owen and Barth, we find that it is therefore not necessary either to be a member of the elect community in history, or to widen the notion of election in Christ to include all human beings, in order to speak of being represented before God. Rather, all are represented before God precisely through election. This is so because the elect community shares in the same dynamic as is established in God's self-election for us in Jesus Christ: the bearing of the apparently rejected in the self before God in order that the alienated other might be held in the sphere of God's promised blessing.

Intercessory Prayer Once Again

Intriguingly, despite Barth's insisting that the only act of representation possible for the church is to represent God to others in witness, there is a place in his theology where he holds out a very different possibility. With it, we return to a topic that has surfaced several times in the course of previous chapters. In his brief discussion of intercessory prayer Barth does indeed point to the church's existence as also entailing representing the other to God.[24]

24. This forms part of his profound treatment of prayer in *CD* III/4, §53, 3.

In the context of discussing the fact that there is no isolated praying "I," but only the "I" who prays as part of the "we" of the believing community, Barth remarks that in turn, those whom Christ has summoned to pray with him in the fellowship of the church cannot be considered as forming an "exclusive circle." On the contrary the praying "we" of the church are "united . . . among ourselves in order that we may be responsible for the world around us *representing our Lord among them and them before our Lord*."[25]

That which the believing community has and others lack is the knowledge of what God has done for all in Christ, as our Lord and theirs. As such, "we" may believe in the midst of the others while they do not yet believe, doing so *"provisionally in their place,"* and so holding a position that they may never have occupied or may have abandoned.[26] The "genuinely universal character" of prayer is that the community "believes, prays and asks only as *the representative of . . . mankind and the world*."[27] As believers pray in community we do so in anticipation with and for all others. Hence the one who prays *"does not merely represent himself, or the community in the world, but mankind and the world as a whole before God*."[28]

Barth is careful to clarify that this does not make us co-redeemers or fellow reconcilers with God — God "neither compromises Himself nor does He overload us."[29] God simply commands us to pray, as that which is the proper expression of our relation to him, and in and through our asking accomplishes his purposes, so that our prayer is our "modest participation in the work of Jesus Christ."[30] As for the question of the "necessity" for such participation, it is, says Barth, quite simply that God wills that we pray and this is part of his unfolding purpose. "If God is not God without us, if He wills to have us with Him in His work of salvation and universal lordship," then it is to refuse God's grace — and his command — to refuse to come to him with our requests.[31]

Ironically we may turn again at this point to Barth's comments when insisting that the *only* active role for the church in salvation history is to witness. Here too, he is careful to point out that Christ the True Witness

25. *CD* III/4, p. 102, my italics.
26. *CD* III/4, pp. 102 and 103 respectively, my italics.
27. *CD* III/4, p. 103, my italics.
28. *CD* III/4, p. 103, my italics.
29. *CD* III/4, p. 104.
30. *CD* III/4, p. 104.
31. *CD* III/4, p. 96.

and one Prophet of his own work does not *need* the participation of the church for the accomplishing of his ends. He chooses, however, not to exercise this office alone, setting apart the church by the Spirit who indwells them particularly for this task.[32] The necessity of the church's role in the unfolding of Christ's prophetic ministry in the world — and also, Barth has briefly conceded, in sharing in Christ's continuing ministry of intercession — is therefore not laid upon God, but upon the church. It is quite simply commanded and ordained to this participation.

While Barth relates the concept of representing others to God only to the intercessory prayer of the church, and while this is only a small thread in the vast tapestry of the *Church Dogmatics,* Barth comes close here to the heart of the dynamic of election to representation as we have outlined it. It is with this in mind that we close by returning to our three scriptural principles, in dialogue with Owen and Barth, to draw out more fully where the agreements and disagreements lie, paying particular attention to the pneumatological questions with which this undertaking began.

Owen and the Priority of the One Elect Community

Recalling our account of Owen in Chapter 1, the elect in Christ are those, and only those, who are united to Christ by the Spirit through the Spirit's gift of faith. This is situated within a *filioque*-shaped Trinitarian logic that is concerned both to speak of the Spirit's completing and perfecting role in election as the expression of inner divine relations, and to see an overall unity in the work of the Son as co-author of the decree, as the one who in his incarnate life, death, and resurrection effects all that is necessary to accomplish the salvation of those elect in him, and who in his ascended mediation bestows the Spirit upon those whom he and the Father have chosen.

The elect are therefore those to whom the Spirit is efficaciously given in accordance with the eternal decree, and are thus united to Christ to

---

32. *CD* IV/3/2, pp. 607-10, where Barth asks, "Apart from the prophetic work of Jesus Christ Himself, does there have to be this ministry of His Word by the church?" (p. 607). To which the answer is that Christ is his own Revealer and Proclaimer of the reconciliation of the world, and it is the church that has need of Christ to fulfill its proclamation, and not vice versa. It is simply the reality that in its unity with Christ, this proclamation is the meaning and principle of its existence. It is the expression of the free grace of God that the church has its part to play in the unfolding of Christ's prophetic ministry, and by its very existence, the church cannot help but participate in it.

share in his election; the reprobate are those upon whom the Spirit is not bestowed and who have therefore been determined to remain in their sin, apart from Christ. Thus, the Spirit's work is decisive in the economy of election, and at the same time is bound to and dependent upon the work of Christ.

With this in mind, if we were to bring Owen's presentation of election into dialogue with the three guiding principles that provide the scriptural contours for election to representation, we would be well advised to begin with the last: that election is a meaningful term only in the context of a clearly delineated community set apart as the covenanted people of God. Here Owen and Reformed orthodoxy are emphatic and unequivocal, and in strong accord with the thrust of the contemporary biblical scholarship that we have outlined. As we have noted, at the heart of this from a New Testament perspective is the Spirit's role as the one whose work is the boundary marker of the elect people of God in Christ.

To begin with the last of the guiding principles, however, is not simply to point out the most obvious area of agreement; it is also to suggest that for Reformed orthodoxy this becomes the all-encompassing defining principle of election. The determination of each human being's destiny either to salvation or to reprobation within or outside the covenant community is the content of God's electing decision, such that individual soteriology becomes the entire compass of the doctrine. Reformed orthodoxy sees in the very existence of the elect the basis upon which to construct its fearsomely coherent interpretation of the first two guiding principles — continuity in the purpose and dynamic of election. The triune God's purpose in election is to bring to salvation those eternally chosen for redemption in Christ; the entire unfolding of human history is the outworking of this particular aim.

The biblical scholarship upon which the approach to election offered here is based suggests a somewhat different shape to God's electing purpose. Rather than concluding that this is to be understood primarily in terms of the determination of a few to salvation and the decision to abandon the rest to the consequences of their sin, election is seen as the means of furthering God's wider purpose of blessing.

The third of our scripturally derived principles, in other words, cannot be allowed to take precedence over the way in which the other two are to be understood. Rather, it is given its meaning in the context of the other two. As we have noted, election cannot be considered solely as a soteriological end in itself. The dynamic of election as representing God to others and others to God places the focus radically elsewhere. God sets apart his elect in human history, not as the enclave of those predestined to be saved, but as the chosen means by which God works out his blessing for those outside the elect community, in order to bring about his reconciling and saving will in and for the world.

Barth and the Priority of Election as Blessing

With this we turn to Barth, whose overwhelming priority in his account of election corresponds to the way in which contemporary biblical scholarship has led us to formulate the first guiding principle: that God's election is fundamentally for the sake of blessing. In Barth's christological reorientation of the doctrine we find just such an identification of election and blessing expressed in terms of the very being of God. The triune God quite literally *is* the God who blesses by means of election. Chapter 2 reminded us of the radical move made by Barth in which the election of God is not the decision for or against individual human beings but the primary ontological category by which God is who he is. In the language of Seitz, election is indeed the means God uses to bring about his purpose of blessing, now understood not simply as God's choosing a particular people for himself, but as God's self-election to be God-for-us in the person of Jesus Christ.

Moreover, Barth's description of the nature of Christ's election takes us to the core of the way in which the second of our guiding principles — the representational dynamic of election — has been presented. Christ's election fundamentally entails taking into himself the rejection of the alienated other, in order that the apparently rejected may be held in the sphere of God's promised blessing. He exhausts in himself the "No" of sinful humanity to God, and God's "No" to sinful humanity, for the sake of God's redeeming and reconciling "Yes."

It is the way in which Barth develops this account of the concentration of the whole of election in the person of Christ, however, as the one elect as well as the only truly rejected person, that leads to serious difficulties. We have already discussed some of the scriptural issues raised by his presentation of the all-encompassing twofold nature of Christ's election, and by the relationship between christology and pneumatology within this. In the present context, any suggestion that election — and its corollary of being "in Christ" — is a christologically determined *a priori* of theological anthropology is profoundly at odds with the third of our scriptural guiding principles. This emphatically denies that election is a term that can be given any kind of universal reference or applicability. Instead, it refers firstly to Christ and then to the covenant community set apart in a unique relationship to God and the world. These relations quite simply *are* what election means with regard to us; it is not possible to be "elect" apart from them.[33]

Election to Representation: One Community for the Blessing of the World

Election to representation therefore strongly upholds the exclusivity of the concept of election, insisting with Owen and the historic Reformed tradition and *contra* Barth that to speak of the elect is to refer, after the resurrection of Christ, only to those who are united to Christ by the Spirit through faith. Along with the implications of the New Testament witness, it maintains that to be elect is now to be "in Christ," and there is no union with Christ apart from the work of the Spirit. Like Reformed orthodoxy, therefore, this approach offers full scope for a robustly scriptural and trinitarianly consistent election pneumatology, in unity-in-distinction with the work of Christ.

The dynamic within which election to representation adheres to this third guiding principle, however, highlights a considerable departure from

---

33. This renders problematic Barth's account of the election of the individual in which the elect who belong to the believing community and the rejected who do not are christologically united (both are elect in Christ) but pneumatologically divided (the former has the gift of the Spirit but the latter does not). It also calls into question his other basic twofold division within humanity's election: the suggestion that Israel and the church together constitute the two sides of the one community that is particularly designated "elect" within the general inclusion of humanity in Christ's election. For the earlier account of these twofold divisions, see Chapter 2, 45-47, and Chapter 3, 60-63. As Chapters 4 and 5 have made clear, the preference here has been to follow the New Testament scholarship that maintains that faith in Christ alone is the badge of membership of the elect new covenant community. The identity of the elect community is to be understood in the light of the New Testament's understanding that a change in the eschatological time brings about a corresponding change in the way that the covenant community is to be understood. After the life, death, and resurrection of Christ, the covenant in person, it is by union with Christ through the Spirit that one is adopted into the eschatological family of Abraham as the community that remains in continuity with the covenant promises.

both Owen and Barth. For Owen, *that* individuals should come to actualize their election *is* the purpose of God's election to salvation, and that they do not is the enacting of his decree of reprobation. There is no other intent in God's electing than this. Barth's attempt to avoid the double decree by refusing to confine the concept of election in Christ to the one clearly delineated community stems at least in part from the fact that he is working within the same framework as the tradition. For Barth as much as for Reformed orthodoxy, only those to whom the term "elect" can be applied may be considered as the objects of God's reconciling action in Christ. Therefore, a way must be found to declare that *all* may be described as elect in Christ and so held within the sphere in which hope for all becomes thinkable.[34]

By contrast, the argument here is that the pattern of election — which may be discerned in Israel's self-understanding, is made manifest in Christ, and is now enacted through the church — suggests that it is not those who may be designated the "elect" who are the sole object of God's reconciling action. Rather, the elect exist to be the channel of God's reconciling activity for the world. That the uniquely covenanted chosen people is set apart to be the elect of God therefore does not in any way suggest the lesser significance or worth of others before God, but is the very means by which God chooses to bring about his wider purpose of blessing beyond the elect community. It is for this reason that the singular (in every sense of the word), utterly exclusive particularity of election is its *sine qua non*.

As such, this representational election dynamic shares with Barth and *contra* Reformed orthodoxy the insistence that the foundational purpose of election is blessing, and is grounded in God's electing self-determination to be God-for-us in Christ. In spite of the fact that his christological reworking of the doctrine raises profound scriptural and Trinitarian difficulties, Barth's fundamental insight cannot be relinquished: that in the person of Jesus Christ, Electing God and Elect Man, we see God's self-determination to be God-with-us and God-for-us; we see that election is radically for the sake of blessing.

34. So, e.g., *CD* II/2, p. 325, where, in Barth's view, to be unable to proclaim to the rejected their election in Christ is at best to leave them in a "neutral" place with regard to Christ, and at worst, to exclude them from Christ's redemptive work entirely. The polarization is between the historic tradition, with its understanding of the elect for whom Christ's work avails and the rejected as those "for whom in actual fact he means nothing," and Barth's conviction that we must be able to speak of the rejected as elect in Christ if we are also to speak of them as the objects of God's grace (pp. 325-26).

As the previous chapter made clear, we also affirm that in Jesus Christ the nature and purpose of election is revealed, enacted, and proleptically fulfilled. As such, the election of the community and of individuals has no independent reality apart from Christ's, but is embraced within and expressive of his. The elect community participates secondarily and derivatively in Christ's election as the means by which the once-for-all work of Christ is worked out in the world.

This understanding of election also insists that we be consistent in seeing in our election the same pattern that is revealed in Christ. It is not that the many participate in the two sides of the one election of Christ, but that the full dynamic of election as it is made known in Christ is concentrated first in Israel and then in the new covenant community in Christ, each of which has been called to enact in human history the representational ontology of election that Christ reveals to be at the heart of the purposes of God for the world. As is suggested in Israel and definitively made known in the incarnate Son, and as we must affirm continues to be the case with the church, God deals with humanity through his elect, working out his purpose of blessing for the many through the uniquely covenanted one.

The Spirit and the Dynamic of Election to Representation

It is the role of the Spirit in election to representation which provides a way of securing that which Barth seeks above all to safeguard — the inclusion of humanity as a whole within the sphere of God's self-election in Christ — and it does so within a fully Trinitarian dynamic in which that role is theologically and scripturally consistent. This is most clearly illustrated by returning once more to the question of the relationship between the "elect" and the "rejected" as Barth presents it.

His desire is to see both as inseparably bound to each other through election in Christ. Their different roles are tied to the concept of representation and the work of the Spirit. The elect believers represent the reality of God's saving purposes in Christ to the rejected, as the outer circle of election in Christ, and the outer represents that which God in Christ has overcome to the elect, although all the while being unaware of either aspect of the representational dynamic in which it is involved.

In both cases, representation signifies "showing forth." The elect represent God's saving purpose (and recognize that which the rejected represent) because of the Spirit's work in enabling proclamation and faith. The rejected remain in the outer circle precisely because, not illuminated by the Spirit, they do not recognize that which the elect manifest. Not having been given the Spirit in this way, they are deaf to the proclamation and incapable of faith.

In the strictest sense, therefore, "representation" as Barth understands it in this context does not embrace the outer community in any way that is meaningful to themselves, and pneumatology in fact *divides* the two communities, although they are ontologically united in Christ. As has been suggested throughout, however, it is in fact extremely difficult to reconcile any notion of being found to be "in Christ" with the absence of the Spirit's work. If the two communities are really to be considered in terms of the integral relation to each other that Barth requires, this must be a pneumatological reality as well as a christological one.

The twofold dynamic of representation as we have formulated it holds out just such a possibility. The elect not only represent God to the rest of humanity, but represent the rest of humanity *to* God, such that, through and through, both the elect in Christ and those who are *not* elect in Christ are related to each other and to God *in Christ by the Spirit.*

As this indicates, what is being envisaged here is a considerably more radical participation of the elect community in the dynamic by which God's electing purposes unfold than either Barth or Owen allows, and with this, a richer role for the Spirit. We cannot think of the Spirit's role in election primarily in terms of separating the elect from the reprobate, as Reformed orthodoxy posits; neither can we suggest, with Barth, that it is Christ who unites and the Spirit who divides the elect and the rejected within their election in Christ. Rather, the fullness of the Spirit's role in election includes the binding together of the elect and the rest of humanity in the representational dynamic through which the very function of the one elect community whom the Spirit sets apart in Christ is to hold those who themselves are not (yet) in Christ within the sphere of God's promised blessing.

As we explored in the previous chapter, the Spirit's work is therefore at the very heart of every aspect of election to representation as we have presented it on the basis of the three scriptural principles. Taking the last of these first, we have emphasized that election entails the setting apart of one clearly delineated community in a unique relationship to God and the world, and it is the Spirit who creates, sets apart, and shapes the new covenant community in Christ.

Having noted the significance of representation for thinking through the nature of election in Israel and Christ, our second guiding principle argued that this must also be seen as central to the way that the church understands its own election. The previous chapter explored the way in which the Spirit constitutes and shapes the unique perichoretic personhood of the elect that binds together the elect community and the rest of humanity. In this way the Spirit plays his particular part in the accomplishing of the purpose of election as we have described it in the first of our guiding principles: that election is the expression of — and the chosen means to further — the triune God's purpose of blessing.

As well as offering an account of election that seeks to take into account some suggested scriptural contours for its nature and purpose, election to representation therefore also endeavors to present an election pneumatology that is in accordance with the New Testament understanding of the Spirit as the one who alone brings about the union with Christ and transformation in Christ-likeness by which election is now to be understood, and as the previous chapter indicated, does so in a way that seeks to take into full account the Trinitarian context of the Spirit's role. The pneumatological dynamic of election to representation is the outworking for election of that which theology discerns from the self-revelation of God to be the nature of the Spirit's person and work.

Election to Representation and the Extent of Salvation in Christ

What, then, of the impasse to which Owen, and Barth's two doctrines of election appear to lead us: that within a Reformed framework, a scripturally consistent and trinitarianly robust account of the Spirit's role in election seems to lead only and inevitably to individual double predestination? As we concluded the previous chapter with an account of election to representation and the parousia, so here we look again at its eschatological implications, this time with the pneumatological problem we posed at the outset particularly in mind.

It must be emphasized once again that this approach considers election to be the means through which God's purpose of blessing is enacted, *not* the way in which the parameters of that blessing are defined. Such an account of election therefore does not seek, and cannot presume, to answer questions about the final scope of salvation in Christ. Nevertheless, the way in which the purpose of election and its pneumatological dynamic are understood allow us to rethink the apparently intractable pneumatological problem with which both Owen and Barth confront us.

As we have seen, for Owen and the early Barth, the Spirit's work sets apart the elect from the reprobate, in the pneumatological logic of individual double predestination. For the later Barth, that all participate in Christ's election, whether or not they have been enabled by the Spirit to acknowledge and live in accordance with this reality, provides the basis for the claim that election is unequivocally "good news" and the sum of the gospel. Within this, we find a pneumatology that struggles to do justice to the scriptural balance between Christ's work and the Spirit's, but which corresponds to his all-inclusive election christology, with its strong inclination towards *apokatastasis*. Where Barth attempts to restore a more scripturally and trinitarianly robust pneumatology, we have seen that he is drawn back towards individual double predestination.

Election to representation cannot be as clear-cut as the historic Reformed tradition: that only the elect community in history, whose union with Christ by the Spirit will be manifest in their calling and faith in this life, are saved. The fundamental contention in the approach to election being developed here is that election is the means by which God furthers his purpose of blessing *beyond* the elect community itself. Central to this election dynamic is the notion that the rest of humanity is provisionally held in Christ by the Spirit awaiting the consummation of God's purposes in the person of Christ and the final outpouring of the Spirit at the parousia.

Like Barth, however, neither can election to representation straightforwardly affirm *apokatastasis*. There are significant differences in the way in which Barth's account and election to representation approach this issue, however, and these differences lie in the respective understandings of the "field of tension" that the doctrine of election is required to inhabit.

Scripturally and theologically, election to representation insists *both* that in Christ we see the content of God's electing decision to be God-for-us, *and* that there is no sharing in that promise of blessing apart from the Spirit's work in uniting us to Christ. Now and at the eschaton, only those upon whom the Spirit is bestowed to this effect are united to Christ and so drawn into the dynamic of the triune life, and this work of the Spirit is entirely the free, unconditioned, gracious gift of God. These are the poles that define the "field of tension" for election to representation.

In contrast, with Barth's insistence that all are elect in Christ, that his salvation avails for all, and that it is impossible *actively* to participate in this ontological reality apart from faith, but that faith itself is not essential to being "in Christ," Barth has described a "field of tension" that struggles to do full justice to key elements of the New Testament witness to the Spirit in particular, and leads to the difficulties that have been delineated in this chapter and in Chapter 3. With regard to the issue in hand, that all are elect in Christ as the fundamental truth of their being, and yet that there remains a possibility that some might ultimately be rejected, remains an incomprehensible mystery which is not to be resolved.

Within election to representation, however, we cannot maintain that election in Christ is a universal given of theological anthropology. Instead, it affirms simply that the elect in Christ, united to him by the Spirit through faith, are set apart as those through whom God's purpose in election — that blessing may come even to the apparently rejected — shall be accomplished. Strictly speaking, therefore, with its attempt to place equal emphasis upon Christ as the manifestation and enacting of God's self-election to be God-for-us and upon the necessity of the Spirit's work, *both* individual double predestination *and apokatastasis* are possible (and indeed, are the *only* two possibilities for a Reformed understanding) within the dynamic of election to representation.[35]

Clearly, however, this way of understanding election inclines more towards the latter than the former. Whereas with the historic Reformed position, the central mystery of election is why God has determined to save some but not others, for election to representation, as for Barth, the central mystery is whether any will ultimately be excluded. Election to representation therefore indwells the same paradox as Barth: If election signifies the bearing of rejection for the sake of God's intention to bless, how then is it possible for any to fall outside God's purpose of blessing? By seeking to do fuller justice to the implications of the New Testament witness concerning the nature and necessity of the Spirit's role, however, and to the balance between pneumatology and christology, it also avoids some of the contradictions to which the outworking of Barth's concept of election "in Christ" give rise.

If, as Barth suggests, *apokatastasis* is that for which we may hope, the three scriptural guidelines that shape election to representation — that election is for the sake of blessing, that there is continuity in the representational dynamic as well as the purpose of election, and that election entails setting apart a clearly delineated community to be and do what no

---

35. As noted in Chapter 3, n. 64, a clear presentation of these as the only two possibilities within an Augustinian-Reformed theological framework can be found in Oliver D. Crisp, "Augustinian Universalism," *International Journal for Philosophy of Religion* 53 (June 2003): 127-45.

other can be and do — offer a somewhat different angle from which to think through the possibility. At the same time, this approach to election also suggests that there is after all another answer to the pneumatological question posed by a Reformed approach to election. With election to representation as it has been developed here, we see that it is indeed possible to offer a strong, coherent role for the Spirit that does not lead us only and inexorably to a form of individual double predestination, but holds out the possibility of a hope for all that is pneumatologically shaped as well as christologically grounded.

As the previous chapter makes clear, however, we will not know what the fullness of Christ's representational work itself actually means, and therefore we will not know what the outcome of the church's secondary and derivative representational work will be, or what the final unfolding of election for the sake of wider blessing will ultimately entail, until the parousia brings the dynamic of God's electing purpose to its fulfillment and consummation. All that the approach to election being offered here can do in the meantime is continue to reiterate what has been made known to us of the purpose of election and the dynamic by which it unfolds.

What can be said on the basis of the pneumatological dynamic of election to representation is that the being and doing of the elect new covenant community, as it lives out its calling and grows into the image of God, lies at the heart of God's purposes for the countless multitudes from every tribe and tongue who will come to find their true eschatological identity and personhood in Christ by the Spirit. It does so in ways that preserve the robust pneumatology of Reformed orthodoxy, wholly bound to the work of Christ and shaped by a consistent account of the person and work of the Spirit in the Trinity. It also does so in agreement with fundamental aspects of Barth's radical reworking of the doctrine, but in ways that Barth's election pneumatology cannot envisage, and to which his election christology itself cannot lead us if we are to remain faithful to the New Testament insistence that it is only by the Spirit that we are found to be "in Christ."

Glancing Backward, Looking Forward

In the preceding chapters, I have presented an account of election from a Reformed perspective, with the difficulties raised by the gift and work of the Holy Spirit particularly in mind. Building upon the issues and questions raised by Owen and Barth, the aim has been to look again at some suggestive scriptural themes to guide us towards an alternative formulation of the doctrine.

On the basis of this, I have endeavored to establish some foundations, and sketch some contours, for the notion that the concept of representation might offer a fresh and helpful category for rethinking the nature and purpose of election. This approach to the doctrine seeks to follow the implications of the scriptural witness, both in maintaining election's exclusivity in denoting one clearly defined community set apart to be and to do what no other can be and do, and also in the suggestion that this very "being and doing" of the elect is radically and intrinsically for the sake of the other, as the chosen means by which God's purpose of wider blessing unfolds in human history.

As we have seen, the understanding of election being developed here therefore reflects similarities with and asks some questions of both the historic Reformed tradition, exemplified by Owen, and Barth's mature account of the doctrine. It also shares with both Owen and Barth the recognition that it is neither the purpose of any account of election, nor is it possible for any account of election to resolve all of the mysteries and problems raised by the doctrine. What I have attempted to outline is a potentially fruitful alternative framework for indwelling and exploring them, and in particular, a way of doing so that suggests an alternative answer to the pneumatological question posed with such clarity by the various formulations of Owen and Barth. Election to representation presents us with a Reformed doctrine of election that does not force us to choose between the christological *shape* of election as it is so richly set forth in Barth's mature presentation of the doctrine and a pneumatological *dynamic* of election that lies, as the older tradition rightly discerned, at the heart of the New Testament understanding of what it is to be "in Christ," and so of what it means to be elect "in Christ."

In closing, I would like to look forward, offering some hopes and suggestions for where the concept of election to representation as I have begun to develop it here might lead. First, it seems to me that the representational dynamic of election I have been suggesting here might hold the potential to enrich Jewish-Christian conversation and Christian ecumenical discussion on this most difficult and divisive of doctrines. Second, I hope that it might have a role to play in renewing the church's self-understanding with regard both to its shared life and worship, and to its engagement with the wider world.

Election to Representation: Possibilities for Dialogue

There are few more sensitive and problematic areas for Jewish-Christian dialogue than the concept of election. As we have seen in Chapter 4, this is a theme of considerable interest to contemporary Jewish biblical scholars and theologians, both in terms of furthering an understanding of election within Judaism and in exploring how this relates to Christian understandings. The convergence of biblical scholarship upon which I have drawn here suggests some possibilities for enriching the ongoing conversation on this shared theological theme.

It is through a range of Old Testament scholarship, including both Jewish and Christian perspectives, that it has been possible to discern how we might speak of election in such a way as to include a "being-for" the other that does not impose New Testament categories and judgments upon Israel's own self-understanding. It is on the basis of the various strands of Old Testament scholarship on which I have drawn in Chapter 4 that the concept of representation — in terms of representing God to others, and, although only tentatively and implicitly, of representing others to God — emerges as a way in which to think about the nature of election, and its present and eschatological purpose.

The close relationship noted between this way of understanding Israel's election and a Pauline approach to election in Israel and in Christ allows Christian theology to begin to express the church's election in a way that seeks to do justice *both* to the integrity of the scriptural witness to Israel's own understanding of its election *and* to the radical reinterpretation of Israel's election entailed by the death and resurrection of Christ.

Thus, just as it was suggested in Chapter 4 that representation, as a category rooted more clearly in the scriptural narrative, might assist biblical scholarship to move the discussion of election beyond the unhelpfully freighted terminology of "particularism" and "universalism," so this rootedness in both Jewish and Christian scripture might allow the concept of representation to illuminate Jewish as well as Christian approaches to election. Here we might find a shared category through which to explore our respective understandings of election, and what these might mean for our communities, even if we cannot reach shared conclusions.

Turning to the question of ecumenical discussion, it might seem at first sight that an account of the doctrine so explicitly rooted in the Reformed tradition has little to offer on a subject that has divided the Reformed communion from other Protestants, as well as from Roman Catholicism and Eastern Orthodoxy. What we find, however, is that with its focus upon the intention of election, seen as God's chosen means to further his purpose of wider blessing, and in its suggestion that this takes place particularly as the elect represent God to others and others to God, election to representation bypasses some of the fiercest loci of debate on the subject between the Reformed tradition and other approaches. While these loci remain of the utmost theological importance, the approach outlined here allows the nature and purpose of election to be discussed in ways that hold out significant possibilities for convergence, rather than in ways that issue in immediate polarization.

So, for example, I have indicated my own view from the outset: that election is to be seen as the outcome of the sheer, mysterious, unconditioned sovereign grace of God. I have thereby eschewed any possibility of finding a "solution" to the problems raised by the doctrine through anything that might suggest a synergistic interpretation of the relationship between God and humanity. From my perspective, there is no help to be found in resolving the difficulties of election in the concept of "foreseen" faith, for example, and indeed, there is no response of faith that is not in itself divinely enabled, in the liberation of the will for God by God. In upholding this position, I follow the trajectory of Reformed thinking from Calvin and the early Calvinist tradition *contra* Lutheran developments and the Arminian controversy, and from Schleiermacher through Barth to contemporary expressions of the centrality of these Reformed insights by such as Gunton.

Nevertheless, while the questions and priorities of a Reformed approach have shaped the critical and analytical task here, the representational dynamic of election that I have suggested does not absolutely require a Reformed framework. Its contours are patient of other interpretations of the relationship between God and human beings. In the three scriptural guiding principles and the twofold dynamic of representation by which this account of election is shaped, there are prospects for illuminating and enriching the approaches of the various traditions that uphold theological perspectives other than my own.

As such there is the possibility of a much wider overlap in the ellipses of our interpretations of what it means to speak of election. This offers the hope that to raise the question of election might no longer mean the closing down of conversation, but instead a summons to a fresh exploration of what it means for the whole church, as the elect new covenant people of God in Christ, to be called out to be and do for the world what no other community can be and do.

Election to Representation:
Reclaiming the Doctrine for the Church

In turn, this points to the possibilities for a positive reappropriation of the doctrine in the wider life of the church. The prospects for this might well seem bleak. In 1991 David Fergusson made the need to revisit the doctrine of election the subject of his inaugural lectures at the University of Aberdeen. Given the way in which the doctrine has influenced Scottish church culture and life, he remarked that the most common reactions to any mention of the doctrine were likely to be ridicule or loathing.[1] I suspect that this still holds true. In the other contexts of church life with which I have been most familiar, however (England and Australia), election rarely seems to arise as a topic of reflection for long enough to provoke either reaction. Outside the sphere of academics who engage sympathetically or critically with Barth's account there seems to be an unspoken agreement that it is not necessary to revisit the doctrine, and indeed, that

---

1. David Fergusson, "Predestination: A Scottish Perspective," *SJT* 46 (1993): 457-78.

to mention it at all would be a fearful breach of etiquette in polite church company. A fear of waking this particular sleeping theological giant seems to have become embedded deep in the ecclesial psyche. In my new context of the United States, I am increasingly aware of the deep and often polarizing passions the doctrine can arouse.

It seems, then, that the doctrine of election has often been either an all-too-powerful and profoundly damaging force, scarring the ecclesial landscape, or that the subject is rarely mentioned, as one too arcane and divisive to be allowed to deflect attention from the task of being the people of God in the world. The irony, of course, is that here we have a central doctrine for that very purpose, and every time the church attempts to reflect on such matters it is already working with an implicit understanding of the concept. As has been clear throughout this undertaking, election is an inescapable and supremely important scriptural category for shaping the self-understanding of the people of God, and for discussing the nature of God's dealings with the created order as a whole. Therefore while the reality that the church at times uses the doctrine to wreak havoc is a scandal, it is also a scandal if the alternative is a conspiracy of silence.

Driving my undertaking has been a refusal to allow this doctrine to be relegated to a theological optional extra, and instead to set election in its rightful place at the heart of an attempt to speak of the purposes of God in and for the world. Although the predominant thrust of my work here has been to probe some of the difficulties raised by accounts of the doctrine, and then to lay the foundations for and begin to develop an alternative formulation, my wider hope is that in looking afresh at the scriptural and theological contours of election, the church as a whole might be enabled positively to reclaim a difficult but central doctrine as one intended to shape and enrich the church's understanding of its own life and its engagement with the wider world.

On the one hand, as we have seen, election to representation entails a strong affirmation of the church's singular particularity, in its unique identity as the elect people of God in Christ. To be elect is to exist in the particular set of relations that make this representational dynamic a reality, and as such, there is no way to speak of being elect "in Christ" apart from the work of the Spirit in uniting us to Christ by faith. On the other, as I have reiterated throughout, this third scriptural principle cannot be seen in isolation from the other two: that the representational dynamic of election is the means through which God's wider purpose of blessing unfolds in the face of human sin. To be elect therefore means to be set apart to be *for* the rest of humanity, as the elect one set apart for the sake of the alienated many.

It will be recalled that at the heart of election to representation lies the notion that it is intrinsic to what it means to be a member of the elect community self-consciously and unself-consciously to represent God to others and others to God, and that in doing so, election entails holding those who are apparently rejected within the sphere of God's promised blessing. What might this representational ontology of election mean for our approach to worship? How might such an understanding of election inform our conception of what the triune God intends and accomplishes through the adoration, confession, proclamation, thanksgiving, intercession, praise, and blessing that the elect are summoned and enabled to offer, in the gift of participating through the Spirit in the Son's communion with the Father, and in his continuing ascended ministry?[2]

Election to representation insists that the elect are those through whom God's purpose of blessing unfolds, partially and proleptically, in the sphere of human history. What might this mean as the church considers its role towards those as yet outside the community of believers, although not outside its embrace? In particular we might recall Wright's insistence that the representational shape of the church's election, following that of Christ and Israel, means that it exists as the community through whom that which God has made known and accomplished in Christ is to be worked out in the world.[3] God's purpose in electing a people for himself is that God's loving justice and salvation might reach to the ends of the earth. Election to representation offers one reminder among many that proclaiming the good news of God's salvation accomplished in Christ cannot be separated from seeking out and endeavoring to bring healing to those situations in which the pain and grief of continuing injustice and lovelessness cry out to be assuaged.

Moreover, as Wright also reminds us, Paul insists that we cannot think only of the human sphere when we consider the church's election. The wider creation awaits its own liberation in the consummation of the redemption of the people of God. We must also ask how election to representation might contribute to the recognition that the historical and es-

2. As this indicates once again, there is considerable scope for reflecting on the implications of election to representation in relation to J. B. Torrance's account of worship as the unfolding of the Trinitarian summary statement reiterated here. See Chapter 6, pp. 153-54 above.

3. See especially Chapter 5, pp. 115-16; 131-34 above.

chatological destiny of the created order as a whole is bound up with our own. Although only an occasional marginal theme in the preceding chapters, the way is open to explore the implications of this approach to election for our stewardship of the earth, and for the long tradition of considering human beings as the "priests" of creation.

In asking how the concept of election to representation might play out in various aspects of the church's life, Colin Gunton's hopes for a renewed doctrine of election come to mind in these concluding reflections, as they did in the Introduction. His claim is that rightly understood, "the doctrine of election . . . should serve the cause of a proper ecclesial self-confidence."[4] This is not a confidence based solely on the individual assurance of salvation, and it is not confidence *in* the church, but rather, a confidence based on the church's role in the purposes of God, and "in a call to ecclesial faithfulness."[5] It is just such a confidence that the approach to election I have been developing here seeks to express, and to which it seeks to summon the church. Likewise, from the continued probing of what could be seen historically as a peculiarly Reformed theological obsession may come a possibility of so conceiving of election that, in Gunton's words once again, the Reformed tradition is able to offer "a genuinely universal contribution to the Church's calling."[6]

4. Colin Gunton, "Election and Ecclesiology in the Post-Constantinian Church," *SJT* 53 (2000): 212-27, p. 213.

5. Gunton, "Election and Ecclesiology," p. 213.

6. Gunton, "Election and Ecclesiology," p. 213.

Bibliography

Austin, Mary C. "Joy in the Moment: Immediacy and Ultimacy in Dementia." In *Spirituality and Ageing*, edited by Albert Jewell, pp. 115-34. London: Jessica Kingsley, 1999.

Barth, Karl. *The Göttingen Dogmatics: Instruction in the Christian Religion*. Translated by G. W. Bromiley; edited by Hannelotte Reiffen. Grand Rapids: Eerdmans, 1991.

————. *Church Dogmatics*. Edited by G. W. Bromiley and T. F. Torrance. Edinburgh: T. & T. Clark, 1956-1975.

Bauckham, Richard. *The Bible and Mission: Christian Witness in a Postmodern World*. Carlisle: Paternoster, 2003.

Berkouwer, G. *The Triumph of Grace in the Theology of Karl Barth*. Translated by H. R. Boer. London: Paternoster, 1956.

Bettis, J. D. "Is Karl Barth a Universalist?" *Scottish Journal of Theology* 20 (1967): 423-36.

Boesel, Chris. *Risking Proclamation, Respecting Difference: Christian Faith, Imperialistic Discourse, and Abraham*. Eugene, OR: Cascade Books, 2008.

Bowman, Donna. *The Divine Decision: A Process Doctrine of Election*. Louisville: Westminster/John Knox Press, 2002.

Brand, Chad Owen, ed. *Perspectives on Election: Five Views*. Nashville: B. & H. Publishing, 2006.

Brueggemann, Walter. *Theology of the Old Testament: Testimony, Dispute, Advocacy*. Minneapolis: Fortress, 1991.

Burns, Robert. *Poems and Songs*. Edited by J. Kinsley. Oxford: Oxford University Press, 1969.

Busch, Eberhard. "The Covenant of Grace Fulfilled in Christ as the Foundation of the Indissoluble Solidarity of the Church with Israel: Barth's Position on the Jews During the Hitler Era." Translated by James Seyler. *Scottish Journal of Theology* 52 (1999): 476-503.

Calvin, John. *Institutes of the Christian Religion.* Translated by Ford Lewis Battles; edited by John T. McNeill. Philadelphia: Westminster Press, 1960.

————. *The First Epistle of Paul the Apostle to the Corinthians.* Translated by John W. Farmer; edited by David W. Torrance and Thomas F. Torrance. Edinburgh: Oliver & Boyd, 1960.

Canlis, Julie. "Calvin, Osiander and Participation in God." *International Journal of Systematic Theology* 6 (April 2004): 169-84.

————. "The Ascent of Humanity in Calvin: Anthropology, Ascension and Participation. Continuity with an Irenaean Theme?" Ph.D. Diss., University of St. Andrews, 2005.

Carswell, John. *The Porcupine: The Life of Algernon Sidney.* London: John Murray Press, 1989.

Chung, Sung Wook. "A Bold Innovator: Barth on God and Election." In *Karl Barth and Evangelical Theology: Convergences and Divergences,* edited by Sung Wook Chung, pp. 60-76. Milton Keynes: Paternoster / Grand Rapids: Baker Academic, 2006.

Clifford, Alan. *Atonement and Justification: English Evangelical Theology 1640-1790.* Oxford: Clarendon Press, 1990.

Colwell, John E. *Actuality and Provisionality: Eternity and Election in the Theology of Karl Barth.* Edinburgh: Rutherford House Books, 1989.

————. "The Contemporaneity of the Divine Decision: Reflections on Barth's Denial of 'Universalism.'" In *Universalism and the Doctrine of Hell: Papers Presented at the Fourth Edinburgh Conference on Christian Dogmatics, 1991,* edited by N. M. de S. Cameron, pp. 139-60. Carlisle: Paternoster, 1992.

Crisp, Oliver. "On Barth's Denial of Universalism." *Themelios* 29, no. 1 (2003): 18-29.

————. "Augustinian Universalism." *International Journal for Philosophy of Religion* 53 (June 2003): 127-45.

Davis, J. C. "Cromwell's Religion." In *Oliver Cromwell and the English Revolution,* edited by John Morrill, pp. 181-208. London: Longman, 1990.

Dunn, J. D. G. *Romans 9–16.* Word Biblical Commentary 38B. Dallas: Word, 1991.

————. *The Epistle to the Galatians.* Peabody, MA: Hendrickson, 1993.

————. *The Theology of Paul the Apostle.* Edinburgh: T. & T. Clark, 1998.

Eddy, Paul R. "The (W)Right Jesus: Eschatological Prophet, Israel's Messiah, Yahweh Embodied." In *Jesus and the Restoration of Israel: A Critical Assessment of N. T. Wright's Jesus and the Victory of God,* edited by Carey C. Newman, pp. 40-60. Carlisle: Paternoster, 1999.

Engel, Mary Potter. *John Calvin's Perspectival Anthropology.* Atlanta: Scholars Press, 1988.

Erskine, Thomas. *The Doctrine of Election.* 2nd edition. Edinburgh: David Douglas, 1878.

Farrow, Douglas. *Ascension and Ecclesia: On the Significance of the Doctrine of the*

Ascension for Ecclesiology and Christian Cosmology. Edinburgh: T. & T. Clark, 1999.

Fee, Gordon D. *The First Epistle to the Corinthians.* New International Commentaries on the New Testament. Grand Rapids: Eerdmans, 1987.

———. *God's Empowering Presence: The Holy Spirit in the Letters of Paul.* Peabody, MA: Hendrickson, 1994.

Ferguson, Sinclair B. *John Owen on the Christian Life.* Banner of Truth Trust: Edinburgh, 1987.

Fergusson, David A. S. "Predestination: A Scottish Perspective." *Scottish Journal of Theology* 46 (1993): 457-78.

Gleason, Randall C. *John Calvin and John Owen on Mortification: A Comparative Study in Reformed Spirituality.* New York: Peter Lang, 1995.

Gockel, Matthias. "New Perspectives on an Old Debate: Friedrich Schleiermacher's Essay on Election." *International Journal of Systematic Theology* 6 (July 2004): 301-18.

———. *Barth and Schleiermacher on the Doctrine of Election: A Systematic-Theological Comparison.* Oxford: Oxford University Press, 2007.

Goldsmith, Malcolm. *In a Strange Land . . . People with Dementia and the Local Church: A Guide and Encouragement for Ministry.* Southwell, UK: 4M Publications, 2004.

Grenz, Stanley J. *The Social God and the Relational Self: A Trinitarian Theology of the Imago Dei.* Louisville: Westminster/John Knox Press, 2001.

Gunton, Colin E. "Karl Barth's Doctrine of Election as Part of His Doctrine of God." *Journal of Theological Studies* 25, no. 2 (1974): 381-92.

———. *The Promise of Trinitarian Theology.* Edinburgh: T. & T. Clark, 1991.

———. "Trinity, Ontology and Anthropology: Towards a Renewal of the Doctrine of the *Imago Dei.*" In *Persons, Divine and Human,* edited by Christoph Schwöbel and Colin E. Gunton, pp. 47-61. Edinburgh: T. & T. Clark, 1991.

———. *The One, the Three and the Many: God, Creation and the Culture of Modernity.* The 1992 Bampton Lectures. Cambridge: Cambridge University Press, 1993.

———. *The Triune Creator: A Historical and Systematic Study.* Grand Rapids: Eerdmans, 1998.

———. "Salvation." In *The Cambridge Companion to Karl Barth,* edited by John Webster, pp. 143-58. Cambridge: Cambridge University Press, 2000.

———. "Election and Ecclesiology in the Post-Constantinian Church." *Scottish Journal of Theology* 53 (2000): 212-27.

Hall, Basil. "Calvin against the Calvinists." In *John Calvin. Courtenay Studies in Reformation Theology No. 1,* edited by G. E. Duffield, pp. 19-37. Abingdon, UK: Sutton Courtenay Press, 1966.

Helm, Paul. *Calvin and the Calvinists.* Edinburgh: Banner of Truth Trust, 1982.

Hendry, George. "The Freedom of God in the Theology of Karl Barth." *Scottish Journal of Theology* 31 (1978): 229-44.

Holmes, Stephen R. *Listening to the Past: The Place of Tradition in Theology.* Carlisle: Paternoster, 2002.

Hunsinger, George. *How to Read Karl Barth: The Shape of His Theology.* Oxford: Oxford University Press, 1991.

———. *Disruptive Grace: Studies in the Theology of Karl Barth.* Grand Rapids: Eerdmans, 2000.

———. *The Eucharist and Ecumenism: Let Us Keep the Feast.* Cambridge: Cambridge University Press, 2008.

Jenson, Robert. *Alpha and Omega: A Study in the Theology of Karl Barth.* Edinburgh: Thomas Nelson, 1963.

———. "The Holy Spirit." In *Christian Dogmatics,* edited by Carl E. Braaten and Robert W. Jenson, pp. 101-78. Philadelphia: Fortress Press, 1984.

———. "You Wonder Where the Spirit Went." *Pro Ecclesia* 28, no. 3 (1993): 296-304.

———. *Systematic Theology.* 2 vols. Oxford: Oxford University Press, 1997, 1999.

Jewell, Albert. *Spirituality and Ageing.* London: Jessica Kingsley, 1999.

Jewett, Paul K. *Election and Predestination.* Grand Rapids: Eerdmans, 1985.

Kaminsky, Joel S. *Corporate Responsibility in the Hebrew Bible.* Journal for the Study of the Old Testament Supplement Series 196. Sheffield: Sheffield Academic Press, 1996.

———. "The Concept of Election and Second Isaiah: Recent Literature." *Biblical Theology Bulletin* 31, no. 4 (2001): 135-44.

———. *Yet I Loved Jacob: Reclaiming the Biblical Concept of Election.* Nashville: Abingdon Press, 2007.

Kapic, Kelly M. *Communion with God: The Divine and the Human in the Theology of John Owen.* Grand Rapids: Baker Academic, 2007.

Keck, David. *Forgetting Whose We Are: Alzheimer's Disease and the Love of God.* Nashville: Abingdon Press, 1996.

Kendall, R. T. *Calvin and English Calvinism to 1649.* Oxford: Oxford University Press, 1979.

Krötke, Wolf. "The Humanity of the Human Person in Karl Barth's Anthropology." Translated by Philip G. Ziegler. In *The Cambridge Companion to Karl Barth,* edited by John Webster, pp. 159-76. Cambridge: Cambridge University Press, 2000.

Levenson, Jon D. *The Death and Resurrection of the Beloved Son: The Transformation of Child Sacrifice in Judaism and Christianity.* New Haven: Yale University Press, 1993.

———. "The Universal Horizon of Biblical Particularism." In *Ethnicity and the Bible,* edited by M. G. Brett, pp. 143-69. Leiden: Brill, 1996.

MacDonald, Nathan. *Deuteronomy and the Meaning of "Monotheism."* Tübingen: Mohr Siebeck, 2003.

————. *"The Imago Dei* and Election: Reading Genesis 1:26-28 and Old Testament Scholarship with Karl Barth." *International Journal of Systematic Theology* 10 (July 2008): 303-27.

MacLeod Campbell, John. *The Nature of the Atonement.* 1856. Reprint, with introduction by J. B. Torrance. Grand Rapids: Eerdmans, 1996.

McCormack, Bruce. *Karl Barth's Critically Realistic Dialectical Theology: Its Genesis and Development 1909-1936.* Oxford: Clarendon, 1995.

————. "Grace and Being." In *The Cambridge Companion to Karl Barth,* edited by John Webster, pp. 92-110. Cambridge: Cambridge University Press, 2000.

————. "What's at Stake in Current Debates over Justification? The Crisis of Protestantism in the West." In *Justification: What's at Stake in the Current Debates,* edited by Mark Husbands and Daniel J. Treier, pp. 81-117. Downers Grove, IL: InterVarsity Press, 2004.

McDonald, Suzanne. "Barth's 'Other' Doctrine of Election in the *Church Dogmatics,*" *IJST* 9 (April 2007): 134-47.

————. *Dementia and a Theology of Holy Saturday.* MHA Aspects of Ageing Papers No. 1. Derby, UK: Methodist Housing Association, 2003.

————. "The Pneumatology of the 'Lost' Image in John Owen." *Westminster Theological Journal* 71, no. 2 (Fall 2009): 323-35.

McKim, Donald K., ed. *God Never Forgets: Faith, Hope and Alzheimer's Disease.* Louisville: Westminster/John Knox Press, 1997.

Molnar, Paul D. *Divine Freedom and the Doctrine of the Immanent Trinity.* London: T. & T. Clark, 2002.

————. "The Trinity, Election and God's Ontological Freedom: A Response to Kevin W. Hector." *International Journal of Systematic Theology* 8 (July 2006): 294-306.

Muller, Richard. *Christ and the Decree: Christology and Predestination in Reformed Theology from Calvin to Perkins.* Durham, NC: Labyrinth Press, 1986.

————. "Calvin and the Calvinists: Assessing Continuities and Discontinuities between the Reformation and Orthodoxy." *Calvin Theological Journal* 30, no. 2 (1995): 345-75; 31, no. 1 (1996): 125-60.

————. *The Unaccommodated Calvin: Studies in the Foundation of a Theological Tradition.* Oxford: Oxford University Press, 2000.

Newbigin, Lesslie. *The Open Secret: An Introduction to the Theology of Mission.* Rev. ed. London: SPCK, 1995.

Novak, David. *The Election of Israel: The Idea of the Chosen People.* Cambridge: Cambridge University Press, 1995.

Owen, John. *The Works of John Owen.* 24 vols. Edited by William H. Gould. London: Johnstone & Hunter, 1850-1855.

Pannenberg, Wolfhart. *Human Nature, History, and Election.* Philadelphia: Westminster Press, 1977.

Payne, Jon D. *John Owen on the Lord's Supper.* Edinburgh: Banner of Truth Trust, 2004.

Perkins, William. *The Workes of . . . William Perkins.* Vol. 1. Cambridge, 1609.

Prins, Richard. "The Image of God in Adam and the Restoration of Man in Jesus Christ: A Study in Calvin." *Scottish Journal of Theology* 25 (1972): 32-44.

Rehnman, Sebastian. *Divine Discourse: The Theological Methodology of John Owen.* Grand Rapids: Baker Academic, 2002.

Robinson, H. Wheeler. *Corporate Personality in Ancient Israel.* 2nd ed. Philadelphia: Fortress, 1980.

Rogers, Eugene F. "Supplementing Barth on Jews and Gender: Identifying God by Anagogy and the Spirit." *Modern Theology* 14 (January 1998): 43-81.

———. "The Eclipse of the Spirit in Karl Barth." In *Conversing with Barth,* edited by John C. McDowell and Mike Higton, pp. 173-90. Aldershot: Ashgate, 2004.

Rosato, P. J. *The Spirit as Lord: The Pneumatology of Karl Barth.* Edinburgh: T. & T. Clark, 1981.

Rowley, H. H. *The Biblical Doctrine of Election.* London: Lutterworth Press, 1950.

Sapp, Stephen. "Memory: The Community Looks Backward." In *God Never Forgets: Faith, Hope and Alzheimer's Disease,* edited by Donald McKim, pp. 38-54. Louisville: Westminster/John Knox Press, 1997.

Saunders, James. *Dementia: Pastoral Theology and Pastoral Care.* Cambridge: Grove Books, 2002.

Schleiermacher, Friedrich. "Über die Lehre von der Erwählung, besonders in Bezichung auf Herrn Dr Bretschneiders Aphorismen." In *Theologisch-dogmatische Abhandlungen und Gelegenheitschriften. Kritische Gesamtausgabe,* vol. I/10, edited by H.-F. Traulsen and M. Ohst, pp. 145-222. Berlin: De Gruyter, 1990.

———. *The Christian Faith.* Edited by H. R. Mackintosh and J. S. Stewart. Edinburgh: T. & T. Clark, 1928.

Seitz, Christopher. *Figured Out: Typology and Providence in Christian Scripture.* Louisville: Westminster/John Knox Press, 2001.

Sharp, Douglas R. *The Hermeneutics of Election: The Significance of the Doctrine in Barth's Church Dogmatics.* Lanham, MD: University Press of America, 1990.

Sonderegger, Katherine. *That Jesus Christ Was Born a Jew: Karl Barth's "Doctrine of Israel."* University Park: Pennsylvania State University Press, 1992.

Soulen, R. Kendall. "Karl Barth and the Future of the God of Israel." *Pro Ecclesia* 6, no. 4 (1997): 413-28.

———. "YHWH the Triune God." *Modern Theology* 15 (January 1999): 25-54.

Spence, Alan. *Incarnation and Inspiration: John Owen and the Coherence of Christology.* London: T. & T. Clark, 2007.

Thompson, Andrew. "The Life of Dr Owen." In *The Works of John Owen*, edited by William H. Gould, vol. 1, pp. xix-cxxii. London: Johnstone & Hunter, 1850.

Thompson, John. *The Holy Spirit in the Theology of Karl Barth*. Allison Park, PA: Pickwick Publications, 1991.

Toon, Peter. *God's Statesman: The Life and Work of John Owen, Pastor, Educator, Theologian*. Exeter, UK: Paternoster, 1971.

Torrance, J. B. "Covenant or Contract? A Study of the Theological Background of Worship in Seventeenth-Century Scotland." *Scottish Journal of Theology* 23 (1970): 51-76.

————. "The Incarnation and 'Limited Atonement.'" *Evangelical Quarterly* 55 (1982): 83-94.

————. "Strengths and Weaknesses of the Westminster Theology." In *The Westminster Confession in the Church Today*, edited by A. I. C. Heron, pp. 40-54. Edinburgh: St. Andrew Press, 1982.

————. *Worship, Community and the Triune God of Grace*. Carlisle: Paternoster, 1996.

Torrance, T. F. *Calvin's Doctrine of Man*. Grand Rapids: Eerdmans, 1957.

Trueman, Carl R. *The Claims of Truth: John Owen's Trinitarian Theology*. Carlisle: Paternoster, 1998.

————. *John Owen: Reformed Catholic Renaissance Man*. Aldershot: Ashgate, 2007.

Turretin, Francis. *Institutes of Elenctic Theology*. Vol. 1, translated by George Musgrave Giger; edited by J. T. Dennison. Phillipsburg, NJ: Presbyterian & Reformed Publishing, 1992.

Volf, Miroslav. *Exclusion and Embrace: A Theological Exploration of Identity, Otherness, and Reconciliation*. Nashville: Abingdon Press, 1996.

————. *After Our Likeness: The Church as the Image of the Trinity*. Grand Rapids: Eerdmans, 1998.

Webster, John. *Word and Church: Essays in Christian Dogmatics*. Edinburgh: T. & T. Clark, 2001.

————. *Barth's Earlier Theology*. London: T. & T. Clark, 2005.

————. "The Church and the Perfection of God." In *The Community of the Word: Toward an Evangelical Ecclesiology*, edited by Mark Husbands and Daniel J. Treier, pp. 75-95. Downers Grove, IL: InterVarsity Press, 2005.

————. "The Visible Attests the Invisible." In *The Community of the Word: Toward an Evangelical Ecclesiology*, edited by Mark Husbands and Daniel J. Treier, pp. 96-113. Downers Grove, IL: InterVarsity Press, 2005.

Witherington III, Ben. *The Jesus Quest: The Third Search for the Jew of Nazareth*. Downers Grove, IL: InterVarsity Press, 1995.

Wright, N. T. *The Climax of the Covenant: Christ and the Law in Pauline Theology*. Edinburgh: T. & T. Clark, 1991.

————. *Jesus and the Victory of God*. Volume 2 of *Christian Origins and the Question of God*. London: SPCK, 1996.

―――――. "The Letter to the Romans: Introduction, Commentary and Reflections." In *New Interpreter's Bible in Twelve Volumes,* vol. 10, pp. 393-770. Nashville: Abingdon Press, 2002.

―――――. *Paul: Fresh Perspectives.* London: SPCK, 2005.

Wyschogrod, Michael. "A Jewish Perspective on Karl Barth." In *How Karl Barth Changed My Mind,* edited by Donald K. McKim, pp. 156-61. Grand Rapids: Eerdmans, 1986.

―――――. *The Body of Faith: God in the People Israel.* 2nd ed. Northville, NJ: Jason Aronson Inc, 1996.

―――――. "Israel, the Church and Election." In *Abraham's Promise: Judaism and Jewish-Christian Relations,* edited by R. Kendall Soulen. Grand Rapids: Eerdmans, 2004.

Yu, Anthony C. "Karl Barth's Doctrine of Election." *Foundations* 13, no. 3 (1970): 248-61.

Index of Names and Subjects